CHICKEN COOKERY

by Ceil Dyer

HPBooks

Table of Contents

Creative Cookery with Chicken 3
Poultry Pointers 4
Poultry Cutting Know-How 9
Appetizing Ways with Chicken 15
Best of All Soups & Stews 25
Main Dishes—Sautéed, Braised & Steamed 37
Poultry—Roasted, Stuffed & Broiled 57
Perfect Fried Chicken 77
Stir-Fried Chicken 89
Easy Casserole & Oven Cookery 97
Cooked Poultry Used Great Ways 109
Superb Salads & Sandwiches 127
Flavorful Backyard-Cooked Poultry 139
Perfect Poultry Accompaniments 148
Index 157

ANOTHER BEST-SELLING VOLUME FROM HPBooks®

Publisher: Rick Bailey; Executive Editor: Randy Summerlin; Editorial Director: Elaine Woodard;
Editor: Retha M. Davis; Art Director: Don Burton; Production Coordinator: Cindy Coatsworth;
Typography: Michelle Carter; Food Stylist: Carol Flood Peterson;
Poultry-Cutting Consultant: Anthony J. Russo; Photography: deGennaro Associates

NOTICE: The information contained in this book is true and complete to the best of our knowledge. All recommendations are made without any guarantees on the part of the author or HPBooks. The author and publisher disclaim all liability in connection with the use of this information.

Published by HPBooks, A Division of HPBooks, Inc.

P.O. Box 5367, Tucson, AZ 85703   602/888-2150
ISBN 0-89586-054-6
Library of Congress Catalog Card Number 82-83657
©1983 HPBooks, Inc.   Printed in the U.S.A.
4th Printing

Cover: Roast Chicken, pages 58-59,
surrounded with roasted vegetables
Photo by Tom Eglin Studio

Creative Cookery with Chicken

If you enjoy cooking, serving and eating chicken, you may already know many ways to prepare it. But, if you limit your repertoire to a few familiar recipes, you are missing some delicious eating. In addition to hundreds of creative chicken dishes, there are many new and exciting ways to cook chicken. Some are faster and easier—with fewer calories. There are also ways to make chicken even more economical. And best yet, you will learn how to make this versatile bird more flavorful than you ever thought possible.

Nearly everyone enjoys chicken because they can have it just the way they like it: roasted, fried, stewed or poached. Chicken can be served plain or in hundreds of combinations. It takes on the flavor of seasonings, and its character will change each way it's prepared. Glance through this book and note the wonderful selection of recipes. Flavors range from delicate to hearty; character from simple to elegant.

Chicken may be the most-versatile meat you can buy. For a festive occasion or a family dinner, chicken is likely to be your first choice. Chicken can be fried or baked in a very basic way, or you can create an elegant roast chicken with stuffing and various trimmings. Chicken cookery is easy and predictably good. You can be assured of pleasing those you serve.

Faced with escalating food prices, today's shopper can turn to poultry for some budget relief. In the 1930's, poultry was viewed as "chicken on Sunday" and "turkey on Thanksgiving." Fortunately, those are days of the past. Modern production techniques have made poultry very affordable and readily available in a variety of forms. Consumers can enjoy poultry often and in the form they choose. No matter what the price, poultry has great flavor and goodness.

The light, delectable taste of chicken and turkey gives no clue to the fact that they are nutritional heavyweights. Both are excellent sources of protein and low in fat—two important considerations for those with a keen interest in nutrition. Poultry also provides such essential nutrients as iron and B vitamins. An average serving of chicken or turkey contains fewer calories than an average serving of most other meats. Poultry can be prepared without additional fat, and it takes well to low-calorie seasonings. It appeases even the hearty appetite. With all of its good-for-you qualities, poultry satisfies more than just hunger. It provides tasty pleasant eating—who could ask for more?

Over 200 tempting recipes are in this book. Along with chicken, you will find recipes for turkey, goose, duck and Cornish hen. To complete the book, there is a chapter on sauces, garnishes and a few of my favorite poultry accompaniments. There is no end to the variety of ways you can prepare poultry.

Ceil Dyer

Ceil Dyer is a graduate of Louisiana State University. She has served as food editor and publicist for several food and wine companies in New York. Ceil has written a syndicated column with quick gourmet entertaining ideas. An enthusiasm for travel has taken her throughout Europe studying regional cuisines. A fluent writer, Ceil has authored over 30 cookbooks including the best-selling *Wok Cookery* and its sequel, *More Wok Cookery.* A thrifty up-bringing is demonstrated in the practicality and usefulness of Ceil's recipes.

Poultry Pointers

TYPES OF POULTRY

The U.S. Department of Agriculture has established guidelines and classifications for poultry including chicken, turkey, duck and goose. All poultry moving in interstate commerce is required by law to be inspected according to department guidelines. That is your assurance of a wholesome product. Poultry may also be graded through a voluntary program. When buying poultry, you may find the grade mark, a shield carrying the grade letter A, B or C, on the packaging material. This is your assurance of the quality of the bird.

The following list gives the types and approximate ready-to-cook weights of the poultry classes.

CHICKEN	
Rock Cornish Hen	not over 2 lbs.
Broiler/Fryer	3/4 to not over 3-1/2 lbs.
Roaster	2-1/2 to over 5 lbs.
Capon	4 to 8 lbs.
Stewing Chicken, Hen or Fowl	2-1/2 to over 5-1/2 lbs.
TURKEY	
Fryer or Roaster (very-young turkey)	4 to 8 lbs.
Young Turkey	8 to over 24 lbs.
Mature Turkey	8 to over 24 lbs.
DUCK	
Broiler or Fryer Duckling	3 to over 5 lbs.
Roaster Duckling	3 to over 5 lbs.
Mature Duck	3 to over 5 lbs.
GOOSE	
Young Goose	4 to over 14 lbs.
Mature Goose	4 to over 14 lbs.

POULTRY CLASSES

Poultry is divided into classes with the same physical characteristics. These are primarily associated with age. Age affects the tenderness of poultry and dictates the cooking method to use.

Young birds are tender-meated and suitable for roasting, broiling, frying, rotisserie cooking, barbecuing and baking.

Older, mature birds are less tender-meated. They need long, slow cooking with water or steam to make them tender and to develop a full flavor. These birds are preferred for simmering, steaming, braising and pressure cooking.

Poultry must be labeled with the proper class name. This enables shoppers to select the bird which will best meet their needs.

Classes of Young Chickens

Cornish Game Hen—a young immature chicken, about 5- to 6-weeks old, not more than 2 pounds ready-to-cook weight.
Broiler or Fryer—a young chicken, usually under 13-weeks old, of either sex.
Roaster—a young chicken, usually 3- to 5-months old, of either sex.
Capon—a young surgically unsexed male chicken, usually under 8-months old.

Classes of Mature Chickens

Hen, Fowl, Baking Chicken or Stewing Chicken—a mature female chicken, usually more than 10-months old.
Cock or Rooster—a mature male chicken with coarse skin, toughened and darkened meat.

Classes of Young Turkeys

Fryer-Roaster Turkey—a young immature turkey, usually under 16-weeks old.
Young Turkey—a young turkey, usually under 8-months old, and somewhat less tender than a fryer-roaster turkey.

Classes of Mature Turkeys

Yearling Turkey—a fully matured turkey, usually under 15-months old.
Mature Turkey—an older, mature turkey, usually over 15-months old with coarse skin and toughened flesh.
NOTE: The designation of sex—hen or tom—with the class name on the label is not required and does not affect the tenderness.

BASICS OF BUYING

What type and how much should you buy? A chart of servings per pound cannot tell you exactly how much to purchase. It can only give an approximation. The amount of poultry you will need depends on how many people you plan to serve, the type of poultry you are buying, how you plan to cook it, when and how it will be served and what will accompany it.

Here are some general guidelines for buying poultry. When preparing a whole bird, allow 3 to 4 ounces of cooked meat per serving. This does not include bone, therefore buy 1/2 to 2/3 pound per serving. For boneless cuts, such as a turkey roll or roast, buy 1/3 pound per serving. When serving cut-up chicken, a serving is generally considered 1 breast half or 1 leg or 2 drumsticks or 2 thighs or 4 wings.

When buying prepackaged poultry, be aware of moisture loss. The drier the package, the fresher the poultry. Most suppliers date packaged poultry with the last date it should be sold. Check this date before buying. Avoid purchasing torn or broken packages. Use fresh poultry as soon as possible, or package and store in your freezer.

STORAGE—FRESH OR FROZEN

Like any fresh meat, poultry is very perishable and should be refrigerated at all times. Tray-packed poultry should be stored in its original wrapping in the coldest part of the refrigerator. Cold, raw poultry should be used within 1 to 2 days. If poultry is purchased in wrapping other than transparent plastic wrap, unwrap it. Remove giblets. Place poultry on a platter or tray. Cover with waxed paper or plastic wrap. Cover giblets and refrigerate separately.

Uncooked poultry may be frozen whole or in pieces. Be sure to use moisture- and vapor-proof material suitable for freezing. This includes heavy-duty foil, freezer paper or plastic freezer bags. Press air out of the package before sealing.

Cooked poultry should be prepared for freezing the same way except when made with gravy or sauce. Then, it is best packaged in rigid containers with tight-fitting lids. Be sure to label all packages with the date and contents.

Freezer storage time depends on the quality of poultry when frozen, packaging material and storage temperature. Quality of poultry can be maintained, but it will not improve. Poultry quality will decrease if handled incorrectly.

DEFROSTING

Frozen poultry is generally thawed before cooking. However, whole poultry or frozen poultry parts may be cooked without thawing. Cooking time will be longer than for thawed or fresh poultry.

There are three basic methods for defrosting poultry products: in the refrigerator, in cold water and at room temperature. Select a method according to the amount of time and space available.

Thawing in the refrigerator—Place whole, original-wrapped poultry on a tray or platter. Place in the refrigerator 1 to 2 days or until pliable. Whole frozen chicken under 4 pounds require 12 to 16 hours refrigerator time to thaw. Allow 4 to 9 hours for chicken pieces. Turkey over 18 pounds may take 3 days to thaw.

Thawing in cold water—For more rapid thawing, place poultry in watertight wrapping in cold water. Change water frequently to hasten thawing. Small birds require about 1 hour. Larger birds require 6 to 8 hours. Thaw until pliable. You can also combine defrosting methods. Start by defrosting in the refrigerator, then complete the process in cold water.

Thawing at room temperature—When time does not allow you to use the methods above, poultry can be safely thawed in a cool room away from heat. Leave poultry in the original wrapping. Place poultry in a closed, double-wall paper bag or wrap poultry in newspaper. This helps keep the surface temperature of the bird cool during thawing. Thaw poultry until pliable.

Thawing and refreezing poultry is not recommended as it reduces both quality and flavor. You can freeze cooked chicken which was frozen in the uncooked form with satisfactory results.

COOKED-CHICKEN POINTERS

People often ask how long cooked chicken is safe unrefrigerated. Experts say chicken cooked without sauces such as fried, baked or broiled, after proper cooling, is safe up to 6 hours at a cool room temperature. Always keep chicken salad, creamed chicken or similar dishes refrigerated until ready to reheat or serve cold.

BASIC PREPARATION

To prepare poultry for cooking, rinse whole bird or parts in cool water. Drain well. Pat dry with paper towel. Trim off any excess body fat, if desired. IF FRYING OR DEEP-FRYING, BE SURE POULTRY IS COMPLETELY DRY. Water drops in hot oil cause spattering.

To avoid any cross-contamination to other foods or surfaces in the kitchen, wash hands thoroughly after handling poultry. Always clean and sanitize any equipment, knives, cutting boards or other items used in preparing poultry.

After basic preparation, poultry can be cooked in an unlimited number of ways. It can be baked, broiled, braised, stewed, sautéed, fried, barbecued, stuffed and stir-fried. It can be prepared using a conventional range, microwave oven, slow-cooking pot, clay pot, outdoor grill, electric frying pan, wok, deep-fryer and others.

If yours is the average kitchen, you have all the basic equipment needed to prepare any of the recipes in this book. One of the most essential elements is you—your hands, eyes and taste buds.

One unique piece of equipment referred to in the chapter on roasting is the *culinary injector.* It is used to inject butter, seasoned oil or a combination of flavorful liquids into poultry before roasting. Injectors may be purchased in a gourmet kitchen shop or the houseware section of a department store.

Poultry is a very versatile product, giving the preparer the opportunity to create a new dish each time it's served.

U.S.D.A. Maximum Suggested Storage Times at 0F (−20C).	
	Months
Uncooked poultry:	
Chicken and turkey	*12*
Duck and goose	*6*
Giblets	*3*
Cooked poultry (slices or pieces):	
Covered with broth or gravy	*6*
Not covered with broth or gravy	*1*
Poultry meat sandwiches	*1*
Cooked-poultry dishes	*6*
Fried chicken	*4*

CHICKEN STOCK

A frequent concern of consumers is the difference between *stock* and *broth*. Basically, the two terms are interchangeable. They really mean the same product. Throughout this book, when stock is called for, I mean strained clear stock. You can substitute canned broth, if you wish.

Homemade stock is much richer than canned broth. Homemade stock is the basis for many of the elegant sauces that give French cooking its fine reputation. A well-seasoned stock, reduced by boiling to intensify flavor, will give any sauce or soup a delectable flavor. Stock is also low in calories because it requires little additional thickening with butter, flour, eggs or cream. Canned broth, although convenient and good, cannot produce a sauce that is both light and delicate, while superbly rich in flavor.

When fresh stock is not available, I use a good-quality canned product. However, I do not use or recommend using bouillon. Bouillon is generally very salty. This is unacceptable for flavor reasons and may be unadvisable for health reasons.

It is both easy and convenient to select canned broth; however, there is nothing difficult about making your own. It must cook slowly for several hours to release the rich flavor and gelatin from the bones, but the actual work time is minimal. If you poach chicken, make stock from the bones as in Poached Chicken & Rich Stock. It requires no more effort, and often less, than preparing any other type of chicken dinner. Though the stock must indeed simmer a long time, who says you have to stand there and simmer along with it? Stock practically makes itself.

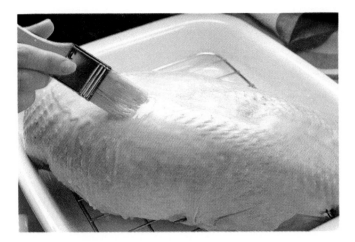

TURKEY TIPS

Select fresh turkey whenever available. Although more expensive than frozen, fresh turkey usually is more juicy and flavorful, and well worth the extra cost. Fresh turkey is generally available during the traditional holiday season and by special order through your local supplier. Frozen turkey is of good quality and is generally available year-round. It is an excellent choice any time of year.

Choose your turkey by size. If it is to be the star of the meal—the only meat—allow 1/2 to 3/4 pound per person. Served with other meats or on a buffet, allow 1 pound per 6 to 8 guests.

When selecting fresh turkey, look for creamy-beige skin and firm flesh. Skin should be tight over the breast and drumstick areas. Because of packaging, you cannot select a frozen bird by these guidelines. Therefore, be sure to buy a well-known brand or from a reliable supplier. Be sure the wrapping has not been torn. There should be no apparent ice crystals—a sure sign that the turkey was partially thawed and refrozen for some reason.

Turkey comes in a wide range of sizes: small, 5 to 10 pounds; medium, 10 to 16 pounds; and for the family holiday feast, the large, 16 to 24 pounds. Although small birds are meaty and delicious and a good buy for a small family, I prefer medium even when I plan to serve only a small group. This gives me perfect roast turkey for the occasion and plenty for using as leftovers in casseroles, sandwiches and stir-fry dishes. Select the size most appropriate for you and your needs.

GOOSE & DUCK

Both goose and duck are available whole in fresh-frozen or fresh-chilled form. The majority are sold frozen. Although traditionally thought of as holiday meats, they are now available throughout the year. Both forms of poultry have all dark meat and contain larger portions of fat than do chicken or turkey. The fat layer under the skin acts as a self-baster during roasting.

Duck is marketed at a 7- to 8-week age as duckling or young duck. Goose is marketed at 4 to 5 months and ranges in size from 6 to 14 pounds. Average goose size is 7 to 11 pounds. Duck and goose are marketed young because weight gained after 3 to 4 months is mostly fat.

MICROWAVE TIPS

Poultry is an ideal product for microwave cooking. It is naturally tender and juicy, resulting in excellent dishes. Most poultry can be cooked on high or full power. Larger birds such as turkey are generally started on full power, then reduced to medium about half-way through the cooking period.

During cooking, it is important to turn or rearrange poultry pieces to ensure even cooking. When placing chicken pieces in a dish for microwave cooking, arrange meaty portions to the outside of the dish. This allows more even cooking of all pieces.

Chicken pieces cook rapidly in the microwave, resulting in a minimum of browning. To enhance the color, select a sauce, glaze or crumb-coating appropriate to the dish. Microwave chicken pieces, skin-side down, in sauce for the first half of the cooking time. Then, turn pieces over and microwave the remaining time.

When preparing a stuffed bird in the microwave, select a light bread stuffing rather than a heavy stuffing, such as cornbread. A light stuffing will allow the heat to penetrate more quickly and the stuffing will be done when the bird is finished.

When preparing crumb-coated chicken, microwave pieces on a rack so the chicken doesn't stew in pan juices. Microwave uncovered to prevent steaming. **Do not try to deep-fry in the microwave.**

Poultry can be defrosted quickly in the microwave. Defrosting is done at medium-low or 30% power at an average of 4 minutes per pound. Then the power is reduced to 10% or low and microwave 5 minutes per pound. Let poultry stand in cold water to complete defrosting.

Defrosting Poultry in Microwave

	30% power or medium/low	10% power or low
Turkey breast or whole chicken, turkey, duck, and Cornish hen	4 minutes per lb.	5 minutes per lb.
Turkey wings, turkey hindquarter	5 minutes per lb.	7 minutes per lb.

Turkey larger than 10 pounds should be defrosted and cooked conventionally. They tend to defrost and cook unevenly in the microwave oven. Many microwave ovens cannot accommodate the large baking dish necessary to hold larger birds.

For additional information on preparing poultry in the microwave oven, refer to your microwave oven Use & Care Guide or *Microwave Cookbook—The Complete Guide,* published by HPBooks.

Rendered Chicken Fat & Cracklings (Grebenes)

Rendered chicken fat, *schmaltz,* can be used in place of oil or butter when preparing sautéed chicken, chicken gravies or sauces. Paprika may be added for both flavor and color.

Cracklings, or *grebenes,* are a bonus. Crisp and flavorful, they may be served as an appetizer or used in place of bacon as an ingredient or garnish for other recipes.

Cut off all visible fat and extra skin from chicken before cooking. Wrap fat and skin in foil, or place in an air-tight plastic bag. Store in freezer until you have 1-1/2 to 2 cups or enough to prepare. Because fat never freezes completely, store no longer than 1 month.

Trim off and discard any bits of meat from fat or skin. Place in a large heavy skillet over very low heat. Add 1 cup water. Simmer gently until water has evaporated and clear yellow liquid fat begins to collect. As soon as there are 2 to 3 tablespoons of rendered fat, spoon it from skillet into a storage container with a lid. Continue until all fat has been rendered and skin becomes crisp golden cracklings. Do not let fat brown. Drain cracklings on paper towel. Serve or use within 1 to 2 hours or they become soggy. Store fat in refrigerator. Use within 8 to 10 days.

Poultry Cutting Know-How

There are a number of ways to cut food costs without reducing quality or quantity. When selecting chicken, buy whole birds. Then, cut them into serving pieces yourself. Pound for pound, whole chicken is generally priced about 10% below an equal amount of precut chicken. Buying broiler-fryers on sale can save as much as 20% to 25%. When buying turkey, it is more economical to select larger birds. They carry more meat than bone, providing additional servings, generally at a lower cost per-pound.

With some simple know-how, cutting-up a chicken can be a very fast and simple job. Whole chicken can be cut into serving pieces in less than 10 minutes. A chicken breast can be boned in even less time. Plan to divide, package and freeze chicken pieces to suit your needs, combining convenience and economy.

An important consideration when cutting-up any meat is cutlery. Knives are a lifetime investment. They pay for themselves in both time and money saved. An all-purpose 10- to 12-inch knife is ideal for slicing, chopping and cutting. A 6-inch, narrow boning knife is used to cut or bone chickens. A slicing knife with a thin flexible blade is used for carving. A heavy cleaver is great for mincing, chopping and flattening skinned chicken pieces. The most important factor in cutlery is sharpness. Whatever the quality of the knife, if it is not sharp, it will not perform the function it is intended for. Keep your knives sharp by using a steel, a sharpening stone or by having them professionally sharpened on a regular basis.

How to Cut-Up a Chicken

1/Place chicken on side. Holding wing, move it back and forth until joint connecting it to body pops up. Cut behind joint, moving knife under wing and cutting at an angle to remove it. Remove wing-tip section, if desired. Repeat to remove second wing.

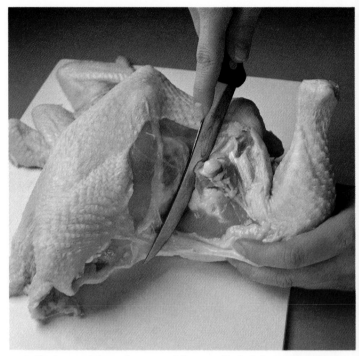

2/Place chicken breast-side up. Pull 1 leg away from body. Cut through top skin and flesh. Place your fingers under thigh and press up until hip joint pops up and separates from body. Cut leg-thigh section away from bird. Repeat to remove second leg-thigh section.

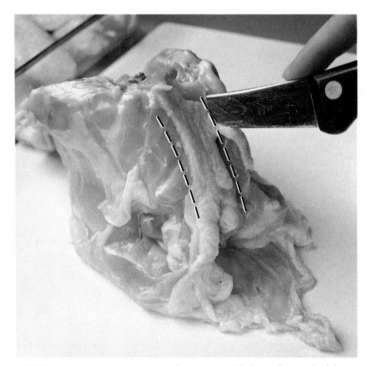

5/To remove upper back, turn chicken breast-side down. Using a sawing motion, cut along both sides of spinal column, completely removing it from chicken.

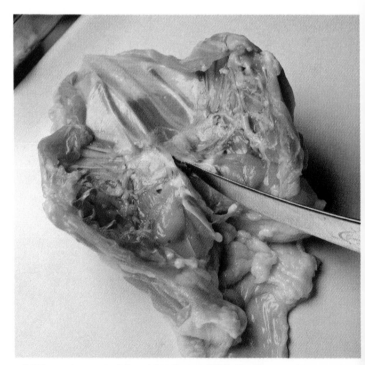

6/Place breast skin-side down. With knife, cut through white cartilage at neck-end of *keel* or breast bone.

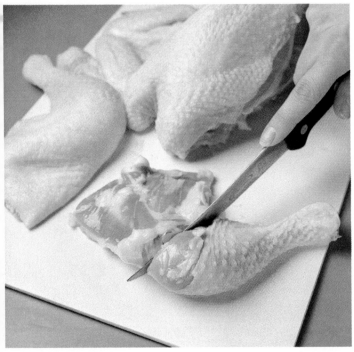

3/To separate thigh from leg, if desired, bend piece to locate knee joint. Place skin-side down. Cut through knee joint on each piece.

4/To remove lower back, cut between breast and back, slanting knife, until reaching rib bones. Break piece away from chicken through spinal column.

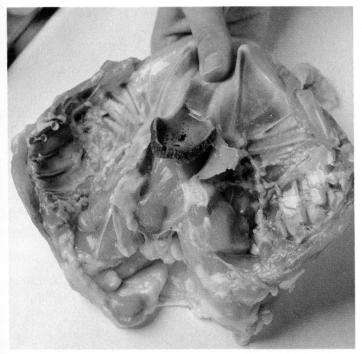

7/Bend breast back, exposing end of keel bone. Loosen keel bone by running thumb or index finger around both sides of the bone. Pull out keel bone.

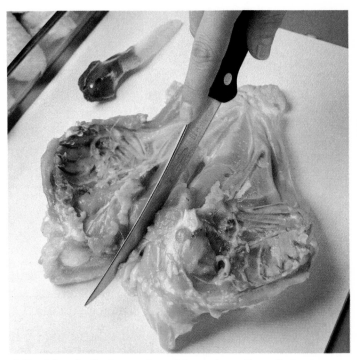

8/Position knife in center of breast section. Cut completely through center.

11

How to Bone a Chicken Breast

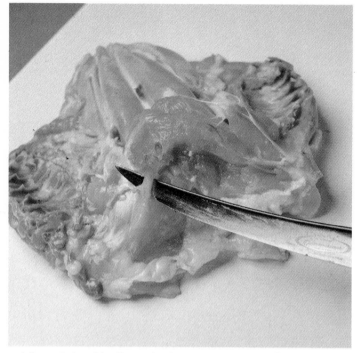

1/Insert tip of knife under long narrow bone. Completely remove this bone. Repeat on other side.

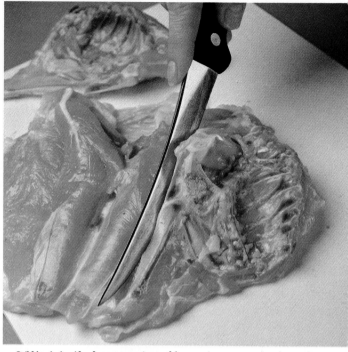

2/Work knife from center of breast area under long bone and rib section. Separate meat from rib cage. Repeat for other side.

How to Bone a Chicken Breast

1/To remove keel bone, place breast skin-side down. With knife, cut through white cartilage at neck-end of keel bone. Bend breast back, exposing end of keel bone. Loosen keel bone by running thumb or index finger around both sides of the bone. Pull out keel bone. Refer to photos 6 and 7, pages 10 and 11.

2/Position wide portion of breast toward you. Working with 1 side of breast, insert tip of knife under long narrow bone. Completely remove this bone. Repeat on other side.

3/Work knife from center of breast area under long bone and rib section. Separate meat from rib cage. Turn breast and repeat for other half of rib cage.

4/If desired, remove white tendons on either side of breast and pull skin off.

How to Bone a Chicken-Breast Half

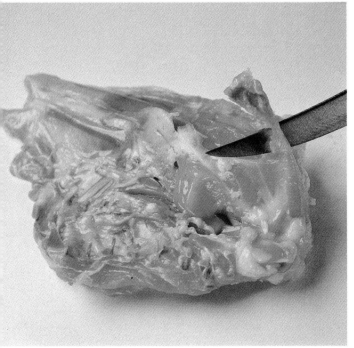

1/Insert tip of knife under long narrow bone. Completely remove this bone.

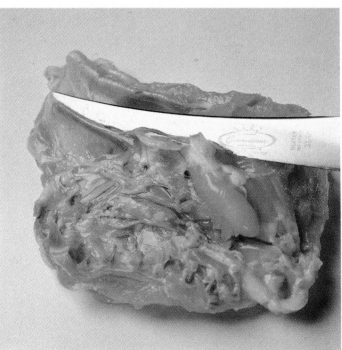

2/Work knife from center of breast half under long bone and rib section. Separate meat completely from rib cage.

How to Bone a Chicken-Breast Half

1/If not already removed by the butcher, remove keel bone by running thumb or finger under to loosen bone. Lift from breast.

2/Position wide portion of breast toward you. Insert tip of knife under long narrow bone. Completely remove this bone.

3/Work knife from center of breast half under long bone and rib section. Separate meat completely from rib cage.

How to Cut Chicken in Halves or Quarters

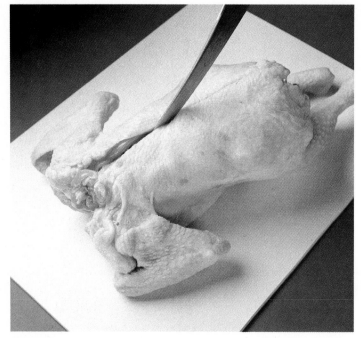

1/Place chicken breast-side down. Starting at neck-edge, cut down 1 side of backbone to tail.

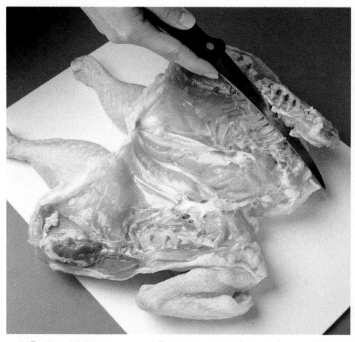

2/Pull chicken open. Remove backbone by cutting down other side of backbone from neck to tail. Reserve backbone for stock or soup.

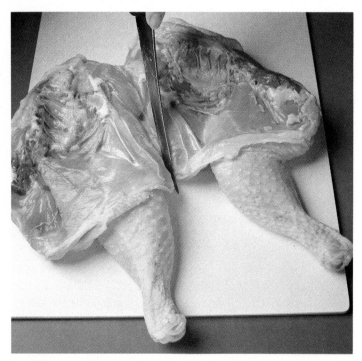

3/Remove keel bone by running thumb under keel. Lift out to remove as in boning breasts, page 12. Cut through center of breast.

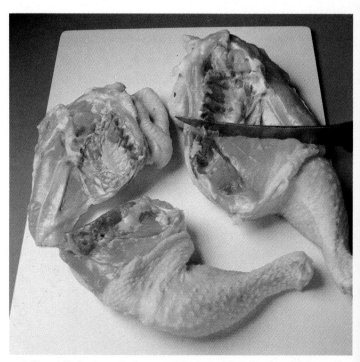

4/To split halves into quarters, position knife at base of rib section on a slight angle. Cut through piece just below ribs.

Appetizing Ways with Chicken

Great-tasting appetizers are small taste-tempting morsels that play a key role in entertaining. Chicken appetizers are adaptable to all types of occasions and are sure to please your guests. They go well with a variety of beverages and other good foods.

This chapter will become a favorite when planning an appetizer buffet for a crowd or when expecting a few friends for a casual visit. These recipes help make a delicious first course for a small dinner party or a light and quick snack.

Try serving a Jewish delight, Chopped Chicken Livers, on crisp lettuce leaves with thinly sliced dark bread. It's something you and your guests will remember.

To add extra dimension and interest to a buffet-party menu, choose Mustard-Honey Mini-Drumsticks or Spiced Chicken Wings. Both disappear quickly, so always make plenty. They are inexpensive and can be prepared well ahead of guests' arrival.

When you want something out of the ordinary, serve flaky, light Puffy Tarts. They are incredibly good and easy to prepare. You don't even have to make pastry. Best of all, you can make them ahead. They go from freezer to oven and on to your guests in a matter of minutes.

In this chapter you will find specially flavored pâtés and spreads. For easy serving, simply mound them on a small plate and surround with toast points, crackers or thin slices of tart apple. Another good choice is to serve slices of raw turnip or jicama. People like the crisp, crunchy texture and the low-calorie goodness.

You will enjoy planning menus using many of these appetizers. With these great recipes ready and waiting, why not plan a party today?

Housewarming Party
Skewered Chicken with Pineapple,
page 20
Puffy Tarts, page 22
Chicken-Liver Pâté, page 16
Fresh Apple & Turnip Slices
Assorted Cheeses
Crackers, Toasted Pita Wedges
Wine

15

Chicken-Liver Pâté   Photo on page 21.

Smooth, rich and elegant served with crackers or fruit.

1/2 lb. chicken livers
2 tablespoons vegetable oil
2 tablespoons butter
1 small onion, minced
1/2 teaspoon curry powder
1/4 teaspoon paprika
1 teaspoon salt
1/4 cup chicken stock

2 (8-oz.) pkgs. cream cheese,
   cut in 1-inch cubes, room temperature
1 cup toasted chopped walnuts
Crisp lettuce leaves
Paprika
Raw apple and vegetable slices or
   unsalted crackers

Drain livers; blot dry with paper towel. Remove and discard any connective tissue. Cut chicken livers in quarters. Heat oil in a wok or large heavy skillet over high heat. When very hot, add livers. Stir-fry livers 4 to 5 minutes or until crisp and browned, but still slightly pink in the center. Be sure not to overcook livers. Remove livers; set aside. Melt butter in wok or skillet over medium heat. Add onion; sauté 2 to 3 minutes or until tender. Stir in curry powder, 1/4 teaspoon paprika and salt. Add stock; stir to blend. Pour stock mixture into a blender or food processor fitted with a steel blade. Add stir-fried livers; process until smooth. In a medium bowl, combine liver mixture and cream cheese. Beat until smooth. Cover and refrigerate several hours. At serving time, stir in nuts. Line a small bowl with lettuce leaves. Spoon pâté into lettuce-lined bowl. Sprinkle lightly with paprika. Serve with apple and vegetable slices or unsalted crackers. Makes 3 cups.

Chopped Chicken Livers

A favorite and irresistibly good Jewish recipe.

1/4 cup butter or rendered chicken fat,
   page 8
1 large sweet onion, chopped
1 lb. chicken livers, cut in half, if large
2 hard-cooked eggs, cut in quarters
2 teaspoons salt
1/4 teaspoon coarsely ground pepper

Crisp lettuce leaves
Cracklings,
   if desired, page 8
Chopped or thinly sliced white radishes
Matzos, unsalted crackers or
   cocktail rye rounds

Lightly oil inside of a small bowl; set aside. Place butter or chicken fat in a large heavy skillet over medium heat. When butter or fat is hot, add onion. Sauté 2 to 3 minutes or until tender. Using a slotted spoon, transfer sautéed onion to a food processor fitted with a steel blade or a chopping bowl. Add 1/4 of the chicken livers to remaining butter or fat in skillet. Sauté 2 to 3 minutes or until lightly browned. Repeat with remaining chicken livers. Place browned livers in food processor or chopping bowl. Add eggs and any remaining fat from skillet to livers. If using a food processor, process until finely chopped, not pureed. If using a chopping bowl, finely chop ingredients. Season with salt and pepper. Place in oiled bowl. Cover and refrigerate several hours to blend flavors. Arrange lettuce on a small plate. Unmold liver mixture onto center of lettuce. Sprinkle with cracklings, if desired, and surround with radishes. Serve with matzos, unsalted crackers or cocktail rye rounds. Makes 8 appetizer servings.

Smoked-Turkey Pâté

A tasty pâté, similar to those sold in Paris food shops.

1/2 cup chopped walnuts
1 cup diced cooked turkey
2 tablespoons soft butter
1/2 teaspoon hickory-smoked salt

1 tablespoon Cognac or brandy
Raw apple and vegetable slices or
   unsalted crackers

In a blender or a food processor fitted with a steel blade, combine walnuts and turkey. Process until finely ground. Add butter, salt and liquor. Process until blended. Place in a small bowl. Cover and refrigerate several hours. Serve with apple and vegetable slices or unsalted crackers. Makes 1-1/2 cups.

Chicken & Pineapple Spread   *Photo on page 21.*

Make this delicious mixture with leftover roast chicken or turkey.

1 (8-oz.) can crushed pineapple
   in natural juices
2 cups diced cooked chicken or turkey
1/2 cup coarsely chopped walnuts

1/4 cup mayonnaise
1 teaspoon cider vinegar
Salt and coarsely ground pepper to taste
Crackers or Belgian endive, if desired

Drain pineapple well, reserving juice for another use; set aside. Place chicken or turkey in a food processor fitted with a steel blade. Process until finely minced. Or, finely chop meat in a chopping bowl. Add pineapple, nuts, mayonnaise and vinegar. Process or stir until blended. Season with salt and pepper. Serve with crackers, or core and stuff individual leaves of Belgian endive, if desired. Makes about 3 cups.

Variation

Substitute 1 (8-ounce) can chopped mango or mandarin-orange segments for crushed pineapple.

Rumaki

Even people who say they don't like chicken livers will like this appetizer.

1/2 cup soy sauce
1/2 cup dry sherry
1/2 cup packed light-brown sugar
1 lb. chicken livers, about 16 large livers

8 water chestnuts, cut in halves
8 bacon slices, cut in halves
1/2 cup water

In a large bowl, combine soy sauce, sherry and sugar. Add livers, stirring to coat well. Cover and refrigerate several hours, stirring occasionally. Place broiler rack 6 inches below heat. Preheat broiler to high. Drain livers; blot dry with paper towel. Remove and discard any connective tissue. Wrap a liver around a water-chestnut half. Wrap half a bacon slice around liver. Secure with a wooden pick. Repeat with remaining livers, water chestnuts and bacon. Place prepared livers in a single layer on a rack in a shallow roasting pan. Pour water in pan. Broil 10 minutes or until bacon is crisp, turning often. Serve hot. Makes 16 appetizer servings.

Rumaki can be prepared up to 1 hour ahead. Broil just before serving.

Chinese Chicken Mini-Drumsticks

A great appetizer to make ahead and refrigerate or freeze. Reheat to serve.

24 mini-drumsticks
1/2 cup soy sauce
1/2 cup dry sherry
1 garlic clove, crushed
1 (1-inch) cube gingerroot, crushed or
   1 teaspoon ground ginger
1 cup all-purpose flour

1/2 teaspoon salt
1 teaspoon coarsely ground pepper
2 eggs
1 tablespoon water
1 cup fine dry breadcrumbs
Oil for deep-frying

Place prepared drumsticks in a large plastic bag. In a small bowl, combine soy sauce, sherry, garlic and ginger. Pour soy-sauce mixture over drumsticks. Seal bag tightly and place in a large bowl. Refrigerate several hours or overnight. To prepare, drain drumsticks, reserving marinade. Discard garlic and gingerroot. In a pie plate, combine flour, salt and pepper. In a small bowl, beat eggs and water. Spread breadcrumbs in a second pie plate. Roll ball of meat, not bone, in flour mixture; shake off excess. Dip meat in egg mixture; drain over bowl. Roll meat in breadcrumbs. Press breadcrumbs evenly onto meat. Place coated chicken on a wire rack. Repeat with remaining drumsticks. Let stand 20 to 30 minutes at room temperature to firm coating. Preheat oven to 350F (175C). In a wok or deep skillet, pour oil to a 1-1/2-inch depth. Heat oil to 375F (190C). Fry 5 or 6 prepared drumsticks in hot oil 1 to 2 minutes or until evenly browned, turning with tongs as necessary. Drain on paper towel. Repeat with remaining drumsticks. Place drumsticks in a single layer in a 13" x 9" baking dish. Bake 10 to 12 minutes. Serve hot or at room temperature. To freeze for later use, place cooked drumsticks in a single layer on a baking sheet or foil. Place in freezer until firm. Remove from freezer; place in a plastic bag. Return to freezer and store up to 1 month. To serve, reheat in 350F (175C) oven 25 minutes. Makes 24 appetizer servings.

Mustard-Honey Mini-Drumsticks

Spicy-sweet chicken on a stick; fun to eat and easy to make ahead.

16 mini-drumsticks
1/2 cup dry white wine or vermouth
1 tablespoon white-wine vinegar
2 garlic cloves, crushed
1 (2-inch) cube gingerroot, crushed or
   2 teaspoons ground ginger
1/4 teaspoon dried leaf thyme

1/4 teaspoon dried leaf marjoram
1/4 teaspoon dried red-pepper flakes
1/4 cup honey
1 cup Dijon-style mustard
2 cups fine dry whole-wheat breadcrumbs
Oil for deep-frying

Fill a steamer pot or wok with a steamer rack with water to 1 inch below rack. Bring water to a boil. Place drumsticks on rack. Cover and steam 10 to 12 minutes. Remove and cool; set aside. In a small saucepan, combine wine or vermouth, vinegar, garlic, ginger, thyme, marjoram and red-pepper flakes. Bring to a boil over medium heat. Reduce heat and simmer until reduced to 2 tablespoons, about 5 minutes. Strain through a fine sieve into another small saucepan. Stir in honey and mustard. Cook over low heat 2 minutes; cool slightly. Spread breadcrumbs in a pie plate. Dip meaty portion of a drumstick into honey mixture; drain over saucepan. Roll meat in breadcrumbs. Press breadcrumbs evenly onto meat. Place coated chicken on a wire rack. Repeat with remaining chicken drumsticks. Let stand 20 to 30 minutes at room temperature to firm coating. In a wok or deep skillet, pour oil to a 1-1/2-inch depth. Heat oil to 375F (190C). Fry 5 or 6 prepared drumsticks in hot oil 1-1/2 minutes or until evenly browned. Drain on paper towel. Repeat with remaining drumsticks. Serve hot or warm. Makes 16 appetizer servings.

How to Make Mini-Drumsticks

1/Cut through skin and cartilage connecting 2 larger wing sections.

2/Holding larger wing portion, push meat and skin to top of bone. Shape in a ball.

How to Make Mini-Drumsticks

1/Hold 1 wing between both hands, flex 2 larger sections back and forth to break cartilage connecting mini-drumstick and 2-part wing-tip section.

2/Use a knife or cleaver to cut through skin and cartilage connecting the 2 larger sections. Reserve 2-part wing-tip section for stock or soup.

3/Use a small knife to cut cartilage loose from cut-end of mini-drumstick. Holding drumstick in 1 hand, push meat and skin to top of bone. Shape into a compact ball.

Buffet-Party Chicken   *Photo opposite.*

Finger-food with an exciting blend of flavors.

12 chicken thighs, boned, cut in
   1-inch pieces, page 47, steps 1 and 2
3 large garlic cloves, crushed
1/4 cup lemon juice
1 teaspoon salt
Coarsely ground pepper to taste

1/2 teaspoon Italian herb seasoning
2 tablespoons olive oil
3/4 cup freshly grated Parmesan cheese
   (2-1/4 oz.)
1/4 cup minced parsley

Preheat oven to 350F (175C). Rub each chicken piece with garlic. Place chicken, skin-side up, in a single layer in a 13" x 9" baking dish. Season chicken with lemon juice, salt, pepper and herb seasoning. Drizzle oil over chicken. Bake 25 to 30 minutes. Place broiler rack 6 inches below heat. Preheat broiler to high. Turn chicken pieces skin-side down. Sprinkle chicken with 1/4 cup cheese. Broil chicken 3 to 4 minutes. Turn chicken skin-side up. Sprinkle chicken with remaining 1/2 cup cheese. Broil chicken 3 to 4 minutes or until crisp. Place chicken on a platter. Sprinkle with parsley. Let stand 10 to 15 minutes before serving. Serve with wooden picks. Makes 12 to 14 appetizer servings.

Skewered Chicken with Pineapple

Equally delicious as an appetizer or main course.

8 chicken thighs, boned,
   page 47, steps 1 and 2
Salt and coarsely ground pepper to taste
1 (15-1/4-oz.) can pineapple chunks
   in heavy syrup

1/2 cup soy sauce
1/2 cup honey
2 tablespoons ketchup
1 garlic clove, minced

Preheat oven to 350F (175C). Cut across each thigh, making 3 nearly equal pieces. Place chicken, skin-side up, in a 13" x 9" baking dish. Season with salt and pepper. Drain pineapple chunks, reserving syrup. In a small bowl, combine pineapple syrup, soy sauce, honey, ketchup and garlic. Blend well; pour mixture over chicken. Cover tightly with foil. Bake 20 minutes, turning chicken occasionally and basting with sauce. Add pineapple chunks. Bake, uncovered, 10 minutes or until tender. On a small skewer, place 3 chicken pieces and 2 or 3 pineapple chunks. Repeat with remaining chicken and pineapple chunks. Serve as an appetizer or main course over seasoned rice. Makes 8 appetizer servings or 4 entree servings.

Variation

Substitute 1 (15-1/4-ounce) can mandarin-orange segments in syrup for pineapple.

Front, left to right: Buffet-Party Chicken, page 20; Miniature Chicken Strudels, page 23; center, Chicken-Liver Pâté, page 16; back, Chicken & Pineapple Spread, page 17.

Puffy Tarts

Frozen puff pastry and easy fillings let you put these appetizers together in minutes.

Florentine-Style Filling or
  Chicken-Mushroom Filling, see below

1 (17-1/4-oz.) pkg. frozen puff pastry
1 egg white, slightly beaten

Florentine-Style Filling:
2 tablespoons butter
1 (10-oz.) pkg. frozen chopped spinach
  or broccoli, thawed, drained
1/2 cup shredded Cheddar or
  Swiss cheese (2 oz.)

1/4 teaspoon salt
1 egg yolk
1/4 cup minced cooked ham
1 cup minced cooked chicken or turkey

Chicken-Mushroom Filling:
2 tablespoons butter
1 medium onion, finely chopped
1 cup minced cooked chicken or turkey
1 egg yolk, slightly beaten
1 (3-oz.) can chopped mushrooms,
  drained

1/4 cup pimiento-stuffed olives,
  chopped
1/2 cup shredded Monterey Jack
  or Cheddar cheese (2 oz.)
1/4 teaspoon salt
1/8 teaspoon coarsely ground pepper

Prepare choice of filling. Thaw puff-pastry sheets at room temperature 20 minutes or until pliable but still cold. On a lightly floured surface, roll a pastry sheet to a 13-inch square. Divide square into 4 equal parts. Repeat with second sheet. Divide filling equally between 8 pastry squares, leaving a 1 inch border on all sides of each square. Brush borders generously with egg white. Fold squares diagonally in half to form triangles. Press edges firmly together. Press sealed edges with a fork to seal securely. Brush tops with egg white. Pierce center of each tart with a knife for steam to escape. Arrange tarts 1 inch apart on ungreased baking sheets. Place in freezer while oven heats. Preheat oven to 450F (230C). When ready to bake, reduce oven temperature to 400F (205C). Transfer frozen tarts to room-temperature ungreased baking sheets. Cold metal will retard crisping of pastry. Bake 20 minutes or until puffed and golden brown. Serve hot or at room temperature. Tarts can be completely frozen on baking sheets. Then, remove and wrap individually in freezer wrap. Store up to 3 weeks in freezer. To serve, extend baking time to 30 minutes for frozen tarts. Makes 8 appetizer servings.

Florentine-Style Filling:
Melt butter in a small skillet. Add spinach or broccoli; sauté 2 minutes. In a medium bowl, combine sautéed spinach or broccoli, cheese, salt and egg yolk. Cover and refrigerate until cold. Stir in ham and chicken or turkey. Cover and refrigerate until ready to use.

Chicken-Mushroom Filling:
Melt butter in a small skillet over medium heat. Add onion; sauté 2 to 3 minutes or until tender. Cool slightly. In a medium bowl, stir together sautéed onion, chicken or turkey, egg yolk, mushrooms, olives, cheese, salt and pepper. Cover and refrigerate until ready to use.

Variation
Substitute 4 patty shells for frozen puff pastry. Roll each patty shell into a 6'' x 12'' rectangle. Cut in half, making 8 (6-inch) squares. Follow stuffing instructions as given above.

1/Spoon chicken mixture along 1 short side of buttered filo sheets, making a strip of filling about 1 inch wide.

2/Using a knife, score top of roll crosswise, making cuts about 1/4 inch deep and 1 inch apart.

Miniature Chicken Strudels   *Photo on page 21.*

These flavorful appetizers are made with buttery filo-pastry sheets.

1 (10-oz.) pkg. frozen chopped spinach, thawed
1-1/2 cups diced cooked chicken or turkey
1 cup ricotta cheese (8 oz.)
2 tablespoons Parmesan cheese
1 egg yolk

1/2 teaspoon salt
1/4 teaspoon coarsely ground pepper
16 filo-pastry or strudel sheets, thawed
1/2 cup butter, melted
1 cup Italian-seasoned breadcrumbs

Preheat oven to 375F (190C). Squeeze spinach to remove all moisture. In a medium bowl, combine spinach, chicken or turkey, cheeses, egg yolk, salt and pepper. Blend well; set aside. Unroll filo or strudel sheets. Place 1 sheet on a flat surface. Cover remaining sheets with plastic wrap or a slightly damp kitchen towel to prevent sheets from drying. Brush 1 sheet with melted butter. Sprinkle with 1 tablespoon breadcrumbs. Place another sheet over the first. Brush with melted butter. Sprinkle with 1 tablespoon breadcrumbs. Repeat, using 2 more sheets. Spoon 1/4 of the chicken mixture along 1 short side of stacked buttered sheets, making a strip of filling about 1 inch wide. Roll up sheets to enclose filling; tuck ends under. Using a knife, score top of roll crosswise, making cuts about 1/4 inch deep and 1 inch apart. Brush roll with melted butter. Using a spatula, place roll, seam-side down, on a baking sheet. Cover loosely with plastic wrap or a slightly damp kitchen towel. Repeat using remaining ingredients to make a total of 4 rolls. Remove plastic wrap or kitchen towel. Bake strudels 15 minutes or until golden brown. Slice into serving pieces along markings. Serve hot. Filled rolls can be frozen before baking. Place each roll on a flat surface in freezer until firm. Then, wrap individually in plastic wrap. Store in freezer up to 2 months. Bake frozen rolls 20 to 25 minutes. Makes about 48 appetizers.

Crunchy Chicken Nuggets

These crunchy appetizers disappear like magic at any festive gathering.

1 (12-oz.) jar dry-roasted mixed nuts
1/4 cup cornstarch
1 teaspoon salt
1/2 teaspoon sugar
2 tablespoons dry sherry

2 egg whites
8 chicken-breast halves, boned,
   skinned, cut in 1-inch pieces
Oil for deep-frying

Place nuts in a blender or food processor fitted with a steel blade. Process until finely ground. Spread ground nuts on waxed paper; set aside. In a small bowl, combine cornstarch, salt and sugar. Stir in sherry. In a medium bowl, beat egg whites until foamy. Stir in cornstarch mixture. Dip each chicken piece in egg-white mixture. Roll each piece in ground nuts. Press nuts evenly onto pieces. Place coated chicken on a wire rack. Let stand 20 to 30 minutes at room temperature to firm coating. In a wok or deep skillet, pour oil to a 1-1/2-inch depth. Heat oil to 375F (190C). Fry 6 to 8 chicken pieces in hot oil 1 minute or until golden brown. Drain on paper towel. Repeat with remaining pieces. Serve warm with wooden picks. Makes about 40 pieces.

Spiced Chicken Wings

Just the right blend of spices makes these chicken wings a tasty treat.

1 teaspoon salt
1/2 teaspoon coarsely ground pepper
1/4 teaspoon ground allspice
1/4 teaspoon ground ginger

1 teaspoon ground nutmeg
1/4 teaspoon ground cloves
12 chicken wings

Preheat oven to 400F (205C). Lightly oil an 11'' x 7'' baking dish. In a small bowl, combine salt, pepper, allspice, ginger, nutmeg and cloves; set aside. Remove wing-tip section by cutting through wing joint which was farthest from chicken body; reserve wing-tips for soup or stock. Cut 2-part wing pieces apart by cutting through remaining joint. Place wing pieces in a single layer in oiled baking dish. Bake 15 minutes. Turn each piece over. Sprinkle wing pieces evenly with salt mixture. Bake 35 to 40 minutes or until juices run clear when pierced with a fork. Serve hot or at room temperature. Makes 24 appetizer servings.

Chicken-Lettuce Rolls

Your weight-watching friends will love you for this one.

1 (8-oz.) bottle Thousand-Island or
   Russian salad dressing
24 strips cooked chicken or turkey,
   1/4 inch thick and 1/2 inch long

24 crisp lettuce leaves

Pour dressing into a small bowl. Dip each meat strip in dressing; drain over bowl. Roll each strip in a lettuce leaf or half of a lettuce leaf. Secure with a wooden pick. Arrange on a platter. Cover and refrigerate until ready to serve. Makes 24 appetizer servings.

Best of All Soups & Stews

We all remember Grandma's steamy hot chicken soup. It's a favorite when the weather is cold or when you are not feeling well. Like Grandma's soups, these are not meant to be served in thin china cups. These soups are hearty and filling. All make totally satisfying meals, the kind you enjoy coming home to after a hard day's work. Many can be made ahead, adding convenience and flexibility to meal planning.

You may think something as good as homemade soup would be difficult to prepare, but it isn't. Soup-making requires very little work and few skills. An all-time favorite is New-Fashioned Chicken Soup. It offers several variations for those who enjoy a vegetable or noodle soup. You will like it because there's no fat floating on the surface. Chicken has a fatty skin, so I remove it before making soup. I also skim any fat from the soup before it is served, leaving only the goodness for my guests to enjoy.

Some soups are easy adaptations of longtime favorites. Each is internationally known for its unique qualities and its pleasurable combination of ingredients. For a treat from the Far East, try Oriental Chicken Soup accented with Chinese vegetables. From Scotland, you will find the classic Cock-a-leekie—Chicken & Leek Soup.

For your summer dining, switch to cold soup. Serve the elegant, cold creamy Singhalese Soup. It's a tasty combination of chicken or turkey and tart apple seasoned with curry and chili powder.

Chicken is also a favorite in savory stews. Brunswick Stew is a hearty winter-type dish filled with a variety of vegetables and plenty of chicken. Even the biggest appetite will be truly satisfied.

Make your kitchen the home of satisfying soups. Many can be made more quickly with canned broth; however, they are doubly good when made with homemade stock. No matter how you choose to make chicken soup, it is sure to be a family favorite.

Après-Ski Dinner
Brunswick Stew over Steaming Rice,
page 31
Parmesan-Cheese Rolls
Creamy Butterscotch Pudding
Hot Beverages

Basic Chicken Stock

This blend of ingredients produces a mild, richly flavored stock.

2 to 3 lbs. chicken backs,
   wing-tips and necks
Water
2 medium onions, cut in quarters
1 garlic clove, unpeeled
2 celery stalks, cut in 2-inch pieces
2 to 3 parsley sprigs
1 (1-inch) strip lemon peel

1/2 cup mushroom stems or
   2 to 3 large mushrooms,
   cut in quarters
1 cup dry white wine
1/4 teaspoon dried leaf thyme
1/4 teaspoon dried leaf rosemary
2 teaspoons salt
4 to 6 peppercorns

Remove skin from neck and back pieces; discard. Place chicken in a large pot. Add water to within 3 inches of rim. Bring to a boil over high heat. Skim foam from surface until surface is clear. Reduce heat and add remaining ingredients. Simmer, partially covered, 3 to 4 hours. To cool stock quickly, fill your sink half full with cold water. Place pot of stock in water. When cooled, lift fat from surface and discard. Strain stock through a colander into a large bowl. Discard chicken and vegetables. Or, strain hot stock, discarding solids. Refrigerate stock until fat congeals on surface. Lift fat from surface; discard fat. Ladle strained stock into storage jars or other containers. Cover and refrigerate or freeze until ready to use. Store stock in refrigerator up to 2 days. To freeze, fill containers no more than 3/4 full. Cover and seal containers air-tight. Store in freezer up to 3 months. Before using refrigerated or frozen stock, bring to a full boil. Makes 3 to 4 quarts.

Variation

For a clear stock, strain again through a fine sieve lined with cheesecloth. Cover and refrigerate until fat congeals on the surface. Lift fat from surface; discard. The stock will have jellied. Place stock in a large pot. Bring to a full boil. Simmer until reduced by half, if desired. The result will be a concentrated, very flavorful stock.

Brown Chicken Stock

A rich, deep-brown stock, especially flavorful for soups and stews.

4 lbs. chicken wings and backs
Salt and coarsely ground pepper to taste
1 large onion, chopped
1 garlic clove, minced
1/4 to 1/2 cup mushroom stems or
   pieces, chopped

1 cup dry white wine
1 qt. (4 cups) water
1 bay leaf
3 parsley sprigs
1 large tomato, chopped
Leafy celery tops, if desired

Cut wings in half at joint. Cut back pieces in half. Place in a deep heavy pot over medium heat. Cook, stirring frequently, 10 minutes. Chicken will make its own fat. Season with salt and pepper. Add onion, garlic and mushrooms. Cook, stirring frequently, until chicken is browned. Add wine, water, bay leaf, parsley, tomato and celery tops, if desired. Bring to a boil. Cover and reduce heat. Simmer about 1-1/2 hours, stirring frequently. Remove from heat and cool slightly. Strain through a fine sieve; discard solids. Refrigerate stock until fat congeals on surface. Lift fat from surface; discard. Reheat stock. Cool slightly. Ladle stock into storage containers. Cover and refrigerate or freeze until ready to use. Store stock in refrigerator up to 2 days. To freeze, fill containers no more than 3/4 full. Cover and seal containers air-tight. Store in freezer up to 3 months. Before using refrigerated or frozen stock, bring to a full boil. Makes about 3 cups.

Poached Chicken & Rich Stock

Dinner plus stock—all in 1 pot.

2 (3- to 3-1/2-lb.) chickens, cut-up
2 chicken-breast halves, if desired
Water
2 celery stalks
1 large red onion, chopped
1/2 cup chopped mushroom stems or pieces
2 garlic cloves
2 to 3 parsley sprigs

1 teaspoon dried leaf thyme
1 bay leaf
2 teaspoons salt
1 teaspoon coarsely ground pepper
1 cup dry white wine or vermouth
Back, neck and wing-tips from
    a cut-up chicken, if desired

Place chickens and breast halves, if desired, in a large pot. Cover with water to within 3 inches of rim. Bring to a full boil over high heat. Skim foam from surface until surface is clear. Add celery, onion, mushrooms, garlic, parsley, thyme, bay leaf, salt and pepper. Reduce heat and simmer uncovered. Allow 25 minutes for white meat, 35 minutes for dark meat. Remove chicken when tender enough to remove meat easily from bones. Remove skin and bones from chicken and reserve. Serve chicken hot with a seasoned sauce. Or, cut chicken into bite-size pieces and place in a bowl. Cover with a small amount of stock. Cover and refrigerate until ready to use. Return skin and bones to stock. Add wine or vermouth and chicken back, neck and wing-tips, if desired. Add water to within 3 inches of rim. Cover and simmer over low heat 1 to 1-1/2 hours. Cool slightly. Strain stock into a large bowl. Discard bones, skin and vegetables. Refrigerate stock until fat congeals on surface. Lift fat from surface; discard. Ladle jellied stock into storage jars or other containers. Cover and refrigerate or freeze until ready to use. Store stock in refrigerator up to 2 days. To freeze, fill containers no more than 3/4 full. Cover and seal containers air-tight. Store in freezer up to 3 months. Reheat refrigerated or thawed frozen stock to a full boil before using. Makes about 8-1/2 cups stock and 3 cups poached chicken.

Variation

Substitute 1 to 2 cups orange juice for an equal part of water when poaching chicken. Omit the parsley and thyme. Use this orange-poached chicken in salads or sandwich fillings.

Mulligatawny Soup

This soup came to England via India and has remained popular ever since.

6 tablespoons butter
2 celery stalks, thinly sliced
1 medium onion, chopped
1 tart cooking apple, peeled, chopped
2 medium carrots, thinly sliced
1 tablespoon curry powder
1 tablespoon all-purpose flour

1-1/2 qts. (6 cups) hot chicken stock
1 cup diced cooked chicken
1/2 cup whipping cream
1/4 cup shredded coconut, if desired
Salt to taste
3 cups hot cooked rice
Crusty French bread, if desired

Melt butter in a large heavy pot over low heat. Add celery, onion, apple and carrots. Cook 10 minutes or until tender, stirring frequently. Stir in curry powder and flour. Cook 30 seconds, stirring constantly. Slowly add stock, stirring constantly. Partially cover pot. Simmer 5 minutes. Stir in chicken, cream and coconut, if desired. Season with salt. Cook 5 minutes to heat through. Place 1/2 cup hot rice in each of 6 deep soup bowls. Ladle soup over rice with equal amounts of chicken and vegetables. Serve hot with French bread, if desired. Makes 6 servings.

How to Make Old-Time Chicken Stew & Dumplings

1/Drop dumpling batter by tablespoonfuls over surface of hot stock.

2/To serve, spoon chicken, vegetables and some stock into large soup bowls.

Creamed Turkey-Almond Soup

Toasted nuts add both eye and taste appeal.

1 cooked turkey carcass
6 cups water
1 cup coarsely chopped celery
1/2 cup sliced onion
1/2 cup coarsely chopped carrots
1 bay leaf
1 teaspoon salt
6 peppercorns
1 cup half and half or plain yogurt

1 cup milk
1/2 cup chopped cooked artichoke hearts,
   if desired
3 tablespoons butter
3 tablespoons all-purpose flour
1/2 cup chopped almonds, if desired
2 tablespoons chopped pimiento,
   if desired
Toasted slivered almonds for garnish

Break turkey carcass into small pieces. Place carcass pieces in a large pot or Dutch oven. Add water, celery, onion, carrots, bay leaf, salt and peppercorns. Simmer over medium heat, partially covered, about 1-1/2 hours; remove from heat. Strain through a fine sieve or several layers of cheesecloth into a clean pot. Add half and half or yogurt, milk and artichoke hearts, if desired, to stock. Simmer, but do not boil. In a small bowl, cream butter and flour together. Add flour mixture to stock. Cook, stirring constantly, until thickened and smooth. Stir in 1/2 cup almonds and pimiento, if desired. Serve in deep soup bowls garnished with almonds. Makes 6 to 8 servings.

Old-Time Chicken Stew & Dumplings

This old-fashioned dish is just what you need for today's busy lifestyle.

4 chicken-breast halves, skinned
2 qts. (8 cups) chicken stock or
   3 (10-1/2-oz.) cans condensed chicken
   broth with 4 cans water

1 (1-lb.) pkg. frozen mixed vegetables,
   broken apart
Salt and coarsely ground pepper to taste
Cornmeal Dumplings or Herb Dumplings,
   see below

Cornmeal Dumplings:
1-1/2 cups self-rising cornmeal baking mix
   or muffin mix
1/2 teaspoon chili powder

1 egg
2/3 cup milk

Herb Dumplings:
1-3/4 cups sifted all-purpose flour
1 tablespoon baking powder
1/2 teaspoon salt
2 tablespoons minced parsley
2 tablespoons minced chives

1/4 teaspoon dried leaf thyme
1/4 teaspoon dried leaf marjoram
1 egg
2/3 cup milk

Remove any excess fat from chicken; discard. In a large pot or Dutch oven, combine stock or broth and water. Add chicken breasts. Bring to a boil over medium heat. Skim foam from surface until surface is clear. Reduce heat and simmer 30 minutes or until chicken is tender. Remove from heat. Using tongs or a slotted spoon, remove chicken breasts. Cool slightly. Pull meat from bones in bite-size strips; discard bones. Bring stock or broth to a boil. Add chicken strips and mixed vegetables. Season to taste with salt and pepper. Cover and simmer while preparing Cornmeal-Dumpling batter or Herb-Dumpling batter. Bring liquid to a full boil. Drop dumpling batter by tablespoons over surface. Cover and steam 8 minutes. Remove cover and cook 10 minutes or until dumplings are cooked through. To serve, spoon chicken, vegetables and some stock into large soup bowls. Top each serving with dumplings. Makes 6 to 8 servings.

Cornmeal Dumplings:
In a medium bowl, combine cornmeal mix and chili powder. Make a well in center of dry ingredients. Break egg into well. Add milk; with a fork, beat egg into milk. Stir cornmeal mixture into egg mixture to form a stiff batter. Add to stew according to recipe directions.

Herb Dumplings:
In a medium bowl, combine flour, baking powder, salt, parsley, chives, thyme and marjoram. In a small bowl, beat egg with milk until blended. Add egg mixture to flour mixture to form a stiff batter. Add to stew according to recipe directions.

Don't let poultry stand at room temperature for more than 2 or 3 hours—that includes preparation, storage and serving times. Food may not be safe to eat if held longer than this at temperatures at which bacteria grow rapidly.

Simply Delicious Turkey-Noodle Supper

A sensational supper dish which takes less than 15 minutes to prepare.

6 cups water
1 envelope dry onion-soup mix
1 (10-1/2-oz.) can condensed
  chicken broth
1 (10-1/2-oz.) can condensed cream of
  chicken soup

1 to 1-1/2 cups diced cooked turkey or
  chicken
1 (8-oz.) pkg. curly noodles
Grated Parmesan cheese

In a large pot, bring water to a boil over high heat. Stir in soup mix. Add broth and cream of chicken soup. Stir in turkey or chicken. Reduce heat and simmer 5 minutes. Bring to a full boil. Add noodles slowly, so water continues to boil. Boil 8 minutes or until noodles are tender. Serve in large soup bowls. Sprinkle servings with Parmesan cheese. Makes 4 servings.

After-Work Chicken

For busy cooks, this chicken is prepared using the versatile electric slow-cooking pot.

1 (2-1/2- to 3-lb.) chicken, cut-up
1 (1-lb.) can Italian cooking sauce,
  such as Ragú
1/4 cup water
1 tablespoon red-wine vinegar
Salt to taste
1/4 teaspoon coarsely ground pepper

Dash hot-pepper sauce
1 (1-lb.) can chick peas or
  white kidney beans, drained
1 (4-oz.) can sliced or
  chopped mushrooms, drained
8 to 10 pitted black olives, sliced
Grated Parmesan cheese

Place chicken pieces in a slow-cooking pot. In a small bowl, combine Italian cooking sauce, water and vinegar. Season with salt, pepper and hot-pepper sauce. Pour sauce mixture over chicken. Cover pot. Cook on low 6 to 8 hours. Stir in chick peas or beans, mushrooms and olives. Cover and cook about 30 minutes. Serve in large soup bowls. Sprinkle each serving with grated cheese. Makes 4 servings.

Curried Chicken Soup

Just a touch of curry makes this my favorite winter soup.

2 tablespoons butter
1 tablespoon all-purpose flour
1 teaspoon curry powder
1 qt. (4 cups) hot chicken stock
2 to 2-1/2 cups coarsely chopped
  cooked chicken

1/2 teaspoon salt
1/4 teaspoon coarsely ground pepper
1/2 cup bulgur or quick-cooking rice,
  if desired
1/2 cup plain yogurt or whipping cream

Melt butter in a large pot over low heat. Add flour and curry powder. Stir until blended. Add 2 cups stock; stir rapidly with a whisk until smooth. Slowly pour in remaining 2 cups stock. Add chicken, salt, pepper and bulgur or rice, if desired. Bring to a boil. In a small bowl, combine yogurt or cream and 1/2 cup simmering soup. Stir yogurt or cream mixture into remaining soup. Stir to blend. Heat until steaming, but do not boil. Serve hot. Makes 6 servings.

Brunswick Stew

Make ahead for a one-dish party meal; it's even better when reheated.

1/4 cup vegetable oil
2 (2-1/2- to 3-lb.) chickens,
  cut-up, skinned
2 tablespoons butter
2 medium onions, chopped
1 large green pepper, seeded, chopped
4 celery stalks, chopped
1 garlic clove, minced
2-1/2 cups chicken stock
2-1/2 cups water
1 (1-lb.) can stewed tomatoes
1 bay leaf

1 (10-oz.) pkg. frozen okra, broken apart
1 (10-oz.) pkg. frozen lima beans,
  broken apart
1 (10-oz.) pkg. frozen whole-kernel corn,
  broken apart
2 to 3 dashes hot-pepper sauce
1 teaspoon Worcestershire sauce
1 tablespoon cornstarch
1/4 cup water
Salt and coarsely ground black pepper
  to taste
Hot cooked rice

Heat oil in a deep heavy skillet over medium-high heat. Add as many chicken pieces as will fit in a single layer without crowding. Sauté, turning occasionally, 15 minutes or until lightly browned. Place browned chicken pieces in a large pot. Repeat until all pieces have been browned. Pour off oil; discard. Melt butter in skillet over low heat. Add onions, green pepper and celery. Sauté 3 to 4 minutes or until vegetables are crisp-tender. Stir in garlic; cook 30 seconds. Add sautéed vegetables, stock, 2-1/2 cups water, tomatoes, bay leaf and okra to chicken. Simmer over low heat 15 minutes. Add lima beans; continue to simmer 18 to 20 minutes or until all vegetables and chicken are tender. Using tongs or a slotted spoon, remove chicken pieces. Cool slightly. Pull chicken from bones in large pieces; discard bones. Return chicken to pot. Add corn, hot-pepper sauce and Worcestershire sauce. Simmer 5 minutes. In a small bowl, combine cornstarch and 1/4 cup water. Stir cornstarch mixture into simmering stew. Stir until thickened. Season with salt and black pepper. Serve hot over rice. Makes 10 to 12 servings.

Chicken & Leek Soup

Cock-a-leekie is a classic Scottish soup.

2 large leeks
2 tablespoons butter
2 tablespoons vegetable oil
1 (3- to 3-1/2-lb.) chicken, cut-up, skinned
1-1/2 qts. (6 cups) water

1 medium carrot, sliced
1 medium celery stalk, sliced
1/2 cup barley
1 bay leaf
Salt and coarsely ground pepper to taste

Trim leeks; discard green tops. Quarter leeks lengthwise, cutting almost to the root. Wash under cold running water, pulling layers apart so grit is removed. Drain well. Chop washed leeks. Heat butter and oil in a large heavy skillet over medium heat. Add chicken; sauté 10 to 12 minutes or until firm and white. Place cooked chicken in a large pot. Add water; bring to a full boil. Skim foam from surface until surface is clear. Add chopped leeks, carrot, celery, barley and bay leaf. Season with salt and pepper. Reduce heat and simmer 30 minutes or until chicken is tender. Using tongs or a slotted spoon, remove chicken. Cool slightly. Pull meat from bones; discard bones. Cut meat into bite-size pieces. Remove bay leaf from stock; discard. Add chicken to stock. Simmer 5 minutes. Serve hot. Makes 6 servings.

New-Fashioned Chicken Soup

A quick, low-calorie version of an all-time favorite.

1 (3-1/2- to 4-lb.) chicken, cut-up, skinned
2 to 2-1/2 qts. (8 to 10 cups) water
2 celery stalks, cut in halves
1 large carrot, cut in quarters
1 medium onion, cut in quarters
2 garlic cloves, unpeeled
2 bay leaves, crumbled
2 teaspoons dried leaf thyme

1 teaspoon salt
1/2 teaspoon coarsely ground pepper
1/3 to 1/2 cup chopped mushroom stems or
   4 large mushrooms, chopped, if desired
1/2 cup dry white wine
Salt and coarsely ground pepper to taste
Dry sherry, if desired
French or garlic bread

Remove any excess fat from chicken. Place chicken in a large pot. Cover with water. Bring to a boil over high heat. Skim foam from surface until surface is clear. Add celery, carrot, onion, garlic, bay leaves, thyme, 1 teaspoon salt, 1/2 teaspoon pepper and mushrooms, if desired. Reduce heat and cover. Simmer 45 to 50 minutes or until chicken is tender. Using tongs or a slotted spoon, remove chicken. Cool slightly. Pull meat from bones in large pieces. Reserve chicken bones. Place meat in a medium bowl. Pour 1/4 cup liquid from pot over chicken. Cover and refrigerate until ready to use. Return chicken bones to pot with liquid. Add wine; simmer 1 hour. Cool slightly. Strain through a fine sieve or cheesecloth-lined colander into a large bowl; discard bones and vegetables. Let stand 30 minutes. Skim fat from surface. Return stock to a clean soup pot. Add reserved chicken. Heat over medium heat until steaming. Season with salt and pepper. Using a slotted spoon, place some chicken in each soup bowl. Cover with soup. Add 1 tablespoon sherry to each bowl, if desired. Serve with French or garlic bread. Makes 6 to 8 servings.

Variations

Chicken & Vegetable Soup: Prepare soup as above. Bring to a boil. Add 1 (1-pound) package frozen mixed vegetables. Reduce heat and simmer 8 to 10 minutes or until vegetables are tender. Sprinkle servings generously with grated Parmesan or Romano cheese, if desired.
Chicken Soup with Noodles or Rice: Before adding boned chicken, reheat stock to boiling. While stock continues to boil, slowly add 1 (8-ounce) package flat or curly noodles or 1/2 cup uncooked white rice. Boil until noodles are al dente or rice is tender. Add boned chicken. Sprinkle servings generously with grated Parmesan or Romano cheese, if desired.
Cream of Chicken Soup: Prepare soup as above. In a small bowl, beat 2 eggs until pale-yellow in color. Stir in 1 cup whipping cream, plain yogurt or half and half. Reheat soup until warm. Stir about 1/2 cup warm soup into egg mixture. Then, stir egg mixture into remaining soup. Heat until steaming, but do not boil.

Frozen raw or cooked poultry that has thawed may be safely refrozen if it still contains ice crystals or if it is still cold—below 40F (5C)—and has been held no longer than 1 or 2 days at refrigerator temperature after thawing. Thawing and refreezing may decrease the flavor of the food.

Authentic Creole Chicken Gumbo

Filé powder is made from dried sassafras leaves and is used to season and thicken soups and stews.

6 tablespoons margarine or shortening
5 tablespoons all-purpose flour
1 large onion, chopped
1 garlic clove, minced
2 celery stalks, chopped
1 lb. fresh okra, chopped or
   1 (10-oz.) pkg. frozen chopped okra,
   broken apart
1 (1-lb.) can stewed tomatoes
1/4 teaspoon dried leaf thyme
1/4 teaspoon dried leaf rosemary
1/8 teaspoon dried leaf sage
2 bay leaves

2 qts. (8 cups) chicken stock
1 (2-1/2- to 3-lb.) chicken, cut-up, skinned
1 cup minced cooked ham
1/2 teaspoon salt
2 to 3 dashes hot-pepper sauce
1 duck carcass, if available
1/4 to 1/2 lb. crabmeat
1 lb. deveined shelled medium shrimp
1 pint (2 cups) shucked oysters with liquid
Salt and coarsely ground pepper to taste
1 to 2 tablespoons filé powder, if desired
3 to 4 cups hot cooked rice
Thick-sliced French bread

Melt margarine or shortening in a heavy skillet over low heat. Add flour; stir to blend. Reduce heat to very low. Cook, stirring frequently, 30 minutes or until mixture turns deep brown. Keep heat very low. Do not allow mixture to burn. If mixture develops a burnt flavor, discard and start with fresh ingredients. In a heavy pot, combine onion, garlic, celery, okra, tomatoes, thyme, rosemary, sage, bay leaves and stock. Add chicken, ham, salt, hot-pepper sauce and duck carcass, if available. Bring to a boil. Stir in flour mixture until well blended. Reduce heat and simmer, stirring frequently, 1 hour or until vegetables are tender and meat can be easily pulled from bones. Cool slightly. Remove duck carcass; discard. Using tongs or a slotted spoon, remove chicken. Cool slightly. Pull meat from bones; discard bones. Return chicken to pot. Cover and refrigerate 8 to 12 hours to congeal fat and develop flavor. Lift fat from surface; discard. To serve, heat gumbo to a simmer. Add crabmeat, shrimp and oysters. Simmer 10 minutes, stirring often. Season with salt and pepper. Stir in filé powder, if desired. Place 1/2 cup hot rice in each of 6 to 8 deep soup bowls. Ladle hot gumbo over rice. Serve with French bread. Makes 6 to 8 servings.

Gumbo can also be frozen. Do not add filé powder until gumbo has been reheated and is ready to serve.

Chicken Soup Avgolemono

Greeks say this soup is creamy, rich, light and thoroughly satisfying.

1-1/2 qts. (6 cups) chicken stock
1/2 cup uncooked rice
1 cup diced cooked chicken
2 eggs

1 tablespoon lemon juice
Salt to taste
Lemon slices
Chopped parsley

Bring stock to a boil in a large saucepan over medium heat. Reduce heat and add rice. Simmer 15 minutes or until rice is nearly tender. Stir in chicken. In a small bowl, beat eggs until nearly double in volume. Stir in lemon juice. Slowly pour 1 cup simmering stock into egg mixture, stirring constantly until blended. Stir egg mixture into remaining stock. Stir over low heat until thickened. Season with salt. Increase heat and stir until steaming, but do not boil. Ladle into soup bowls. Top each serving with a lemon slice; sprinkle lightly with parsley. Makes 6 to 8 servings.

1/Cook flour mixture over low heat, stirring constantly, 30 minutes or until mixture turns deep brown.

2/Using your fingers or a fork, pull cooled chicken from bones in long strips. Discard bones.

Singhalese Soup

Here's an elegant cold, creamy soup to serve at a midsummer celebration.

2 tablespoons butter
1 small tart apple, peeled, chopped
1 small onion, chopped
2 to 3 teaspoons curry powder
1/4 teaspoon chili powder, if desired
1 qt. (4 cups) chicken stock
1 teaspoon salt

1/4 teaspoon white pepper
1 cup whipping cream
1 to 1-1/2 cups finely diced cooked chicken
   or turkey breast, chilled
Crushed ice
Minced chives or paprika

Melt butter in a medium saucepan over low heat. Add apple and onion. Sauté 5 minutes or until tender. Stir in curry powder and chili powder, if desired. Add 1/2 cup stock; stir to blend. Pour apple mixture into a blender or food processor fitted with a steel blade. Process until pureed. Return apple mixture to saucepan. Add remaining stock; bring to a boil. Reduce heat and simmer 5 minutes. Season with salt and white pepper. Place mixture in a storage container. Cover and refrigerate. To serve, beat cream in a small bowl with a whisk to lighten slightly. Do not beat until stiff. Stir cream into chilled stock mixture. Add chicken or turkey. Serve in chilled bowls, surrounded with crushed ice. Sprinkle each serving with chives or paprika. Makes 4 to 6 servings.

Variation

Substitute half and half or plain yogurt for whipping cream.

Oriental Chicken Soup

Oriental egg rolls are a great accompaniment to this soup.

2 tablespoons vegetable oil
1 (3- to 3-1/2-lb.) chicken,
   cut-up, skinned
1-1/2 qts. (6 cups) chicken stock
3 tablespoons soy sauce
1 (1-inch) cube gingerroot, crushed or
   1 teaspoon ground ginger

1 garlic clove, crushed
2 teaspoons sugar
1 (1-lb.) pkg. frozen mixed Chinese
   vegetables, broken apart
Additional soy sauce, if desired
3 to 4 cups hot cooked rice

Heat oil in a large heavy pot over medium-high heat. Add chicken; cook 10 to 12 minutes or until firm and white. Using a bulb-baster, remove any oil from pot; discard oil. Add 3 cups stock, 3 tablespoons soy sauce, ginger, garlic and sugar. Bring to a boil. Reduce heat and cover. Simmer 30 minutes or until tender. Using tongs or a slotted spoon, remove chicken. Cool slightly. Pull meat from bones; discard bones. Cut meat into bite-size pieces; set aside. Add remaining 3 cups stock to pot. Bring to a boil. Remove and discard gingerroot and garlic. Add Chinese vegetables; cook 5 minutes or until vegetables are crisp-tender, stirring occasionally. Return chicken to pot. Season with additional soy sauce, if desired. Place 1/2 cup hot rice in each of 6 to 8 deep soup bowls. Ladle soup over rice with equal amounts of chicken and vegetables. Makes 6 to 8 servings.

Pasta Fagioli

Serve this thick stew-like soup in old-fashioned shallow soup bowls.

2 tablespoons butter
1 tablespoon olive oil
3 chicken-breast halves,
   skinned, boned, diced
1 large onion, chopped
1 garlic clove, minced
1 qt. (4 cups) chicken stock
1 cup water
1 (8-oz.) pkg. elbow macaroni

1 (1-lb.) can Italian-style tomatoes
   with basil, undrained
1 (1-lb.) can red kidney beans or
   pinto beans
1/4 to 1/2 teaspoon Italian herb seasoning
1 teaspoon salt
1/4 teaspoon coarsely ground pepper
Grated Parmesan cheese

In a large pot, heat butter and oil over medium heat until foamy. When foam subsides, add chicken, onion and garlic. Cook 5 minutes, stirring occasionally. Add stock and water. Bring to a boil. Add macaroni. Reduce heat and simmer, uncovered, 10 minutes or until macaroni is al dente and chicken is tender. Add tomatoes, beans, herb seasoning, salt and pepper. Simmer 5 minutes, stirring occasionally. Ladle hot soup into bowls. Sprinkle each serving generously with cheese. Makes 6 to 8 servings.

Main Dishes— Sautéed, Braised & Steamed

In the kitchen of a fine French restaurant, one of the first things an apprentice chef learns is how to sauté a chicken. A chicken, simply sautéed, looks and tastes great without further embellishment.

To sauté, cut a whole chicken into the size and shape pieces you prefer. Heat vegetable oil or butter over medium heat in a heavy skillet or sauté pan. Arrange the chicken in the skillet. There are two basic ways to sauté. One calls for the chicken to be cooked until it is golden brown. For the other method, the skin is removed. Then the meat is seared and cooked until golden in color. For both methods, turn pieces frequently during cooking. Season with salt and coarsely ground pepper. Reduce heat and cover. Steam 5 to 10 minutes. This first steaming helps to seal in juices and plumps the meat.

The next step is adding a small amount of liquid such as stock, white wine, vermouth or sherry. Or, add juice from canned tomatoes or any other liquid compatible with the recipe. Vegetables for seasoning, including onions, green onions or mushrooms, can be added at this time. The skillet is then covered. Steam the chicken in this liquid until it is juicy and tender. To finish, transfer the chicken to a heatproof platter or baking dish and place in a warm oven while making any accompanying sauce.

Once basics are mastered, your creativity is unleashed. A sautéed chicken can be transformed into any number of different, yet equally delicious entrees. If you add 1 cup of liquid after browning, you have changed the recipe to braised chicken.

Steamed chicken is an easy way to prepare tender, juicy flavorful meat to serve hot, cold or in recipes calling for cooked chicken. Try Steamed Chicken & Garlic for a mellow flavor. Don't be surprised at the amount of garlic used in the recipe. Remember the garlic flavor loses strength in cooked dishes.

However you season, sauté or steam it, your chicken is certain to be succulent, tender and very tasty.

Birthday Dinner
*Chicken in Champagne Sauce,
pages 50-51
Carrots, Turnips & Peas, page 153
Croissants
Double-Rich Devil's-Food Cake*

Perfect Sautéed Chicken

This chicken is tender, moist and very juicy.

1/4 cup butter
1/4 cup vegetable oil
1 (3- to 4-lb.) chicken, cut-up

Salt and coarsely ground pepper to taste
1/4 cup dry white wine or chicken stock
1 tablespoon lemon juice

Blot chicken dry with paper towel. Place 2 tablespoons butter and 2 tablespoons oil in a deep heavy skillet. Heat over medium-high heat until foamy. When foam subsides, add chicken wings and breast. Sauté, turning frequently, 6 to 8 minutes or until skin is golden brown and breast is firm and white. Season with salt and pepper. Remove from skillet; set aside. Pour off butter and oil; discard. Add remaining butter and oil. When hot, add remaining chicken. Sauté, turning frequently, 10 minutes or until golden brown on all sides. Season with salt and pepper. Return wings and breast to skillet, placing breast pieces on top of other pieces. Reduce heat to low. Cover skillet; steam 5 minutes. Pour in wine or stock and lemon juice. Cook, covered, 25 to 30 minutes. Place chicken on a platter. Serve hot. Makes 4 to 6 servings.

Variation

Chicken Mole: Substitute 2 to 3 tablespoons mole paste and 1 cup chicken stock for white wine and lemon juice. Combine mole paste and stock in a small bowl. Pour mixture over chicken. Cook, covered, 25 to 30 minutes. Place chicken on a platter. Sprinkle with 2 tablespoons toasted sesame seeds.

Chicken Thighs au Poivre

A classic French creation coats chicken with crushed peppercorns.

8 chicken thighs, skinned, boned,
   page 47, steps 1 and 2
Salt to taste
2 tablespoons whole peppercorns,
   coarsely crushed
1/4 cup peanut oil

1/4 cup butter
2 tablespoons finely chopped shallots or
   green onions, white part only
1/4 cup dry white wine
1/2 cup whipping cream

Using a heavy cleaver or meat mallet, flatten each thigh to about 1/4 inch thick. Season each piece lightly with salt. Evenly coat each piece with crushed peppercorns. Using your fingers, press pepper firmly onto chicken. Heat 2 tablespoons oil and 1 tablespoon butter in a deep heavy skillet over high heat. When hot and nearly smoking, add 4 chicken pieces. Cook 3 minutes on each side. Place cooked chicken pieces on a platter. Pour off oil and butter; discard. Heat remaining oil and 1 tablespoon butter. When hot, add remaining chicken pieces; cook as above. Place on platter. Pour off oil and butter; discard. Melt remaining 2 tablespoons butter over low heat. Add shallots or green onions; sauté 2 to 3 minutes or until slightly softened. Return chicken to skillet. Pour in wine. Cook, spooning wine over chicken, 3 to 4 minutes. Place chicken on a platter. Increase heat under skillet to high. Add cream; cook, stirring constantly, 1 minute or until slightly thickened. Pour sauce over chicken. Serve hot. Makes 4 to 6 servings.

Chicken in Red-Wine Sauce

Traditionally known as Coq au Vin.

1/2 lb. salt pork, cut in 1/4-inch cubes
Water
3 lbs. mixed chicken parts, skinned
1/2 teaspoon salt
1/4 teaspoon coarsely ground pepper
1 large yellow onion, chopped
1 garlic clove, minced
1 cup robust dry red wine
1 cup chicken stock

1 tablespoon tomato paste
1/2 teaspoon fines herbes
1/2 teaspoon dried leaf thyme
1 bay leaf
12 to 16 large mushrooms, trimmed
12 to 16 small white onions,
    about 1-inch in diameter
1 teaspoon sugar
Salt to taste

Place salt pork in a medium saucepan. Cover with water. Bring to a full boil. Boil 3 to 4 minutes. Drain well on paper towel; blot dry. Place salt pork in a large heavy skillet over low heat. Cook, stirring occasionally, until fat has cooked out and cubes are browned. Using a slotted spoon, remove cubes from fat. Drain well; set aside. Pour all but 3 tablespoons fat from skillet into a small bowl; set aside. Heat reserved 3 tablespoons fat in skillet over medium-high heat. Add chicken. Cook, turning frequently, 6 to 8 minutes or until meat is firm and white. Transfer chicken pieces to a large pot. Season with salt and pepper; set aside. Add 1 tablespoon reserved fat to skillet. Add yellow onion; sauté 5 minutes or until soft. Add garlic; cook 30 seconds or until fragrant. Spoon off any oil in skillet. Add wine and stock. Simmer 1 minute. Stir in tomato paste, fines herbes, thyme and bay leaf. Bring to a boil and boil 1 to 2 minutes. Pour stock mixture over chicken in large pot. Wipe skillet clean. Add 3 tablespoons reserved fat to skillet. Add mushrooms; sauté over low heat 5 minutes or until tender. Using a slotted spoon, remove mushrooms, draining off any excess fat. Add mushrooms to chicken. Add small onions to skillet. Sauté until lightly browned, adding more reserved oil if necessary. Sprinkle small onions with sugar. Cook onions until slightly glazed. Remove onions with slotted spoon, draining off any fat. Add glazed onions to chicken. Stir chicken mixture to combine ingredients. Partially cover pot. Simmer 30 minutes or until chicken is tender. Adjust seasonings as needed. Spoon onto platter or serving plates. Sprinkle with reserved pork cubes. Makes 4 to 6 servings.

Hawaiian Chicken

A little pre-planning plus your electric slow-cooking pot can add up to an easy party meal.

4 chicken-breast halves, skinned
4 chicken thighs, skinned
1 (8-oz.) can pineapple chunks
1/2 cup ketchup
1/4 cup soy sauce
1 tablespoon brown sugar
1/2 teaspoon dry mustard

1 tablespoon cider vinegar
1-1/2 cups boiling water
1 green pepper, cut in narrow strips
8 to 10 water chestnuts, coarsely chopped
1 tablespoon cornstarch
1/4 cup water
1 cup chopped papaya, if desired

Remove any excess fat from chicken; discard. Place chicken in slow-cooking pot. Drain pineapple, reserving juice. In a large bowl, combine pineapple juice, ketchup, soy sauce, sugar, mustard and vinegar. Add 1-1/2 cups boiling water; stir until blended. Pour over chicken. Set heat at low. Cover pot; cook 6 to 8 hours. Add pineapple chunks, green pepper and water chestnuts. Increase heat to high. Cover; cook 20 to 25 minutes. In a small bowl, combine cornstarch and water. Add cornstarch mixture to pot, stirring until thickened. Stir in papaya, if desired. Serve hot. Makes 6 servings.

Chicken Wings with Garden Vegetables

Especially good for a summer meal with vegetables fresh from the garden.

8 chicken wings
2 tablespoons butter
1 small onion, chopped
1 small green pepper, chopped
1 garlic clove, minced
3 to 4 large juicy tomatoes, chopped
3 medium zucchini, ends trimmed,
   thinly sliced

2 tablespoons water
1/2 teaspoon salt
1/4 teaspoon coarsely ground black pepper
1/4 teaspoon poultry seasoning or
   Italian herb seasoning
Hot cooked rice

Remove small wing-tip section from each chicken wing. Reserve for another use. Cut each wing at joint, making 2 wing pieces. Place wing pieces in a large heavy skillet over medium-high heat. Cook with no additional fat, turning occasionally, 15 to 20 minutes or until browned. Remove from skillet; set aside. Pour off fat in skillet; discard. Melt butter in skillet over low heat. Add onion, green pepper and garlic. Sauté about 1 minute. Place browned chicken wings in skillet. Add tomatoes, zucchini, water, salt, black pepper and poultry seasoning. Stir to blend. Cover and simmer, stirring occasionally, 20 minutes or until tender. Serve hot over rice. Makes 3 to 4 servings.

Sweet & Sour Chicken

Tangy, tart sauce transforms sautéed chicken into a very special dish.

Sweet & Sour Sauce, see below
3 tablespoons butter
1 (2-1/2- to-3-lb.) chicken, cut-up

Salt and coarsely ground pepper to taste
1/4 cup chicken stock

Sweet & Sour Sauce:
1 tablespoon vegetable oil
1 small green pepper, chopped
1 small onion, chopped
1 teaspoon minced fresh gingerroot or
   1/4 teaspoon ground ginger
1 small garlic clove, minced

1 (15-1/4-oz.) can unsweetened pineapple
   chunks in natural juice
1 tablespoon lemon juice
1/4 cup soy sauce
1 tablespoon cornstarch
1/4 cup chicken stock

Prepare Sweet & Sour Sauce. Melt butter in a large heavy skillet over medium heat until foamy. When foam subsides, place chicken, skin-side down, in skillet. Cook, turning frequently, 15 minutes or until browned on all sides. Season with salt and pepper. Cover and steam 5 minutes. Add stock; cover and reduce heat to medium-low. Cook 30 minutes or until tender. Place chicken on a platter. Pour Sweet & Sour Sauce over chicken. Serve hot. Makes 3 to 4 servings.

Sweet & Sour Sauce:
Heat oil in a medium skillet over medium heat. Add green pepper and onion. Sauté 3 minutes or until soft. Add ginger and garlic; sauté 1 minute. Drain pineapple, reserving juice. Add pineapple juice, lemon juice and soy sauce to green-pepper mixture. Simmer 1 minute. In a small bowl, combine cornstarch and stock. Pour cornstarch mixture into skillet, stirring constantly until thickened. Stir in pineapple chunks. Heat until bubbly. Keep warm until ready to use.

How to Make Crumb-Coated Chicken

1/Cover chicken pieces with waxed paper or plastic wrap. Using a heavy cleaver or meat mallet, flatten each chicken piece to about 1/4 inch thick.

2/Dip chicken in breadcrumbs. Press breadcrumbs evenly onto piece. Place coated chicken on a wire rack. Let stand 20 to 30 minutes to firm coating.

Crumb-Coated Chicken

A breadcrumb coating gives chicken a beautiful color.

6 chicken-breast halves, skinned, boned
1 cup all-purpose flour
1 teaspoon salt
1/4 teaspoon coarsely ground pepper
2 eggs
1 tablespoon water
2 cups fine fresh breadcrumbs

1/4 cup or more unsalted butter
1/4 cup vegetable oil
Juice from half a lemon
  (about 1-1/2 tablespoons)
6 very thin lemon slices
6 rolled caper-stuffed anchovy fillets

Using a heavy cleaver or meat mallet, flatten each chicken piece to about 1/4 inch thick. In a pie plate, combine flour, salt and pepper. In a shallow bowl, whisk eggs and water together. Pour breadcrumbs in a second pie plate. Roll a chicken piece in flour mixture; shake off excess. Dip piece in egg mixture; drain over bowl. Roll piece in breadcrumbs. Press breadcrumbs evenly onto piece. Place coated chicken on a wire rack. Repeat with remaining chicken. Let stand 20 to 30 minutes at room temperature to firm coating. Heat 2 tablespoons butter and 2 tablespoons oil in a large heavy skillet over medium-high heat until foamy. When foam subsides, add 3 breast pieces in a single layer. Sauté 3 to 4 minutes or until lightly browned on both sides. Place cooked chicken on paper towel to drain. Sauté remaining breasts in remaining butter and oil. Place chicken on a platter. Sprinkle with lemon juice. Top each breast with a lemon slice. Place a caper-stuffed anchovy in center of each lemon slice. Serve hot. Makes 4 to 6 servings.

Any crumb-coated chicken can be refrigerated prior to deep-frying. Bring chicken to room temperature before frying.

Cajun Chicken

A time-honored braised-chicken recipe from Southern Louisiana.

6 to 8 ears fresh corn or
   1 (10-oz.) pkg. frozen
   whole-kernel corn
1/2 lb. sliced bacon
1 (2-1/2- to 3-lb.) chicken, cut-up, skinned
1 large green pepper, diced
1 large onion, chopped
1 garlic clove, minced
4 large ripe tomatoes, peeled, chopped

1/2 teaspoon salt
1/4 teaspoon coarsely ground black pepper
1/8 teaspoon hot red-pepper flakes, crushed
1/4 teaspoon dried leaf rosemary
1/4 teaspoon dried leaf thyme
1/4 teaspoon dried leaf basil
1 cup chicken stock
4 cups hot cooked rice

If using fresh corn, cut kernels from cobs; set aside. Cut bacon slices in half crosswise. Cook bacon in a large heavy skillet over low heat until crisp. Remove bacon; drain on paper towel. Crumble bacon; set aside. Heat bacon drippings over medium-high heat. Add chicken. Sauté 9 minutes or until browned. Turn and cook 6 minutes. Drain chicken on paper towel. Pour off drippings, reserving 2 tablespoons in skillet. Heat reserved drippings over low heat. Add green pepper and onion. Sauté 5 minutes or until tender. Add garlic; cook 1 minute. Add corn, tomatoes, salt, black pepper, red pepper, rosemary, thyme, basil and stock. Stir until heated through. Add cooked chicken. Cover and simmer 30 minutes or until tender. Stir in cooked bacon. Serve over rice. Makes 4 to 6 servings.

Charleston Company Chicken

Festive chicken and mushrooms in a brandy-cream sauce.

1/4 cup butter
4 chicken-breast halves
Salt to taste
6 to 8 shallots, chopped
1/4 lb. mushrooms, chopped
1/2 cup dry white wine

1/4 cup brandy
2 teaspoons cornstarch
1/4 cup chicken stock
1 cup whipping cream or half and half
Coarsely ground pepper to taste

Melt butter in a large heavy skillet over medium heat until foamy. When foam subsides, add chicken breasts, skin-side down. Sauté 6 minutes or until browned. Turn and sauté 3 minutes. Season with salt. Cover and steam 5 minutes. Add shallots and mushrooms. Stir until evenly distributed. Cook, stirring constantly, 1 to 2 minutes. Add wine; bring to a full boil. Reduce heat and cover. Simmer 20 minutes or until tender but still moist and juicy. Pour brandy into a small saucepan. Warm over low heat until bubbles begin to appear around the edge. Increase heat under chicken to high. When pan juices are sizzling, pour warmed brandy over chicken. Using a long match, carefully ignite brandy. Shake skillet back and forth until flame goes out. Place chicken in a serving dish. In a small bowl, combine cornstarch and stock. Stir cream or half and half into cornstarch mixture. Pour over mushrooms and shallots in skillet. Reduce heat and stir until thickened. Season with pepper. Spoon sauce over chicken. Serve hot. Makes 2 to 4 servings.

To reduce calorie count, substitute 1/2 cup hot fat-free chicken stock for cream.

Chicken with Green Noodles

The blend of color and flavor is quite special in this simply beautiful dish.

4 chicken-breast halves, skinned, boned
1/4 cup butter
1/4 cup chopped shallots or
    green onions, white part only
1 small dried hot red pepper, seeded, minced
1/4 cup amontillado or
    similar pale dry sherry

1 cup whipping cream
2 whole canned pimientos, drained,
    cut in narrow strips
Salt and coarsely ground pepper to taste
1 (1-lb.) pkg. green noodles, cooked
Poppy seeds, if desired

Slice chicken breasts lengthwise in narrow strips. Melt butter in a large heavy skillet over medium heat until foamy. When foam subsides, add chicken. Sauté 2 to 3 minutes or until chicken is firm and white. Add shallots or green onions. Sauté 2 to 3 minutes or until slightly soft. Stir in red pepper. Pour in sherry; bring to a full boil. Add cream and pimientos. Cook, stirring constantly, until thickened. Season with salt and pepper. Place cooked noodles on a platter. Spoon chicken and sauce over noodles. Sprinkle with poppy seeds, if desired. Serve hot. Makes 4 to 6 servings.

Variation

Add 1 cup cooked green peas with cream and pimientos.

Bourbon Chicken with Apples

Southern gourmet cooking at its best.

3 tablespoons vegetable oil
1 (2-1/2- to 3-lb.) chicken, cut-up
Salt and coarsely ground pepper to taste
2 tablespoons butter
2 Granny Smith apples or other tart apples,
    peeled, chopped

1 tablespoon minced chives
1/2 cup chicken stock
1/2 cup bourbon whiskey or apple brandy
2 tablespoons lemon juice
Minced parsley

Heat oil in a large heavy skillet over medium-high heat. Add chicken, skin-side down. Sauté 6 minutes or until lightly browned. Turn and sauté 5 minutes longer. Season with salt and pepper. Cover and steam 5 minutes. Remove chicken from skillet; set aside. Pour off oil; discard. Wipe skillet clean with paper towel. Melt butter in clean skillet over low heat. Add apples; sauté 2 to 3 minutes. Return chicken to skillet. Sprinkle with chives. Add stock and 1/4 cup liquor. Cover and simmer 30 minutes or until tender. Place chicken on a platter. Pour remaining liquor and lemon juice in skillet. Stir constantly 1 minute or until heated. Spoon apples and sauce over chicken. Sprinkle with parsley. Serve hot. Makes 3 to 4 servings.

Reduce calories by removing chicken skin before cooking.

Chicken Breasts Milanese

Serve this chicken in a tasty tomato sauce with noodles and Parmesan cheese.

6 chicken-breast halves, skinned, boned
1-1/2 cups Italian-seasoned breadcrumbs
1/2 cup all-purpose flour
1 teaspoon salt
1/4 teaspoon coarsely ground pepper
2 eggs
2 tablespoons water
1 tablespoon vegetable oil
2 tablespoons butter
1 small red onion, chopped

1/4 lb. mushrooms, chopped
1/2 cup julienne strips baked or boiled ham
1/2 cup chicken stock
1 (8-oz.) can tomato sauce
1/2 teaspoon dried leaf basil or rosemary
2 tablespoons dry sherry
Dash hot-pepper sauce
1 (8-oz.) pkg. flat noodles, cooked
1/4 cup grated Parmesan or
    Romano cheese (3/4 oz.)

Preheat oven to 150F (65C). Using a heavy cleaver or meat mallet, flatten each chicken piece to about 1/4 inch thick. In a pie plate, combine breadcrumbs, flour, salt and pepper. In a shallow bowl, whisk eggs and water together. Dip a chicken piece in egg mixture; drain over bowl. Roll the piece in breadcrumb mixture. Press breadcrumbs evenly onto piece. Place coated chicken on a wire rack. Repeat with remaining chicken. Let stand 20 to 30 minutes at room temperature to firm coating. Heat oil in a large heavy skillet. Add 2 to 3 breast pieces in a single layer. Sauté 3 to 4 minutes or until lightly browned on both sides. Remove as browned and place in a 13" x 9" baking dish. Place in oven to keep warm. Pour off oil; discard. Melt butter in skillet over low heat. Add onion, mushrooms and ham. Sauté 2 to 3 minutes or until onion and mushrooms are tender. Add stock, tomato sauce and basil or rosemary. Simmer, stirring constantly, 10 minutes. Add sherry and hot-pepper sauce. In a large pot, combine noodles and half the tomato mixture. Toss well, coating noodles. Place noodles on a large platter. Arrange chicken breasts over noodles. Top with remaining tomato mixture. Sprinkle with cheese. Serve hot. Makes 4 to 6 servings.

Basque-Style Chicken

A great party dish that can be prepared ahead, then reheated.

3 tablespoons olive oil
1 (2-1/2- to 3-lb.) chicken, cut-up
Salt to taste
1 small onion, chopped
1 large garlic clove, minced
1 cup diced peeled eggplant
1 (1-lb.) can Italian plum tomatoes
1/2 cup dry white wine
1-1/2 cups chicken stock

1 teaspoon salt
1/4 teaspoon coarsely ground pepper
1 tablespoon chopped fresh basil or
    1/2 teaspoon dried leaf basil, crumbled
1/4 cup sliced pitted black olives
1 tablespoon tomato paste
Hot cooked rice
Minced parsley

Heat oil in a large heavy skillet over medium-high heat. Place chicken pieces, skin-side down, in skillet. Cook 6 minutes or until golden brown. Turn and cook other side 5 minutes. Remove chicken. Season with salt; set aside. Reduce heat to low. Add onion, garlic and eggplant. Sauté 2 to 3 minutes or until tender. Add tomatoes with liquid, wine and stock. Season with salt, pepper and basil. Add olives and tomato paste. Place chicken pieces in skillet. Cover; simmer 20 to 30 minutes. Spoon sauce over chicken and rearrange for even cooking. Cover; simmer 15 to 20 minutes or until tender. Serve hot over rice. Sprinkle with parsley. Makes 3 to 4 servings.

Stuffed Chicken Thighs

Italian sausage makes this a delicious and impressive braised-chicken dish.

1/2 lb. sweet or hot Italian sausage
1 medium white or yellow onion, chopped
1 egg yolk
1/2 cup fine fresh breadcrumbs
1/2 teaspoon salt
1/4 teaspoon coarsely ground black pepper
12 chicken thighs, boned
1/4 cup butter

1 large green pepper, cut in strips
1 large red onion, chopped
2 tablespoons all-purpose flour
1/2 teaspoon dried leaf marjoram
1/2 teaspoon chopped parsley
1-1/2 cups chicken stock
1/2 cup dry white wine

Remove sausage casings. Crumble sausages and place in a medium skillet. Add white or yellow onion; cook over medium heat, stirring frequently, 4 to 5 minutes or until fat cooks out and meat is lightly browned. Drain well. Place sausage mixture in a medium bowl; cool. Blend in egg yolk, breadcrumbs, salt and black pepper. Place thighs, skin-side down, on a flat surface. Flatten slightly with a heavy cleaver or meat mallet. Spoon about 2 tablespoons of sausage mixture onto center of each thigh. Bring corners of thigh to center to enclose filling. Tie with string. Melt butter in a large heavy skillet until foamy. When foam subsides, add stuffed thighs, skin-side down. Sauté 8 minutes or until lightly browned. Turn and cook 6 minutes. Remove thighs from skillet; set aside. Add green pepper and red onion to skillet. Cook, stirring frequently, 2 to 3 minutes. Sprinkle with flour, marjoram and parsley. Stir in stock and wine. Bring to a boil. Add sautéed chicken thighs. Reduce heat and cover. Simmer 25 to 30 minutes or until tender. Place chicken on a platter. Remove string from thighs. Skim off fat from sauce. Cook until sauce is reduced by half. Pour sauce over thighs. Serve hot. Makes 8 to 10 servings.

Chicken Cacciatore

An authentic but quick-cooking version of an Italian classic.

1/4 cup olive oil
1 (3- to 3-1/2-lb.) chicken, cut-up
2 tablespoons butter
1 garlic clove, minced
Salt and coarsely ground black pepper
  to taste

1 teaspoon Italian herb seasoning
1 (1-lb.) can Italian-style tomato sauce
  with basil
1/2 cup dry white wine
1 green pepper, cut in strips
Hot cooked pasta

Heat 2 tablespoons oil in a deep heavy skillet over medium heat. Add chicken wings and breast, skin-side down, in a single layer. Sauté, turning occasionally, 8 to 10 minutes or until browned. Breast meat should be firm and white. Remove chicken pieces; set aside. Pour off oil; discard. Heat remaining 2 tablespoons oil in skillet. When hot, sauté remaining chicken pieces 6 to 8 minutes, turning as needed, until browned on all sides. Reduce heat to low and add butter. When melted, return wings and breast meat to skillet, placing breast on top of other pieces. Add garlic; stir it down between chicken pieces. Season with salt and pepper. Add herb seasoning, tomato sauce and wine. Spoon some of the liquid over chicken. Place green-pepper strips on top. Cover and simmer, occasionally basting with sauce, 25 minutes or until tender. Serve with pasta. Makes 4 to 6 servings.

How to Make Stuffed Chicken Thighs

1/Place chicken thigh skin-side down on work surface. Run a sharp knife along each side of the bone.

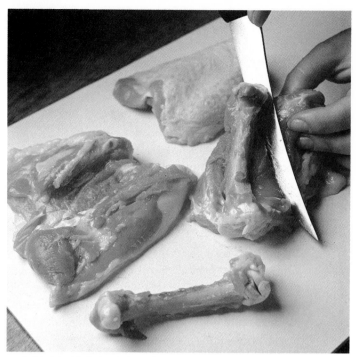

2/Hold thigh in 1 hand at a slight angle. Position knife under thigh bone. Cut closely along bone to remove it.

3/Pull 1 side of thigh up over stuffing.

4/Pull opposite side of thigh over stuffing. Tie securely.

47

Chicken with Taco Sauce

Complete your fiesta with warm tortillas and refried beans.

2 tablespoons butter
1 medium, green pepper, chopped
1 medium onion, chopped
2 tablespoons chopped green chilies
1 garlic clove, minced
1/4 cup all-purpose flour
1 (1-1/4-oz.) envelope taco-seasoning mix
1 teaspoon salt

1 teaspoon coarsely ground black pepper
1/4 cup vegetable oil
1 (2-1/2- to 3-lb.) chicken, cut-up
1 cup chicken stock
1 cup shredded Monterey Jack or
   Cheddar cheese (4 oz.)
1/4 cup pimiento-stuffed olives, chopped

Melt butter in a small skillet over medium heat. Add green pepper, onion, green chilies and garlic. Sauté 3 to 4 minutes or until soft; set aside. In a pie plate, combine flour, 1/2 envelope taco-seasoning mix, salt and black pepper. Roll each chicken piece in flour mixture; shake off excess. Heat oil in a deep heavy skillet. Place chicken, skin-side down, in hot oil. Sauté 6 minutes or until lightly browned. Turn and sauté 5 minutes. Pour off oil; discard. In a small bowl, combine remaining taco-seasoning mix, stock and sautéed green-pepper mixture. Pour over chicken. Cover and simmer 30 minutes or until tender. Place on a platter or serving dish. Sprinkle with cheese and olives. Serve hot. Makes 3 to 4 servings.

Quick Cutlets & Cream Sauce

Almost as fast as commercially prepared entrees and twice as delicious.

2 tablespoons vegetable oil
4 frozen chicken cutlets, opposite
2 tablespoons butter
1 small onion, minced
1/4 cup dry sherry
1 (10-1/2-oz.) can condensed cream of
   mushroom soup

3/4 cup milk
1/2 teaspoon salt
1/4 teaspoon coarsely ground pepper
Salt and coarsely ground pepper to taste
Paprika or sesame seeds, if desired

Heat 1 tablespoon oil in a large heavy skillet over medium-high heat. Add 2 cutlets; sauté 1 minute on each side. Remove from skillet; set aside. Repeat with remaining oil and cutlets. Pour off oil; discard. Melt butter in skillet over medium heat. Add onion; sauté 2 to 3 minutes or until tender. Increase heat to high. Add sherry; bring to a full boil. Reduce heat. Add soup, milk, salt and pepper. Blend well. Return cutlets to skillet. Turn to coat with sauce. Simmer, turning occasionally, 5 minutes or until cooked through and sauce has thickened. Sprinkle with paprika or sesame seeds, if desired. Serve hot. Makes 3 to 4 servings.

Variation

Substitute cream of celery, cream of asparagus, cream of shrimp or Cheddar-cheese soup for cream of mushroom soup.

How to Make Chicken Cutlets

1/Place boned chicken-breast halves on a work surface. Cover with waxed paper or plastic wrap. Using a meat mallet or cleaver, flatten each breast half until about 1/4 inch thick. Cutlets may be frozen for later use.

2/To freeze, place cutlets in a single layer on a baking sheet. Freeze until firm. Stack with waxed paper between each cutlet. Wrap in foil, using drug store fold, or place in an airtight bag. Freeze up to 2 months.

Cutlets Italian-Style

Close your eyes and these flavors will make you think you are in Italy.

2 tablespoons vegetable oil
4 frozen chicken cutlets
2 tablespoons butter
1 garlic clove, minced
1 (1-lb.) can Italian-style tomato sauce
1 tablespoon red-wine vinegar

1 teaspoon Italian herb seasoning
1/4 teaspoon sugar
Salt and coarsely ground pepper to taste
Hot cooked ravioli or other pasta
Grated Romano cheese

Heat 1 tablespoon oil in a large heavy skillet over medium-high heat. Add 2 cutlets; sauté 1 minute on each side. Remove from skillet; set aside. Repeat with remaining oil and cutlets. Pour off oil; discard. Melt butter in skillet over low heat. Add garlic; sauté 2 to 3 minutes or until tender. Add tomato sauce, vinegar, herb seasoning and sugar. Season with salt and pepper. Simmer 5 minutes, stirring often. Return cutlets to skillet. Turn to coat with sauce. Simmer, turning occasionally, 5 minutes or until cooked through. Serve over ravioli or pasta. Sprinkle with cheese. Serve hot. Makes 3 to 4 servings.

Chicken in Champagne Sauce

A superb chicken dish to serve your favorite guests.

3 tablespoons butter
1 (2-1/2- to 3-lb.) chicken,
  cut-up, skinned
1/2 lb. large mushrooms, cut in quarters
1/2 teaspoon salt
1/4 teaspoon coarsely ground pepper
3/4 cup champagne

1 bay leaf
2 tablespoons cornstarch
1/4 cup water
1 cup whipping cream, room temperature
1 (4-oz.) jar chopped pimientos, drained
2 tablespoons capers, if desired

Melt butter in a large heavy skillet over medium heat until foamy. When foam subsides, add chicken. Turn chicken to coat evenly with butter. Sauté, turning frequently, 5 minutes or until meat is firm and lightly browned. Add mushrooms; stir to distribute evenly. Season with salt and pepper. Add champagne and bay leaf. Bring to a full boil. Reduce heat. Cover and simmer 20 minutes or until chicken is tender. Place chicken on a platter. Using a slotted spoon, remove mushrooms. Scatter mushrooms over chicken. Remove bay leaf; discard. In a small bowl, combine cornstarch and water. Stir cream into cornstarch mixture. Stir cream mixture into liquid in skillet. Add pimientos and capers, if desired. Cook, stirring constantly, until thickened. Spoon over chicken. Serve hot. Makes 3 to 4 servings.

Variation

Reduce calories by omitting cornstarch mixture and cream. Boil liquid until reduced by half.

Old-Fashioned Chicken Fricassee

Braised chicken in a cream sauce is a deep-down satisfying dish.

1/4 cup butter
1 (3- to 3-1/2-lb.) chicken, cut-up,
  skinned
1 small onion, chopped
1 pint (2 cups) chicken stock
1/2 cup dry white wine or vermouth

1 egg yolk
1 tablespoon all-purpose flour
1/2 cup whipping cream or half and half
Salt and coarsely ground pepper to taste
1 tablespoon lemon juice
Hot cooked flat noodles

Melt butter in a deep heavy skillet over medium heat. Add chicken; sauté 10 to 12 minutes or until firm and lightly browned. Add onion; stir down between chicken. Sauté 2 to 3 minutes or until onion is soft. Cover and steam 5 minutes. Pour in stock and wine or vermouth. Cover and simmer 30 minutes or until tender. Place chicken in a medium bowl. Spoon some cooking liquid over each piece to keep it moist. Continue to simmer remaining liquid. In a small bowl, beat together egg yolk and flour. Add cream or half and half. Stir until blended. Stir mixture into simmering liquid. Cook, stirring constantly without boiling, 3 to 4 minutes or until thickened. Season with salt and pepper. Stir in lemon juice. Return chicken to sauce. Cook, stirring gently, until reheated. Spoon over noodles. Serve immediately. Makes 4 to 6 servings.

Variation

Serve with broccoli spears, or stir in cooked chopped broccoli when adding lemon juice.

California Chicken

An eye-appealing dish with a sunny California flavor.

3 tablespoons vegetable oil
1 (2-1/2- to 3-lb.) chicken, cut-up
2 tablespoons butter
Juice from half a lemon
 (About 1-1/2 tablespoons)

1/2 cup fresh orange juice
3/4 cup fruity sweet wine or Sauternes
1/2 teaspoon salt or to taste
1 large navel orange, sliced
Paprika

Heat oil in a large heavy skillet over medium-high heat. Add chicken, skin-side down. Sauté 8 to 9 minutes or until chicken is browned. Turn pieces and cook 6 minutes. Cover and steam 5 minutes. Spoon oil from skillet; discard. Reduce heat. Add butter, lemon juice, orange juice and wine. Season with salt. Cover and simmer 20 minutes or until tender. Place on a platter. Pour sauce over chicken. Garnish with orange slices and paprika. Makes 3 to 4 servings.

Dieter's Sautéed Chicken

You'll be surprised at the great flavor of this low-calorie entree.

1 (2-1/2- to 3-lb.) chicken, cut-up
Salt and coarsely ground pepper to taste

1 to 2 tablespoons lemon juice

Remove skin from breast pieces. Heat a large heavy skillet over medium heat. Without adding fat, arrange wings, legs and thighs, skin-side down, in skillet. Without turning, cook until enough fat has been rendered to let pieces move easily in pan. Sauté 8 to 10 minutes or until skin is browned. Turn chicken skin-side up. Add breast pieces. Season with salt and pepper. Reduce heat to medium-low; partially cover skillet. Cook, turning pieces frequently, 25 to 30 minutes or until cooked through but still moist and juicy. Sprinkle with lemon juice before serving. Serve hot. Makes 3 to 4 servings.

Turkey Scallops Fines Herbes

Fresh tarragon enhances the rich flavor.

4 slices (1 lb.) uncooked turkey breast
1/2 cup all-purpose flour
1/4 cup butter
3 tablespoons vegetable oil
1/2 cup chicken stock
2 tablespoons finely chopped green onion
2 tablespoons finely chopped parsley

2 tablespoons finely chopped fresh tarragon
 or 1 teaspoon dried leaf tarragon
2 tablespoons finely chopped chervil
2 tablespoons lemon juice
1/4 cup dry white wine or vermouth
Salt and coarsely ground pepper to taste

Cut each turkey slice in serving pieces. Using a heavy cleaver or meat mallet, flatten each turkey piece to about 1/4 inch thick. Place flour in a pie plate. Roll a turkey piece in flour; shake off excess. Repeat with remaining turkey. Heat 2 tablespoons butter and 1-1/2 tablespoons oil in a deep heavy skillet over medium-high heat until foamy. When foam subsides, add a single layer of turkey. Sauté, turning once, 2 to 3 minutes or until lightly browned and cooked through center. Remove turkey; set aside. Repeat with remaining butter, oil and turkey. When all turkey is sautéed, pour off oil and butter; discard. Add stock; stir, scraping up brown bits from bottom of skillet. Stir in green onion, parsley, tarragon, chervil, lemon juice and wine or vermouth. Season with salt and pepper. Add turkey; heat through. Serve hot with sauce. Makes 3 to 4 servings.

1/Place 2 to 3 tablespoons stuffing on a turkey piece.

2/Roll and tie turkey about 1/2 inch from each end.

Olive-Stuffed Turkey Rolls

Prepare ahead and then reheat for your party.

4 slices (1 lb.) uncooked turkey breast
1/4 cup butter
1 onion, minced
1 garlic clove, minced
1 cup soft fresh breadcrumbs
1/4 cup pimiento-stuffed olives, chopped

1/4 cup minced ham
1 tablespoon vegetable oil
1/4 cup dry white wine or vermouth
1/2 cup chicken stock
2 tablespoons chopped parsley

Cut each turkey slice in serving pieces. Using a heavy cleaver or meat mallet, flatten each piece to about 1/4 inch thick; set aside. Melt 2 tablespoons butter in a medium skillet over low heat. Add onion; sauté 5 minutes or until soft. Add garlic; sauté 30 seconds or until fragrant. Remove from heat. Stir in breadcrumbs, olives and ham. Place 2 to 3 tablespoons stuffing on a turkey piece. Roll and tie with string about 1/2 inch from each end. Repeat with remaining pieces. Heat 2 tablespoons butter and oil in deep heavy skillet over medium heat until foamy. When foam subsides, add turkey rolls. Cook, turning as necessary, 4 to 5 minutes or until meat is firm and white. Tilt pan and spoon or pour off butter and oil. Reduce heat. Add wine and stock. Cover and simmer, turning occasionally, 25 to 30 minutes or until tender. Place turkey rolls on a hot platter. Clip and remove strings. Cook remaining liquid, stirring frequently, until reduced by half. Spoon sauce over turkey rolls. Sprinkle with parsley. Serve hot. Makes 3 to 4 servings.

Neopolitan Chicken & Dumplings

A delightful blend of Italian flavors.

1 cup all-purpose flour
1 teaspoon salt
1/2 teaspoon paprika
1/8 teaspoon garlic powder
1 (3- to 3-1/2-lb.) chicken, cut-up
2 tablespoons butter
1/4 cup vegetable oil
3-1/2 cups chicken stock

1/4 teaspoon Italian herb seasoning
1 (1-lb.) can Italian-style tomatoes
   with basil
1 small onion, chopped
1 tablespoon red-wine vinegar
1 teaspoon light-brown sugar
1/2 teaspoon salt
Sausage Dumplings, see below

Sausage Dumplings:
1/4 lb. spicy pork sausage or
   Italian-style sweet sausage
1 cup buttermilk-biscuit mix

1/3 cup milk
1 teaspoon minced parsley or
   dried leaf basil

In a pie plate, combine flour, 1 teaspoon salt, paprika and garlic powder. Roll each chicken piece in flour mixture; shake off excess. In a large heavy skillet, heat butter and oil until foamy. When foam subsides, add chicken pieces, skin-side down. Cook over medium-high heat 8 to 10 minutes or until lightly browned. Turn pieces and brown other side 8 to 10 minutes. Remove pieces as browned; set aside. Pour off butter and oil; discard. Add 1-1/2 cups stock, herb seasoning, tomatoes with liquid, onion, vinegar, sugar and 1/2 teaspoon salt. Blend well. Place chicken in skillet. Reduce heat and cover. Simmer 25 to 30 minutes or until tender. Remove chicken and keep warm. Skim fat from sauce; discard. Prepare Sausage-Dumpling batter. Add remaining 2 cups stock to skillet. Stir to blend. Bring liquid to a simmer. Spoon small mounds of dumpling batter into simmering liquid. Cook, uncovered, 10 minutes over low heat. Cover and cook 8 to 10 minutes or until dumplings are cooked through. Place chicken and dumplings in a serving bowl. Bring liquid in skillet to a boil. Pour boiling liquid over chicken and dumplings. Serve hot. Makes 4 to 6 servings.

Sausage Dumplings:
Remove sausage casings. Crumble sausages and place in a small skillet. Cook over low heat, stirring frequently, until fat cooks out and meat is browned. Drain well. In a small bowl, combine biscuit mix and milk. Stir in drained sausage and parsley or basil. Set aside until ready to use.

All poultry is perishable. Care and cleanliness should be used in preparation, cooking and serving of poultry products. Hands should always be clean when handling poultry. After handling raw poultry, wash hands, cutting board and utensils with hot soapy water.

Steamed Chicken

A tender, juicy, flavorful meat to serve hot or cold or in any recipe using cooked chicken.

1 (3- to 3-1/2-lb.) chicken	**1/2 small tart apple**
Salt	**1/2 small lemon**
1/2 small onion	

Remove any excess fat from chicken; discard. Season chicken inside and out with salt. Place onion, apple and lemon inside chicken. Place water in a steamer pot or wok to about 1-inch below rack. Bring water to a boil. Place chicken on rack in steamer pan or wok. Cover and steam over simmering water 50 to 55 minutes. Add hot water to pot as necessary to keep water level at 1-inch below rack. Chicken is done when meat thermometer inserted in thickest part of thigh registers 180F to 185F (80C to 85C) or when juices run clear when thigh is pierced with a small knife. Remove chicken from steamer. Let stand 10 to 15 minutes before carving. Carve and serve hot with a favorite sauce. Or, cool to room temperature. Remove skin and bones; discard. Cut meat in bite-size pieces. Place in a storage bowl. Cover and refrigerate until ready to use in casseroles or sandwiches. Makes 4 servings or about 2-1/2 cups cooked chicken.

Steamed Chicken & Garlic

Garlic cloves become mellow and change character completely when steamed.

1 (3- to 3-1/2-lb.) chicken	**1 (1-lb.) loaf crusty French bread**
Salt	**1 tablespoon olive oil**
1 large garlic head (40 cloves)	

Remove any excess fat from chicken; discard. Season chicken inside and out with salt. Remove excess peel from garlic head. Separate garlic into cloves, but do not peel cloves. Place garlic cloves inside chicken. Place a small crumpled piece of foil inside chicken cavity to hold garlic in place. Tie legs together with twine. Pour water into a large steamer to about 1-inch below rack. Place over high heat and bring to a boil. Place chicken on steamer rack. Cover and steam 1 hour or until tender. Remove chicken. Using a slotted spoon, remove garlic from chicken; set aside. Cut chicken in serving pieces. Place on a platter. Season chicken with salt. Cover with foil to keep warm; set aside. Preheat oven to 375F (190C.) Remove peel from garlic by pressing each clove at the root end. Place garlic in a mortar or small bowl. Mash to a paste with pestle or back of a spoon. Stir in oil. Season with salt. Slice bread diagonally to, but not through, bottom of loaf. Separate slices slightly. Spread each slice with garlic mixture. Press loaf back together. Wrap in foil and place in oven 10 minutes or until heated through. Serve with chicken. Makes 4 servings.

Variation

Steamed Chicken with Potatoes & Onions: Substitute 1 large lemon for garlic head. Pierce lemon deeply 10 to 15 times. Place lemon inside chicken. Place a small crumpled piece of foil inside chicken cavity to hold lemon in place. Tie legs with twine. Fill steamer as per recipe. Steam 15 minutes. Place 4 small new unpeeled potatoes around chicken. Steam 10 minutes. Place 4 small white unpeeled onions on steamer rack. Steam 30 minutes or until chicken and vegetables are tender. Serve on a platter with soy sauce.

If you do not have a steamer pot, devise your own. Use a large, heavy pot. Lightly crumple a small sheet of foil. Place it in the bottom of the pot. Place 4 (6-ounce) custard cups upside-down on the foil. The foil keeps the cups in place. Place a cake rack over the cups. Place chicken on the rack. Add boiling water below the rack. Cover and steam as directed in the recipe.

Chicken & Sausage Ragout

A hearty Italian dish made with inexpensive chicken wings.

1/2 lb. sweet Italian sausage
1/2 lb. hot Italian sausage
12 chicken wings
1 tablespoon butter
1 garlic clove, minced
1 large red onion, chopped
1 green pepper, cut in narrow strips
1 sweet red pepper, cut in narrow strips
1 (1-lb.) can Italian tomatoes

2 tablespoons tomato paste
1/4 cup dry white wine
1/4 teaspoon dried leaf basil
1/4 teaspoon dried leaf thyme
1 teaspoon dried leaf oregano
1 (1/2-inch-wide) strip orange peel
1 teaspoon sugar
1/2 teaspoon salt
1/4 teaspoon coarsely ground black pepper

Prick sausages with a fork in several places. Place sausages in a large shallow skillet. Add water to cover. Simmer over low heat 10 minutes. Drain well. Cut sausages in 1/2-inch slices; set aside. Remove small wing-tip section from each chicken wing. Reserve for another use. Place wings in a large heavy skillet over medium heat. Cook with no additional fat, turning occasionally, 15 to 20 minutes or until browned. Place wings in a large pot; set aside. Add sausage slices, about 1/4 at a time, to skillet. Brown in fat from chicken wings. As browned, place sausage in large pot with chicken wings. Melt butter in skillet. Add garlic, onion, green pepper and red pepper. Cook, stirring and scraping up browned bits from bottom of skillet, 5 minutes or until vegetables are tender. Add tomatoes with juice, tomato paste, wine, basil, thyme, oregano, orange peel, sugar, salt and black pepper. Stir to blend well. Pour mixture over sausage and chicken wings. Simmer over medium heat 25 to 30 minutes. Serve hot. Makes 6 to 8 servings.

Chicken & Cream Sauce

Marsala wine adds a new dimension of flavor to this braised dish.

1/4 cup butter
2 tablespoons vegetable oil
1 (3- to 3-1/2-lb.) chicken, cut-up
1 small onion, chopped
1/4 lb. mushrooms, cut in halves or quarters
1/4 teaspoon dried leaf rosemary
1/4 teaspoon dried leaf thyme

1/4 teaspoon dried leaf marjoram
1 cup chicken stock
1/4 cup dry Marsala wine
1/2 cup whipping cream, half and half or
  plain yogurt
1 teaspoon cornstarch
Salt and coarsely ground pepper to taste

Heat 2 tablespoons butter and oil in a large heavy skillet over medium heat until foamy. When foam subsides, arrange chicken pieces, skin-side down, in skillet. Sauté 9 minutes or until lightly browned. Turn pieces and sauté 6 minutes. Place chicken on a platter; keep warm. Pour off butter and oil; discard. Melt remaining 2 tablespoons butter in skillet over medium-low heat. Add onion and mushrooms. Sauté 4 to 5 minutes or until tender. Stir in rosemary, thyme, marjoram, stock and wine. Cover and simmer 10 minutes or until reduced by half. In a small bowl, combine cream, half and half or yogurt and cornstarch. Pour mixture into skillet. Cook 2 to 3 minutes, stirring until thickened. Season with salt and pepper. Spoon sauce over chicken. Serve hot. Makes 4 to 6 servings.

Poultry—
Roasted, Stuffed & Broiled

Along with chicken, other poultry including turkey, duck and goose are now sold year round. The meat department of most markets offers a wide range of poultry items. Recipes for roasting different types of poultry are usually interchangeable.

Don't wait for a party to roast a fine bird. One of the easiest, most satisfactory and delicious meals I ever prepared was for two people. The menu was simple: a 3-pound chicken roasted to perfection and served at room temperature, plus a green salad and delicious French bread.

If you live alone or often dine alone, you can still enjoy a flavorful roasted and stuffed bird. Buy a Cornish hen. Thaw, stuff and roast the bird. Then, serve with vegetables baked in foil.

Have a small family? Cook a large bird. Roast it and enjoy it the first day. Then, wrap and store leftovers in your refrigerator or freezer. The juicy, flavorful meat is superb for sandwiches and salads. Use it as an ingredient in the many quick and easy casserole dishes you will find throughout this book.

Roasting poultry, with or without stuffing, is one of the easiest cooking methods. A basic recipe can be reduced to just a few lines.

The most frequently asked question is how to roast a bird so that white meat will not overcook and become dry before the moist dark meat is cooked. Throughout this section you will find different methods that will help to resolve this problem. All are equally effective in producing moist, juicy meat.

Candlelight Dinner for 4
Cornish Hens with Couscous Stuffing,
page 76
Stuffed Apricots, page 151
Broccoli Spears
Tuscan Green Salad, page 149
Hazelnut-Cream Torte
Expresso

Roasting Poultry

To prepare a bird for roasting, remove giblets and neck from thawed but cold bird. Wash well under cold water. Blot dry with paper towel so oil or butter will stick to the poultry skin. Rub the bird well with butter, oil or other fat as directed in the recipe.

Place the bird in a long shallow pan covered loosely with foil. Refrigerate up to 12 hours. Prepare giblets for broth and stuffing, if desired. Cover and refrigerate giblets in broth along with the bird. You can also prepare the dry ingredients for stuffing 1 day ahead. *Do not add liquid or finish the stuffing mixture more than 2 hours before cooking.*

For easy carving, remove the wishbone before stuffing, if desired. Place bird, breast-side up, on a work surface. Fold back skin from neck cavity. The arching wishbone will faintly appear through the flesh. Using a small boning knife, cut along the outline between the bone and flesh. Press flesh away from the bone with your fingers, easing the bone toward you. Twist it slightly back and forth. It will snap out easily in 1 piece.

When stuffing poultry, stuff just before roasting. Do not fill the cavity completely because stuffing expands during cooking. Allow 1/3 to 1/2 cup stuffing per pound of bird weight, a little less for small poultry. Additional stuffing can be baked separately. Rub the stuffed bird completely with oil, butter or other fat. This helps to form a seal to over the skin to prevent loss of juices during roasting.

How to Truss Poultry

Trussing poultry makes it easy to handle while cooking. It also helps to hold the meat in shape, making it more attractive and easier to carve.

1/Place bird, breast-side up, on work surface. Using a sharp knife or poultry shears, remove wing-tips, if desired.
2/Lift wings up toward neck and fold second joints under back.
3/Place the middle of a 3-to-5 ft. length of string (depending on size of bird) under the tail. Bring the string-ends up and cross over the ends of the drumsticks, bringing string under the drumsticks. Pull drumsticks tightly together and cross string over.
4/Pull string-ends just under the drumsticks along both sides of the bird. Place your thumbs on both sides of the neck and pull the breast forward while pulling up these strings. Turn bird

1/To stuff poultry, place bird in a bowl or sink, neck-end down. Loosely spoon stuffing into cavity. DO NOT PACK BECAUSE STUFFING EXPANDS DURING COOKING.

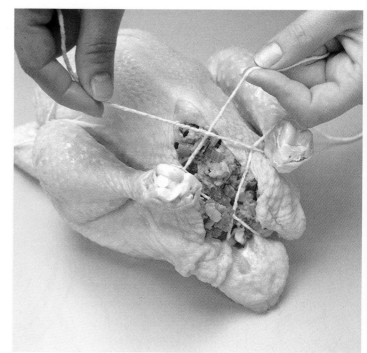

2/Place chicken breast-side up. Place the middle of a 3- to 5-ft. length of string under the tail. Bring string-ends up, crossing over ends of drumsticks, bringing them under drumsticks. Pull tightly together and cross over.

breast-side down. Bring 1 end of the string over 1 wing and over the neck skin. Bring the other end over the other wing and tie the 2 string-ends tightly in a secure knot.

Place poultry on its side on a rack in a shallow roasting pan. Using a rack allows heat to circulate under and around the bird. This results in a crisp, golden-brown skin. Placing the bird on first 1 side and then the other side keeps the juices from draining down and out of the breast.

Roast chicken at a high temperature (425F, 220C). At this temperature, the bird is cooked before it becomes dry. Roast turkey at 425F (220C) until skin is browned. Then, reduce heat and roast until done. Baste often during roasting to keep the skin sealed and meat juicy.

To measure doneness, insert a meat thermometer in the inner-thigh muscle. Poultry is done when the temperature reaches 180F to 185F (80C to 85C). The temperature will rise very little, if any, during standing time. Therefore, it is best to cook poultry to the desired level of doneness. Another way to test doneness is to pierce the inner-thigh muscle with a fork or sharp knife. Juices should run clear. The meat should feel soft, and the drumstick and leg joint move easily. Stuffing temperature should be 165F (75C).

Place roasted poultry on a platter or carving board. Allow it to stand at room temperature 10 to 15 minutes before carving. This allows the juices to settle and prevents excess moisture loss during carving. Serve garnished with your favorite sauce or accompaniments.

U.S.D.A. Poultry-Roasting Guide

Kind	Weight, ready to cook (pounds)	Approximate roasting time at 325F (165C) (hours)
Chicken, whole, stuffed:		
Broiler or fryer	1-1/2 to 2-1/2	1 to 2
Roaster	2-1/2 to 4-1/2	2 to 3-1/2
Capon	5 to 8	2-1/2 to 3-1/2
Duck	4 to 6	2 to 3
Goose	6 to 8	3 to 3-1/2
	8 to 12	3-1/2 to 4-1/2
Turkey:		
Whole, stuffed	6 to 8	3 to 3-1/2
	8 to 12	3-1/2 to 4-1/2
	12 to 16	4-1/2 to 5-1/2
	16 to 20	5-1/2 to 6-1/2
	20 to 24	6-1/2 to 7
Halves, quarters, pieces	3 to 8	2-1/2 to 3
	8 to 12	3 to 4
Boneless roasts	3 to 10	3 to 4

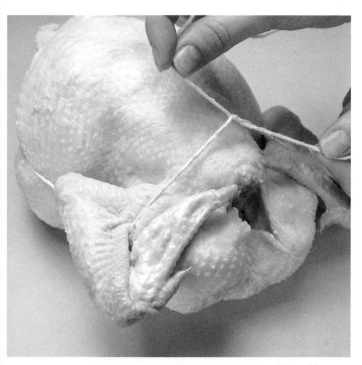

3/Pull string-ends under drumsticks along sides. Turn breast-side down. Bring 1 string over 1 wing and neck skin. Bring other end over other wing. Knot tightly.

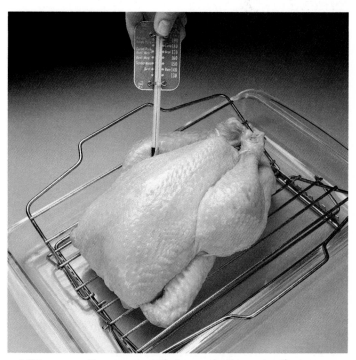

4/Place poultry on a rack in a shallow roasting pan. Insert a meat thermometer in inner-thigh muscle. Poultry should be cooked to 180F to 185F (80C to 85C).

Traditional Carving Method

1/Remove leg and thigh section by pressing leg away from body. Cut through thigh joint, carefully following body contour. Repeat for opposite side of bird.

2/To slice breast, place knife parallel and close to wing. Make a deep base cut into breast to the bone. Slice breast, cutting downward, ending at base cut.

Carving Roast Poultry

Traditional Carving Method

To remove drumstick and thigh, press leg away from body. The leg-to-backbone joint will often snap free or may be severed easily with knife point. Cut dark meat completely from body by carefully following body contour.

To slice dark meat, place drumstick and thigh on a separate plate. Cut through connecting joint. Both pieces may be sliced individually. Tilt drumstick to a convenient angle, slicing towards plate. To slice thigh, hold firmly on the plate with a fork. Cut even slices parallel to the bone.

To slice the breast, place knife parallel and as close to the wing as possible. Make a deep cut into the breast, cutting right to the bone. This is a *base cut*. Breast slices will stop at this vertical cut. Begin to slice the breast, cutting downward, ending at base cut. Start each new slice slightly up on the breast. Cut slices thin and even.

Side Carving Method

Place bird on its side, breast away from carver. Remove wing-tip and first joint. Hold tip firmly, lift up, and sever at joint. Leave second joint of wing attached to bird.

Remove drumsticks. Slice dark meat off drumstick and thigh until thigh bone is exposed. Lift drumstick and cut off at thigh joint. Slice meat from drumstick.

Cut away thigh bone. Steady bird with fork. Run knife point completely around thigh bone, loosening it. Pry one end up, grasp and pull free. With thigh bone gone, generous portions of dark meat can be sliced from bird.

Slice dark meat away from bird just above removed thigh bone. As you work deeper into the meat, you will discover the *oyster*. This choice piece may be lifted whole from spoon-shaped section of backbone.

Make a deep vertical cut in breast just in front of wing joint to serve as base for all breast-meat slices. Start from center of breast and cut toward you, making large, even slices. When more slices are needed, turn bird and repeat process. Remove and serve stuffing.

Old-Fashioned Stuffed Chicken

It never has and never will go out of style.

1 (4- to 5-lb.) chicken	Salt
Giblets and stock for stuffing and gravy, page 62	1/4 cup butter, soft but not melted
Choice of stuffing	2 tablespoons brandy, if desired
1 tablespoon vegetable oil	Giblet Gravy, below, if desired

Remove giblets from chicken. Prepare giblets and stock for stuffing and gravy. Prepare desired stuffing. Place oven rack at the lowest position. Preheat oven to 400F (205C). Remove any excess fat from chicken; discard. Place chicken, neck-side down, in a large bowl. Loosely fill body cavity with stuffing. Spoon remaining stuffing into a 4- to 6-cup casserole dish; set aside. Remove chicken from bowl; blot dry. Truss chicken, if desired. Rub chicken well with oil. Season with salt, rubbing salt into oil with your fingers. Place chicken on its side on a rack in a shallow roasting pan. Insert a meat thermometer in center of inner-thigh muscle, if desired. Roast 20 minutes or until evenly browned. Turn chicken to other side. Spread with softened butter. Roast 20 minutes or until evenly browned. Turn chicken on its back. Spread breast of chicken with butter. Roast 30 to 40 minutes. During final 30 to 40 minutes of cooking, place uncovered casserole of stuffing in oven. Bake 30 to 40 minutes or until firm. Chicken is done when thermometer registers 180F to 185F (80C to 85C) or when juices run clear when a knife is inserted between thigh and breast. Stuffing temperature should register 165F (75C). Place chicken on a platter. Let stand 10 minutes before carving. Serve with stuffing. Pour pan juices into a small saucepan, if desired. Place over medium heat. Add brandy, if desired, and cook, stirring constantly, 2 to 3 minutes. Spoon 1 to 2 tablespoons over each serving or add to giblet gravy, if desired. Makes 4 to 6 servings.

Variations

Substitute 2 (3-pound) chickens for 1 (4- to 5-pound) chicken. Increase roasting time by about 10 minutes. The smaller chickens will provide more serving pieces, making 6 to 8 servings.

Small (6- to 12-pound) turkeys may be prepared as directed above.

Giblet Gravy

Liver strongly flavors gravy or stuffing, therefore use only a small amount to taste.

2 tablespoons butter	Chopped cooked giblets, page 62
2 tablespoons all-purpose flour	2 tablespoons dry sherry or Madeira wine
1 pint (2 cups) hot giblet stock, page 62, or chicken stock	Salt and coarsely ground pepper to taste
Pan juices from roast poultry, if desired	

Melt butter in a large heavy skillet over low heat. Stir in flour. Cook, stirring constantly until blended. Add stock and roasting-pan juices, if desired. Stir with a whisk until smooth. Add chopped gizzard and heart. Stir in sherry or wine until thickened. Season with salt and pepper. Serve hot. Makes 2 cups.

Giblets & Stock for Gravy & Stuffing

Use cooked giblets in gravy or stuffing.

Poultry giblets, including heart,
  liver and gizzard
Water
1 small onion, cut in quarters

1 garlic clove, crushed
1 bay leaf
1/2 teaspoon salt

Place giblets in a medium saucepan. Cover with water; bring to a full boil. Skim foam from surface until surface is clear. Add onion, garlic, bay leaf and salt. Reduce heat and simmer 15 minutes. Using a slotted spoon, remove liver; set aside to cool. Finely chop cooled liver; set aside. Simmer remaining giblets until tender, about 1 hour. Remove remaining giblets from liquid; finely chop giblets. Set chopped giblets aside. Strain cooking liquid; set aside until ready to use. Use cooked giblets and cooking liquid in gravy or stuffing. Also use cooking liquid as stock.

Variation

When adding onion, add 1 celery stalk, cut in 1-inch pieces, if desired.

Leftover cooked poultry, stock, stuffing and gravy should be separated, covered and refrigerated. Use within 1 to 2 days. Freeze for longer storage.

Seasoned Butters

Butter may be seasoned in a variety of ways for use as a baste while roasting, baking or grilling chicken or other poultry.

Combine 1/2 cup butter with any of the following herbs or spices, or create your own basting butter with your favorite seasoning.

1 teaspoon Herbs of Provence
1 teaspoon fines herbes
1 teaspoon dried dill weed
1 teaspoon lemon juice
1 teaspoon chopped parsley
1 teaspoon chopped chives
1 teaspoon dried leaf rosemary

1 teaspoon dried leaf tarragon
1 teaspoon ground rubbed sage
1 teaspoon curry powder
1 teaspoon chopped chervil
1 teaspoon lemon balm
1 teaspoon Italian herb seasoning
1 teaspoon finely chopped mint

Walnut-Cornbread Stuffing

This old-fashioned New England stuffing uses unsweetened homestyle bread.

8 to 10 slices white bread
5 cups crumbled cornbread, page 153
1/2 cup butter
2 medium onions, chopped
1 small green pepper, chopped
4 to 6 celery stalks, chopped
1/2 cup giblet stock, opposite
  or chicken stock
1/4 cup chopped walnuts

1/4 teaspoon poultry seasoning
2 tablespoons chopped parsley
1/4 teaspoon ground ginger
2 large eggs
2 to 3 dashes aromatic bitters or
  hot-pepper sauce, if desired
Chopped cooked chicken livers, if desired
Salt and coarsely ground pepper to taste

Preheat oven to 200F (95C). Cut bread into cubes. Spread bread cubes on a baking sheet. Bake 1 hour or until dry but not browned. Place bread cubes in a large bowl. Add cornbread. Melt butter in a heavy skillet over low heat. Add onions, green pepper and celery. Sauté 3 to 4 minutes or until tender. Add sautéed vegetables to bread mixture. Add stock, walnuts, poultry seasoning, parsley, ginger and eggs. Add bitters or hot-pepper sauce and livers, if desired. Season with salt and pepper. Blend well. Stuff poultry according to recipe directions, or bake stuffing, uncovered, in a 3-quart casserole at 350F (175C) 30 to 40 minutes or until firm. Makes 6 servings or enough to stuff a 4- to 5-pound chicken with a small dish of stuffing for baking.

Variation

Substitute French-bread cubes for cornbread, and add 1 cup cooked chopped spinach and 1/2 cup grated Parmesan cheese.

Fruit Stuffing

Try this stuffing with goose or duck.

1 (6-oz.) pkg. mixed dried fruit
  with raisins
1/2 cup dry sherry
3 cups croutons
1 pint (2 cups) giblet stock,
  opposite, or chicken stock
1 cup water

1/4 cup butter
1 small onion, minced
2 to 3 large mushrooms, minced
1/4 cup chopped walnuts or hazelnuts
2 eggs, beaten
1 teaspoon salt

In a medium bowl, combine fruit with raisins and sherry. Let stand 1 to 2 hours at room temperature. In a large bowl, combine croutons, stock and water. Stir in fruit and any remaining liquid; set aside. Melt butter in a small skillet over low heat. Add onion and mushrooms. Sauté 2 to 3 minutes or until soft. Add onion mixture to crouton mixture, scraping well to remove any brown bits from bottom of skillet. Add nuts, eggs and salt. Blend thoroughly; set aside until ready to stuff poultry. Or, place in a 2-quart casserole dish. Bake, uncovered, in a preheated 350F (175C) oven 40 to 45 minutes or until firm. Makes enough to stuff a 10-pound turkey.

Raisin-Bread Stuffing

Equally good with roast turkey or chicken.

10 to 12 slices whole-wheat raisin bread
1/2 cup butter
1 medium onion, finely chopped
2 to 3 celery stalks, finely chopped
Chopped cooked chicken livers, if desired
1/2 cup chopped pecans, if desired

1/2 cup giblet stock, page 62,
    or chicken stock
1/2 teaspoon salt
1/4 teaspoon coarsely ground pepper
1/2 teaspoon poultry seasoning or
    ground rubbed sage

Preheat oven to 200F (95C). Cut bread into cubes. Spread bread cubes on a baking sheet. Bake 1 hour or until dry but not browned. Place bread cubes in a large bowl. Melt butter in a large heavy skillet over low heat. Add onion and celery. Sauté 3 to 4 minutes or until tender. Add sautéed vegetables to bread cubes. Add livers and pecans, if desired. Stir in stock, salt, pepper and poultry seasoning or sage. Blend well. Stuff poultry according to recipe directions, or bake stuffing, uncovered, in a 2-quart casserole dish at 350F (175C) 30 to 40 minutes or until firm. Makes 6 servings or enough to stuff a 3- to 4-pound chicken with a small dish of stuffing for baking.

Variation

When adding livers, stir in 1 small can of oysters, drained and cut-up, or 1 cup chopped cooked chestnuts or 1/2 cup fresh cranberries.

Sausage & Cornbread Stuffing

An interesting side dish to accompany roast capon or goose.

2 cups crumbled cornbread, page 153
2 cups soft fresh whole-wheat breadcrumbs
1-1/2 cups giblet stock, page 62,
    or chicken stock
1/4 cup butter
1 medium onion, finely chopped

1 celery stalk, thinly sliced
Chopped cooked chicken livers, if desired
1 (1-lb.) pkg. highly seasoned sausage or
    Smithfield ham, finely chopped
2 eggs, beaten
Salt and coarsely ground pepper to taste

Combine cornbread and breadcrumbs in a large bowl. Add stock; mix well. Melt butter in a large heavy skillet over medium heat. Add onion; sauté 3 to 4 minutes or until tender. Add celery; cook 2 to 3 minutes or until celery is crisp-tender. Stir in livers, if desired. Add onion mixture to breadcrumbs. Place ham or sausage in skillet. Cook, stirring over medium heat, 5 to 6 minutes or until no longer pink. Add cooked meat and eggs to breadcrumb mixture. Blend mixture thoroughly. Season with salt and pepper. Stuff poultry according to recipe directions, or bake stuffing, uncovered, in a 2-quart casserole at 350F (175C) 30 to 40 minutes or until firm. Makes 6 servings or enough to stuff a 3-1/2- to 4-pound chicken with a small dish of stuffing for baking.

Variation

When adding eggs, add 1 diced apple or 3/4 cup dried fruit such as apricots, peaches or figs.

Sausage & Apple Stuffing

A good side dish with any meat you are serving.

10 cups bread cubes
  (about 18 slices firm white bread,
  crusts removed, cut in cubes)
1 lb. bulk sausage
1 large onion, chopped

4 small crisp cooking apples,
  peeled, chopped
1 egg, slightly beaten
1/2 to 2/3 cup giblet stock, page 62
Salt and coarsely ground pepper to taste

Preheat oven to 250F (120C). Spread bread cubes evenly on a long baking sheet. Bake, stirring occasionally, 10 minutes or until crisp. Place in a large bowl; set aside. In a large skillet, cook sausage until no trace of pink remains. Remove from skillet with slotted spoon. Add sausage to bread cubes. Pour off all but 2 tablespoons rendered sausage fat. Add onion and apples to fat. Cook, stirring frequently, 5 minutes or until onion is tender. Add onion mixture, egg and stock to bread-cube mixture. Blend well. Season with salt and pepper; set aside until ready to stuff turkey. Makes about 10 cups.

Dinner in a Roasted Chicken

Vegetables roasted in the chicken make an easy, complete meal.

5 small new potatoes,
  cut in 1-1/4-inch cubes
3 medium carrots, cut in 1/8-inch slices
1 teaspoon salt
2 tablespoons vegetable oil
1/4 lb. turkey ham
2 medium onions, cut in quarters
1 (4-1/2- to 5-lb.) chicken

1/2 small lemon
1 teaspoon poultry seasoning or
  1/2 teaspoon ground rubbed sage and
  1/2 teaspoon dried leaf marjoram
2 tablespoons soft butter
Salt
1 pint (2 cups) water

Preheat oven to 450F (230C). In a large saucepan, place potatoes, carrots and salt. Cover with water; bring to a boil over medium heat. Boil 5 minutes. Drain well; set aside. Heat oil in a small skillet over medium heat. Add ham; sauté 1 minute. Remove ham; drain on paper towel. Add ham and onions to potato mixture. Rub body cavity with lemon. Sprinkle chicken with poultry seasoning or sage and marjoram. Lightly stuff body cavity with potato mixture. Place any leftover vegetables in a small baking dish. Top with 1 tablespoon butter. Cover and place in oven during final 30 minutes of roasting. Truss chicken, if desired. Rub chicken with butter. Season with salt. Place chicken, breast-side down, on a V-shaped roasting rack with a non-stick finish or on a rack in a shallow roasting pan. Pour 2 cups water in bottom of pan. Be sure water does not touch chicken. Roast 45 minutes. Turn chicken, breast-side up, adding water to maintain level. Insert a meat thermometer in center of inner-thigh muscle, if desired. Roast 45 minutes longer or until thermometer registers 180F to 185F (80C to 85C) or when juices run clear when a knife is inserted between thigh and breast. Let stand 10 minutes before carving. Scoop out vegetables and place in a dish. Carve chicken and arrange on a large platter. Surround chicken with vegetables. Makes 4 to 6 servings.

Spicy Red Chicken from India

The spicy marinade used in this recipe colors the chicken red.

1 cup plain yogurt
2 teaspoons minced gingerroot or
   1/2 teaspoon ground ginger
1 tablespoon paprika
1 small onion, cut in quarters
1 garlic clove, minced

1 teaspoon dried leaf coriander
1 teaspoon dried leaf cumin
1 teaspoon salt
1 to 2 drops red food coloring, if desired
1 (3- to 3-1/2-lb.) chicken, skinned

In a blender or food processor fitted with a steel blade, combine yogurt, ginger, paprika, onion, garlic, coriander, cumin, salt and food coloring, if desired. Process until smooth. Tie chicken legs together. Using a small knife, pierce flesh at 1-inch intervals over entire chicken. Place chicken in a large bowl. Add yogurt mixture. Spoon some yogurt mixture into body cavity. Cover and refrigerate overnight or up to 24 hours, basting occasionally. Place oven rack at lowest position. Preheat oven to 450F (230C). Remove chicken from marinade. Scrape off excess marinade. Truss chicken, if desired. Place chicken on its side on a rack in a shallow roasting pan. Insert a meat thermometer in center of inner-thigh muscle, if desired. Pour water into bottom of roasting pan. Roast chicken 10 to 15 minutes. Turn to other side and roast 10 to 15 minutes longer. Reduce heat to 375F (190C). Turn chicken on its back and roast 15 minutes longer per pound or until thermometer registers 180F to 185 F (80C to 85C) or until juices run clear when a knife is inserted between thigh and breast. Let stand 10 minutes before carving. Makes 4 servings.

How to use a Vertical Roasting Rack

Vertical roasters hold poultry in an upright position. The roaster is an hourglass-shape wire rack. During cooking, any fat drains off and is collected in a pan placed below the rack. When cooking on a vertical roasting rack, it is not necessary to rotate the bird.

To roast a chicken on a vertical roasting rack, position oven rack at lowest position. Preheat oven to 450F (230C). Remove any excess fat from chicken; discard. Press chicken onto rack according to manufacturer's directions. Set roaster in a round 8- or 9-inch pan. Pour 1/2 cup water into bottom of pan. Insert a meat thermometer into center of inner-thigh muscle. Roast 15 minutes. Reduce heat to 375F (190C). Roast an additional 15 minutes per pound. Roast until thermometer registers 180F to 185F (80C to 85C) or until juices run clear when a knife is inserted between thigh and breast. Let stand 10 minutes before carving. Carve poultry on the rack.

Roast Goose & Peach Stuffing   *Photo on page 68.*

Serve with buttered Brussels sprouts and mushrooms.

Peach Stuffing, see below

Gravy, if desired, see below

1 (9- to 10-lb.) goose, thawed, if frozen

Peach Stuffing:
Goose giblets
2 small onions
3 cups water
1 bay leaf
1/2 teaspoon salt
1/4 teaspoon coarsely ground pepper
1 (29-oz.) can spiced peaches with juice
1/2 cup butter

2 celery stalks, chopped
6 cups soft breadcrumbs
1/2 teaspoon ground rubbed sage
1 egg
1 (3-3/4-oz.) pkg. chopped walnuts
   (about 3/4 cup)
1/4 cup brandy

Gravy:
3 tablespoons goose fat
   from roasting pan
3 tablespoons all-purpose flour
Reserved liquid used to cook giblets

About 1-1/2 cups water
1/4 cup brandy
Salt to taste

Remove giblets from goose; set aside. Prepare Peach Stuffing. Remove any excess fat from goose, reserving 1 piece of fat. Preheat oven to 350F (175C). Loosely fill neck and body cavities with about 4 cups stuffing mixture. Place remaining stuffing in a 1-quart baking dish. Place in oven about 30 minutes before goose is done. Fasten neck skin to back of goose using skewers. Fasten body cavity with skewers; lace with string. Bring tail up between drumsticks. Tie ends of drumsticks and tail together with string. Rub the rack of a shallow roasting pan with reserved goose fat. Prick goose skin all over to let fat drain during roasting. Place goose, breast-side up, on rack in shallow roasting pan. Insert a meat thermometer in center of inner-thigh muscle, if desired. Roast, uncovered, 45 minutes to 1 hour or until skin is well-browned. Pour fat from bottom of roasting pan, reserving 3 tablespoons for gravy, if desired. Loosely place a tent of foil over browned goose. Roast goose 2 to 2-1/2 hours or until thermometer registers 180F to 185F (80C to 85C) or juices run clear when a knife is inserted between thigh and breast. Place roasted goose on a large platter. Let stand 10 to 15 minutes before carving. Prepare Gravy, if desired. Makes 8 to 10 servings.

Peach Stuffing:
Remove and discard tough skin from gizzard. Remove veins from liver. Cut 1 onion in quarters. Chop remaining onion. In a medium saucepan, combine giblets, quartered onion, water, bay leaf, salt and pepper. Bring to a boil. Reduce heat and simmer 10 minutes. Using a slotted spoon or tongs, remove liver; set aside. Continue to simmer remaining mixture until gizzard and heart are tender. Remove gizzard and heart from liquid. Strain, reserving cooking liquid. Finely chop liver, gizzard and heart. Place in a large bowl; set aside. Drain spiced peaches, reserving juice. Finely chop peaches; set aside. Melt butter in a large skillet over low heat. Add chopped onion and celery. Sauté 3 to 4 minutes or until soft. Add peach juice and 1 cup of reserved liquid from cooking giblets. Bring to a boil. Reduce heat; simmer 10 minutes. Add to chopped giblets. Add chopped peaches, breadcrumbs, sage, egg, walnuts and brandy. Blend well.

Gravy:
Heat fat in a large skillet over medium heat. Stir in flour; cook until smooth and bubbly. Slowly add reserved liquid, water and brandy, stirring as added. Cook, stirring until thickened.

Basic Roast Duck   *Photo on page 152.*

Accent roast duck with your favorite sauce or glaze.

Currant-Jelly Glaze, opposite;   **1 (5- to 6-lb.) duck, thawed, if frozen**
  Orange Sauce, below; or   **1/4 cup water**
  Black-Forest Cherry Sauce, opposite

Prepare desired sauce or glaze. Preheat oven to 350F (175C). Remove giblets and neck from duck cavity. Reserve for other use. Remove any excess fat from duck; discard. Prick duck skin all over to let fat drain during roasting. Place duck, breast-side up, on a rack in a shallow roasting pan. Pour water in bottom of roasting pan. Insert a meat thermometer in center of inner-thigh muscle, if desired. Roast duck 2 hours without opening oven door. Or, roast until thermometer registers 180F to 185F (80C to 85C) or until juices run clear when a knife is inserted between thigh and breast. Cool duck slightly. Using kitchen shears or a sharp knife, cut duck into quarters. You should have 2 leg-thigh pieces and 2 breast-wing pieces. Preheat broiler. Place rack 4 to 6 inches below heat. Place duck quarters, skin-side up, on a rack in a shallow roasting pan. Broil until skin is crisp and browned. If serving with Currant-Jelly Glaze, brush with glaze. Broil until skin is well glazed. If serving with a sauce, add browned quarters to prepared sauce in a skillet. Heat over low, spooning sauce over duck. Place duck on a platter. Pour remaining sauce over duck or serve separately. Makes 2 to 4 servings.

Orange Sauce

Orange juice can be substituted for liqueur, if you prefer.

1 large navel orange   **1/4 cup chicken stock**
2 tablespoons sugar   **1 tablespoon cornstarch**
2 tablespoons cider vinegar   **2 tablespoons Grand Marnier or**
1-1/2 cups chicken stock   **other orange liqueur**
2 tablespoons lemon juice   **Salt to taste**
1/2 teaspoon salt

Using a knife or vegetable peeler, cut peel from orange. Cut colored portion of peel into thin strips; discard white portion. Place strips of orange peel in a small saucepan. Cover with water. Bring to a boil over high heat. Reduce heat and simmer 10 minutes. Drain well; set aside. Using a sharp knife, remove white membrane from orange. Cut orange into 1/4-inch slices. Quarter each slice; set aside. In a heavy saucepan, combine sugar and vinegar. Cook over low heat, without stirring, until sugar dissolves. Stir until mixture becomes a deep golden color. Add 1-1/2 cups stock. The syrup will harden immediately. Bring to a boil. Reduce heat and cook, stirring until syrup dissolves. Add lemon juice and salt. In a small bowl, stir remaining 1/4 cup stock into corn-starch. When smooth, add to simmering sauce. Stir until sauce is smooth and thick. Add liqueur, orange peel and orange slices. Makes about 2 cups.

Shown on the preceding pages, Roast Goose & Peach Stuffing, page 67.

Currant-Jelly Glaze

A glaze adds beauty as well as flavor to any roast poultry.

3 tablespoons currant jelly
1 tablespoon soy sauce

1 tablespoon dry sherry

Combine all ingredients in a small saucepan. Cook over low heat until jelly is dissolved. Makes about 1/4 cup.

Variations

Create a variety of glazes using any jam, jelly or preserve. Here are a few combinations.
3 tablespoons apricot jam and 1/2 teaspoon ground ginger
3 tablespoons jellied cranberry and 1 tablespoon orange marmalade
3 tablespoons plum preserves and 1 tablespoon honey
2 tablespoons grape jelly and 2 tablespoons red wine
3 tablespoons citrus marmalade and 1 tablespoon lemon or orange juice

Black-Forest Cherry Sauce   *Photo on page 152.*

Great for roast duck, roast Cornish hen or broiled chicken.

1 (1-lb.) can pitted dark-red
**   sweet cherries in syrup**
2 tablespoons sugar
2 tablespoons lemon juice

1/2 teaspoon ground allspice
1/4 teaspoon ground cloves
1 tablespoon cornstarch
1/4 cup chicken stock

Drain cherries, reserving syrup. In a 1-cup measure, measure syrup. Add enough water to make 1 cup liquid. Pour into a heavy saucepan. Add sugar, lemon juice, allspice and cloves. Cook over low heat, stirring until sugar dissolves. In a small bowl, combine cornstarch and stock. Stir cornstarch mixture into sauce. Cook, stirring constantly, until thickened. Add cherries; heat through. Makes about 1-3/4 cups.

Ducky Bean Casserole

Wonderfully economical, but rich with duck flavor.

1 (1-lb.) pkg. dried Great Northern beans
**   or other white beans**
3 tablespoons tomato paste
1/2 cup dark molasses

1 teaspoon prepared mustard
1 teaspoon salt or to taste
1 cup packed light-brown sugar
Skin from roasted duck, opposite, chopped

Place beans in a large pot; add water to cover by 2 inches. Soak beans 8 to 12 hours or overnight. Drain beans and return to large pot. Cover with fresh water. Simmer over medium heat 35 to 40 minutes or until tender. Preheat oven to 350F (175C). Drain beans, reserving 1/2 cup bean liquid. In a large pot, combine drained beans, reserved liquid, tomato paste, molasses, mustard, salt, sugar and duck skin. Mix thoroughly. Place mixture in a large casserole dish. Cover; bake 1 hour. Remove cover; bake 30 minutes longer. Makes 8 to 10 servings.

Stuffed Turkey Breast

A spectacular treat for a party buffet.

Apple Stuffing, see below
Honey-Soy Glaze, see below
3 tablespoons butter, melted

1 (7- to 9-lb.) whole bone-in or boneless
    turkey breast, thawed, if frozen
2 tablespoons chopped parsley

Apple Stuffing:
1-1/4 cups croutons
2 medium, tart apples, chopped
1/3 cup apple juice or apple cider
2 tablespoons cider vinegar
3 tablespoons butter

1/4 lb. mushrooms, chopped
1 small onion, minced
1 (3-3/4-oz.) pkg. finely chopped walnuts
    (about 3/4 cup)
1/2 teaspoon salt

Honey-Soy Glaze:
1/3 cup honey
2 tablespoons butter

2 tablespoons soy sauce

Prepare Apple Stuffing; set aside. Prepare Honey-Soy Glaze; set aside. Preheat oven to 350F (175C). If using a bone-in breast, place turkey, skin-side down, on work surface. See opposite for boning instructions. Spread boned or boneless breast out flat. Cover with an even layer of stuffing, almost to edge of meat. Sprinkle with parsley. Roll meat up from 1 long side, jelly-roll fashion. Starting at the tail-end, securely fasten roll together with small poultry skewers. Pull loose neck-skin up and over stuffing at end of breast. Fasten to meat with 1 or 2 skewers. Place breast, seam-side down, on a rack in a shallow roasting pan. Brush top generously with melted butter. Roast 20 minutes per pound, basting often with remaining melted butter. Baste frequently with Honey-Soy Glaze during last 15 minutes of roasting. Roast until a meat thermometer inserted in center registers 180F to 185F (80C to 85C) and stuffing reaches 165F (75C). Place on a platter. Let stand 10 to 15 minutes before slicing. Serve hot or at room temperature. Makes 8 to 12 servings.

Apple Stuffing:
In a medium bowl, combine croutons, apples, juice or cider and vinegar. Stir to blend. Let stand until croutons are softened. Melt butter in a small skillet over medium heat. Add mushrooms and onion. Sauté 4 to 5 minutes or until tender. Scrape contents of skillet over crouton mixture in bowl. Add walnuts and salt; blend well. Set aside until ready to use.

Honey-Soy Glaze:
Combine all ingredients in a small skillet. Stir over low heat until blended. Set aside until ready to use. If necessary, stir over low heat to reblend and liquefy mixture when ready to use.

How to Bone and Stuff a Turkey Breast

1/Holding a knife angled toward the keel bone, cut downward until meat has been removed from each side of bone. Lift keel bone and remove it in 1 piece. Spread boned breast flat.

Using a sharp knife, remove ribcage bones from 1 side of breast. Following contour of bones, cut through thin sheathing that holds bone to meat. As you cut, pull bones up from the meat in 1 piece. Repeat on other side of breast. Almost entire bottom half of breast will be covered with the keel bone. Holding your knife angled toward the bone, scrape downward, until all meat has been removed from 1 side of bone. Repeat on other side. Using kitchen shears or a knife, start at the tail end and cut under the center of the bone toward the top of the breast through the cartilage that holds the center of the keel to the meat. Lift it up and remove it in 1 piece.

2/Cover turkey breast with an even layer of stuffing. Sprinkle lightly with chopped parsley.

3/Place rolled turkey breast, seam-side down, on a rack in a roasting pan. Brush top with melted butter.

Roast Turkey in a Bag

A convenient, easy way to prepare moist, tender and delicious turkey.

1 (10- to 12-lb.) turkey, thawed,
   if frozen
Salt
1 medium lemon, cut in halves
1 carrot, cut in thick pieces
1 medium onion, cut in quarters

1 celery stalk, cut in 1-inch pieces
Salt
1 brown paper bag, large enough to
   hold turkey with room to spare
2 tablespoons orange or citrus marmalade

Preheat oven to 400F (205C). Remove giblets and neck from turkey cavity; reserve giblets for Rice & Giblet Casserole. Reserve neck for turkey stock or soup. Rinse turkey under cold running water; blot dry. Sprinkle body cavity with salt. Squeeze lemon, reserving juice and squeezed lemon halves. Stuff turkey with squeezed lemon halves, carrot, onion and celery. Rub turkey with lemon juice. Sprinkle with salt. Place turkey in a brown paper bag. Fold ends of bag over. Close bag with staples or paper clips or bring bag together and tie with kitchen twine. Place bag with turkey on a rack in a shallow roasting pan. Roast 1 hour. Reduce oven temperature to 375F (190C). Continue roasting 2-1/2 hours. Split top of bag open and fold down. Insert a meat thermometer into center of inner-thigh muscle, if desired. Continue to roast turkey until thermometer registers 180F to 185F (80C to 85C) or until juices run clear when a knife is inserted between thigh and breast. Drumsticks will easily move up and down. Evenly spread marmalade over top of turkey. Increase oven temperature to 450F (230C). Roast until surface is glazed, 5 to 10 minutes. Place turkey on a large platter. Let stand 20 to 30 minutes before carving. Serve with Rice & Giblet Casserole, if desired. Makes 10 to 12 servings.

Rice & Giblet Casserole

Bake as a casserole or use as a stuffing for any poultry.

Giblets from 1 (9- to 12-lb.) turkey
3 cups water
1 teaspoon salt
2 to 3 celery tops
1 bay leaf
1 small onion, cut in quarters
1/2 cup butter
1/2 cup chopped onion
1/2 cup thinly sliced celery

1/2 cup thinly sliced carrot
6 to 8 large mushrooms, chopped
5 cups cooked brown rice or wild rice
1 teaspoon poultry seasoning
1/2 cup raisins, if desired
1/2 cup slivered almonds, if desired
2 eggs
Salt and coarsely ground pepper to taste

Butter a 2-quart casserole dish. In a large saucepan, combine gizzard, heart, water, 1 teaspoon salt, celery tops, bay leaf and quartered onion. Simmer 1 hour. Add liver; simmer until tender. Remove giblets. Finely chop giblets; set aside. Strain stock, reserving 1/2 cup. Place remaining stock in a jar. Cover tightly; reserve for later use. Preheat oven to 350F (175C). Melt butter in a small skillet over low heat. Add chopped onion, celery, carrot and mushrooms. Sauté until tender. Place sautéed mixture in a large bowl. Add chopped giblets, rice and poultry seasoning. Add raisins and almonds, if desired. In a small bowl, beat eggs with 1/2 cup reserved stock. Add egg mixture to rice mixture; blend well. Season with salt and pepper. Spoon rice mixture into buttered casserole. Bake 45 minutes to 1 hour. Serve hot. Makes 8 servings.

Cheesecloth-Covered Roast Turkey

Another easy method that guarantees a moist, juicy and flavorful holiday turkey.

Giblet Stock for Gravy and Stuffing,
  page 62
Choice of stuffing, page 63 to 65
1 (10- to 12-lb.) turkey, thawed, if frozen
Salt

1/2 cup butter
1/4 cup peanut oil, safflower oil or
  vegetable oil
Giblet Gravy, page 61, if desired

Prepare stock and stuffing. Rinse turkey under cold water; blot dry. Sprinkle body cavity with salt. Spoon about 1/2 cup stuffing into neck cavity. Smooth neck skin over stuffing and secure to back of bird. Twist wing-tips up and back, flat against skewered neck skin. Lightly stuff turkey. Bring loose skin over cavity; lace with skewers and twine. Loop twine around ends of drumsticks; tie securely together. Place turkey on a rack in a shallow roasting pan. Preheat oven to 325F (165C). Heat butter and oil. Cut a piece of cheesecloth, 3 layers thick, large enough to drape over turkey. Dip cheesecloth into butter mixture. Place cheesecloth over turkey. Roast 3 hours, spooning butter mixture over cheesecloth, as needed. Remove cheesecloth. Insert a meat thermometer into center of inner-thigh muscle, if desired. Roast until browned and thermometer registers 180F to 185F (80C to 85C) or until juices run clear when a knife is inserted between thigh and breast, about 30 minutes. Place turkey on a platter. Let stand 20 to 30 minutes before carving. Serve with Giblet Gravy, if desired. Makes 10 to 12 servings.

Roast Turkey with Fruit Stuffing

Only one basting and no turning makes this juicy bird easy to prepare on a holiday.

Fruit Stuffing, page 63, or
  other stuffing
1 (10- to 12-lb.) turkey, thawed,
  if frozen

1 tablespoon vegetable oil
Salt
2 tablespoons butter, softened
Orange Sauce, page 70, if desired

Prepare Fruit Stuffing. Remove giblets from turkey; reserve for another use. Preheat oven to 400F (205C). Remove excess fat from turkey, especially in tail area. Flatten each fat pad with a heavy cleaver or meat mallet. Cut fat in narrow strips; set aside. Starting at neck opening, carefully lift skin from breast meat on 1 side of breast bone. Using your fingers, pierce the membrane that holds skin to meat. CAREFULLY, slide your hand under the skin, gradually working your fingers around until entire skin has been lifted from breast. Hold the skin up just enough to slide a small knife underneath. Cut 4 long deep slashes, about 1 inch apart, in meat. Force half the fat strips deep into slashes. Repeat on other side of breast. Smooth skin back over breast. Spoon stuffing lightly into neck cavity. Pull neck skin over stuffing. Fasten to back with 2 small skewers. Turn turkey, neck-side down, in a large bowl. Lightly stuff turkey. Close cavity by folding skin over stuffing. Fasten with skewers. Place turkey breast-side up. Lift wings toward neck and fold under the back. Tie tail and end of drumsticks together with string. Rub turkey with oil. Place, breast-side up, on a rack in a shallow roasting pan. Season with salt. Insert a meat thermometer in center of inner-thigh muscle, if desired. Roast 45 to 50 minutes or until browned. Reduce oven temperature to 375F (190C). Loosely cover turkey with a tent of foil. Roast 1 hour. Reduce oven temperature to 325F (165C). Pour 1/2 cup water into roasting pan. Spread butter over turkey. Roast until thermometer registers 180F to 185F (80C to 85C) or until juices run clear when a knife is inserted between thigh and breast. Place turkey on a platter. Let stand 20 to 30 minutes before carving. Serve with stuffing and Orange Sauce, if desired. Makes 12 servings.

Cornish Hens & Onion-Pineapple Stuffing

Onion-soup mix is the special ingredient for the flavorful stuffing.

1 (8-oz.) can unsweetened pineapple chunks
   with juice
1 (8-oz.) pkg. herb-seasoned stuffing
1 envelope dry onion-soup mix
1/2 cup butter
2 to 3 large mushrooms, finely chopped

1-1/2 cups water
4 Cornish hens, thawed, if frozen
1/4 cup butter, melted
Salt
Paprika

Drain pineapple, reserving juice; set juice and pineapple aside. In a medium bowl, combine stuffing and soup mix; set aside. Melt butter in a small saucepan over medium heat. Add mushrooms; sauté 5 minutes. Add water; bring to a boil. Pour mushroom mixture over stuffing mixture. Add pineapple juice; blend well. Preheat oven to 400F (205C). Loosely stuff each hen. Fasten skin over stuffing with skewers. Truss hens, if desired. Spoon remaining stuffing into a 1-1/2- to 2-quart baking dish. Place stuffing in oven 30 minutes before hens are finished. Bake stuffing 20 minutes. Top with pineapple chunks. Sprinkle pineapple with paprika. Bake 10 to 15 minutes longer. Roll each hen in melted butter. Salt each bird lightly. Place each hen on its side on a rack in a shallow roasting pan. Roast 20 to 25 minutes. Turn hens to other side. Brush with melted butter. Roast 20 minutes longer. Turn hens on their backs. Roast 10 to 12 minutes longer or until legs move freely when lifted and twisted. Makes 4 servings.

Cornish Hens with Couscous Stuffing

Flavorful little birds with a Middle Eastern stuffing.

4 Cornish hens, thawed, if frozen
Salt
Paprika
2 tablespoons butter
1 tablespoon vegetable oil
1 medium onion, chopped
1 medium, tart apple, peeled, chopped
1/2 teaspoon salt

1 teaspoon curry powder
1/4 teaspoon saffron threads
2 cups water
1 cup couscous or rice
1/4 cup currants
1/4 cup slivered almonds
1 egg yolk
2 teaspoons cold butter, slivered

Preheat oven to 450F (230C). Season hens, inside and out, with salt and paprika. Heat 2 tablespoons butter and oil in a large saucepan over low heat. Add onion and apple. Sauté 5 to 6 minutes or until very tender. Stir in 1/2 teaspoon salt, curry powder, saffron and 2 cups water. Bring to a full boil. Add couscous or rice, currants and almonds. Cook, stirring occasionally, until water is absorbed, 5 to 6 minutes for couscous, 10 to 12 minutes for rice. Remove from heat; cover and let stand 10 minutes. Fluff mixture with a fork. Stir egg yolk into couscous or rice mixture. Loosely stuff each hen. Fasten skin over stuffing with skewers. Truss hens, if desired. Spoon remaining stuffing into a 1- to 1-1/2-quart baking dish. Place stuffing in oven 15 to 20 minutes before hens are finished. Starting at neck of each bird, slide your fingers under the skin to loosen it from each side of the breast meat. Push slivered butter between meat and skin. Place each hen on its side on a rack in a shallow roasting pan. Roast 10 minutes. Turn hens to other side. Roast 10 minutes longer. Turn hens on their backs. Roast 30 minutes or until legs move freely when lifted and twisted. Birds should be nicely browned. Makes 4 servings.

Perfect Fried Chicken

"The whole secret of good frying comes from the *surprise;* for such is called the action of the boiling liquid which chars and browns, at the very instant of immersion, the outside surfaces of whatever is being fried. By means of this surprise, a kind of glove is formed, which contains the body of food, keeps the grease from penetrating and concentrates the inner juices, which themselves undergo an interior cooking which gives to the food all the flavor it is capable of producing."

These words were written by one of the most knowledgeable gourmets and cookbook authors of all times, Brillat-Savarin. The early-nineteenth-century Frenchman wrote the classic book about food, *Physiology of Taste.* Follow his advice and your fried chicken will be succulent and flavorful and not at all greasy.

For perfect fried chicken, try my recipe for Southern Fried Chicken. This tasty dish will become a permanent item on your family's request list. An old-time favorite of many is Pan-Fried Chicken & Brandied Gravy. Watching calories? That doesn't mean you have to give up fried chicken. Try Calorie-Affordable Fried Chicken for a delicious low-cal treat.

For a more elegant dish, serve chicken thighs as in Spinach-Stuffed Thighs. These are great to make ahead for easy entertaining.

Fried chicken is perfect for a summer picnic or even cold as a late-night snack. No matter what temperature you serve it, your fried chicken will be top quality.

Summer Picnic

Southern Fried Chicken, page 78
French Potato Salad, page 149
Crunchy Raw Vegetables
Butterscotch Cookies
Iced Tea & Lemonade

Southern Fried Chicken *Photo on Cover.*

Perfect fried chicken uses small chickens cut into serving pieces.

2 to 3 (2-1/2- to 3-lb.) chickens,
  cut-up
3 to 3-1/2 cups milk
3 to 4 dashes aromatic bitters or
  hot-pepper sauce

2 to 2-1/2 cups all-purpose flour
2 teaspoons salt
1 teaspoon coarsely ground pepper
1 lb. lard or 3 to 4 cups peanut oil
1/2 cup butter

Place chicken, skin-side down, in 2 or 3 (13" x 9") baking dishes. In a small bowl, combine milk and bitters or hot-pepper sauce. Pour milk mixture over chicken to half cover each piece. Let stand at room temperature 1 hour, turning pieces occasionally. In a pie plate, combine flour, salt and pepper. Remove chicken from milk mixture; drain over plate. Roll chicken in flour mixture; shake off excess. Place coated chicken on a wire rack. Repeat with remaining pieces and flour mixture. Let stand 20 to 30 minutes at room temperature to firm coating. In a deep heavy skillet, heat lard or oil and butter over medium heat to 350F (175C). Place 4 to 5 chicken pieces in hot fat. Avoid crowding or chicken will not brown evenly. Fry, turning with tongs, until evenly browned and cooked through. Allow 25 to 30 minutes for dark meat, 15 to 20 minutes for white meat. To test for doneness, remove 1 piece from hot fat. Pierce meat near bone with point of a knife. Meat should be white but still moist. As each piece is cooked, remove it from fat using tongs or a slotted spoon. Drain on paper towel. Add another flour-coated piece to hot fat. Repeat until all pieces are fried. Serve hot, warm or at room temperature. Makes 10 to 12 servings.

Chicken Cordon Bleu

An entree found on menus throughout the world.

4 chicken-breast halves, skinned, boned
4 thin slices fully cooked smoked ham
4 thin slices Swiss or Gruyère cheese
1/2 cup all-purpose flour
1/2 teaspoon salt
1/4 teaspoon coarsely ground pepper

1 cup dry breadcrumbs
2 eggs
1 tablespoon water
1/2 cup vegetable oil
Lemon wedges
Parsley or watercress

Using a heavy cleaver or meat mallet, flatten each breast half to about 1/4 inch thick. Place 1 slice of ham and 1 slice of cheese on each breast half. Beginning at narrow end, roll up and press meat firmly together. In a pie plate, combine flour, salt and pepper. Spread breadcrumbs in a second pie plate. In a small shallow bowl, beat eggs with water. Roll a chicken piece in flour mixture; shake off excess. Dip piece in egg mixture; drain over bowl. Roll piece in breadcrumbs. Press breadcrumbs evenly onto chicken. Place coated pieces on a wire rack. Repeat with remaining chicken-breast halves. Let stand 20 to 30 minutes at room temperature to firm coating or refrigerate until 30 minutes before frying. In a deep heavy skillet, heat oil to 375F (190C) over medium heat. Fry chicken in hot oil, turning occasionally with tongs, 8 minutes or until golden. Drain on paper towel. Garnish with lemon and parsley or watercress. Serve hot. Makes 4 servings.

Chilled or frozen ready-to-cook poultry may be purchased in various sizes and forms to suit every occasion.

How to Make Chicken Kiev

1/Cut butter in 6 equal pieces. Shape each butter piece in a ball. Roll each butter ball in chive mixture.

2/Place a butter ball in center of each breast half. Roll breast half, pressing meat firmly together.

Chicken Kiev

Make this entree more festive by topping with sour cream and a sprig of fresh tarragon.

6 chicken-breast halves, skinned, boned	**1/2 cup chilled butter**
1 tablespoon finely chopped chives	**1/2 cup all-purpose flour**
1 teaspoon finely chopped parsley	**2 eggs**
1 small garlic clove, minced	**1 tablespoon water**
1/2 teaspoon dried leaf tarragon	**1 cup dry breadcrumbs**
1/2 teaspoon salt	**1 cup vegetable oil**
1/4 teaspoon white pepper	

Using a heavy cleaver or meat mallet, flatten each breast to about 1/4 inch thick. In a small bowl, combine chives, parsley, garlic, tarragon, salt and white pepper. Cut butter into 6 equal pieces. Shape each piece in a ball. Roll each butter ball in chive mixture. Place a butter ball in center of each breast half. Roll each breast half, pressing meat firmly together to enclose butter completely. Place flour in a pie plate. Spread breadcrumbs in a second pie plate. In a small shallow bowl, beat eggs with water. Roll a chicken breast in flour; shake off excess. Dip piece in egg mixture; drain over bowl. Roll piece in breadcrumbs. Press breadcrumbs evenly onto chicken. Place coated pieces on a wire rack. Repeat with remaining chicken. Let stand 20 to 30 minutes at room temperature to firm coating. Pour oil into a deep heavy skillet. Heat oil to 375F (190C). Place chicken rolls in hot oil. Fry, turning occasionally with tongs, 8 minutes or until golden brown. Drain on paper towel. Makes 6 servings.

Variation
Cooked chicken may be placed on a baking sheet and covered with foil. Refrigerate up to 6 hours. Reheat, covered, in a preheated 350F (175C) oven 30 minutes. Uncover and bake 5 minutes.

Batter-Fried Chicken

A quick-and-easy batter guarantees crisp golden goodness.

1 cup chicken stock	**Buttermilk Batter, see below**
1/2 cup dry sherry	**Vegetable oil for deep-frying**
1 (2-1/2- to 3-lb.) chicken,	
cut-up, skinned	

Buttermilk Batter:

1/2 cup buttermilk-biscuit mix	**1/2 teaspoon salt**
1/2 cup all-purpose flour	**3/4 cup club soda**
1 egg	

Combine stock and sherry in a deep heavy skillet. Bring to a simmer over medium heat. Add chicken; simmer 30 minutes. Turn occasionally until cooked through. Remove chicken; set aside. Stock may be reserved for another use. Prepare Buttermilk Batter. Pour oil in skillet to a 1-1/2-inch depth. Heat oil to 350F (175C). Dip a chicken piece in Buttermilk Batter; drain over bowl. Place 4 to 5 pieces batter-dipped chicken in hot oil. Avoid crowding or chicken will not brown evenly. Turn pieces, using tongs, until puffed and evenly browned. Makes 3 to 4 servings.

Buttermilk Batter:
In a blender or food processor fitted with a steel blade, combine all ingredients. Process until smooth. If using a medium bowl, combine biscuit mix and flour. Add egg, salt and club soda. Beat with a whisk until smooth. Set aside until ready to use.

Variations

Cornmeal Batter: In a large bowl, combine 1/2 cup all-purpose flour, 1/2 cup cornmeal, 1/2 teaspoon salt, 1/4 teaspoon pepper and 1 to 2 teaspoons chili powder. Stir in 1 tablespoon vegetable oil, 2 well-beaten egg yolks and 1 cup room-temperature beer. Beat with a whisk until blended. Cover and refrigerate batter 1 to 2 hours. Remove from refrigerator; let stand at room temperature 30 minutes. Add an additional 1/4 cup beer if a thinner batter is desired. Just before using batter, beat 2 egg whites in a small bowl until soft peaks form. Fold into batter.

Beer Batter: In a large bowl, combine 1 cup room-temperature light beer and 1 egg. Beat until blended. Sift 1 cup all-purpose flour, 1/2 teaspoon salt and 1/2 teaspoon paprika, if desired, into beer mixture. Beat until light and smooth. Stir in 1 tablespoon cool melted butter. Let batter stand at room temperature 1 to 2 hours before using, stirring occasionally to keep a film from forming on batter surface.

Determining Frying Temperatures

If you don't have a thermometer to measure the oil temperature when deep-frying, here is a simple way to test the temperature. Drop a 1-inch cube of bread into the hot oil. Time how long it takes bread to turn golden brown. Determine oil temperature based on the following chart:

Oil Temperature	Browning Time
345F to 355F (175C to 180C)	65 seconds
356F to 365F (180C to 185C)	60 seconds
366F to 375F (185C to 190C)	50 seconds
376F to 385F (190C to 195C)	40 seconds
386F to 395F (195C to 200C)	20 seconds

Crumb-Crust Fried Chicken

Fry chicken ahead, bake just before serving.

Choice of crumb coating, see below
1 egg
1 cup milk

6 chicken breast-halves or
   1 (2-1/2- to 3-lb.) chicken, cut-up
Oil for deep-frying

Prepare desired crumb coating. In a shallow bowl, beat egg with milk until blended. Dip a chicken piece in egg mixture; drain over bowl. Roll chicken piece in crumb coating. Press crumbs evenly onto chicken. Place coated chicken on a wire rack. Repeat with remaining pieces. Let stand 20 to 30 minutes at room temperature to firm coating. Or, refrigerate until ready to fry. Bring chicken to room temperature before frying. In a deep heavy skillet, pour oil to a 1-1/2-inch depth. Heat oil to 350F (175C). Fry 2 to 3 chicken pieces in hot oil 2 to 3 minutes or until golden brown on all sides. Drain on paper towel. Place fried chicken, skin-side up, in a long shallow baking dish. Cover and refrigerate until ready to bake, or bake immediately. Preheat oven to 350F (175C). Bake, uncovered, 40 minutes or until cooked through. Serve hot. Makes 3 to 4 servings.

Cracker-Crumb Coating
1-1/2 cups fine dry saltine-cracker crumbs
1/2 teaspoon paprika
1/4 teaspoon coarsely ground pepper

Italian-Style Crumb Coating
1/4 cup grated Parmesan cheese (3/4 oz.)
1 cup Italian-seasoned breadcrumbs

Lemony Crumb Coating
1-1/2 cups crispy rice cereal or cornflakes, finely crushed
1 teaspoon grated lemon peel
1/4 teasoon dried leaf thyme
Salt to taste
1 teaspoon paprika

To make crumb coating, combine all ingredients in a pie plate. Blend well.

Indonesian Oven-Fried Chicken

Chicken with a deliciously different flavor.

1/4 cup creamy peanut butter
1/4 cup orange marmalade
2 tablespoons lemon juice
1 tablespoon soy sauce

1/8 teaspoon ground ginger
1 cup crumbs made from buttery snack
   crackers
4 chicken-breast halves

Preheat oven to 350F (175C). In a shallow bowl, combine peanut butter, marmalade, lemon juice, soy sauce and ginger. Spread cracker crumbs in a pie plate. Dip skin-side of a chicken breast in peanut-butter mixture; drain over bowl. Roll chicken piece in crumbs. Press cracker crumbs evenly onto chicken. Place coated piece, skin-side up, in a 13'' x 9'' baking dish. Repeat with remaining chicken pieces. Bake 30 to 40 minutes or until coating is crisp and brown, and chicken is tender. Makes 3 to 4 servings.

Oven-Fried Chicken Parma

Italian flavor right down to the bone.

1/2 cup olive oil
2 garlic cloves, crushed
1 teaspoon basil
1 (3-lb.) chicken, cut-up

1 cup Italian-seasoned breadcrumbs
1/4 cup freshly grated Parmesan cheese
   (3/4 oz.)
Lemon wedges

Preheat oven to 350F (175C). Pour oil in a large skillet. Add garlic and basil. Cook over low heat until garlic is slightly browned and oil is fragrant; discard garlic. Cool to room temperature. Spoon 1 teaspoon cooled oil in a 13" x 9" baking dish. Spread evenly over bottom of dish; set aside. Add chicken pieces to remaining oil, turning to coat each piece evenly. Using a fork, pierce chicken pieces deeply so oil will penetrate meat. Let chicken stand about 30 minutes. In a pie plate, combine breadcrumbs and cheese. Remove chicken pieces from oil; drain well. Roll each piece in crumb mixture. Press crumbs evenly onto chicken. Place chicken, skin-side up, in a single layer in oiled baking dish. Bake 1 hour or until tender when pierced with a fork and coating is golden brown. Serve with lemon wedges. Makes 3 to 4 servings.

Calorie-Affordable Fried Chicken

Whole-wheat crumbs add extra texture and are good in your diet.

Ice water
Ice cubes
4 to 6 dashes hot-pepper sauce
1 (2-1/2- to 3-lb.) chicken,
   cut-up, skinned
1/2 cup all-purpose flour

1 teaspoon salt
1/4 teaspoon coarsely ground pepper
2 cups fresh whole-wheat breadcrumbs
2 tablespoons butter
3/4 cup vegetable oil
Lemon wedges for garnish

Fill a large bowl with ice water. Add a few ice cubes and hot-pepper sauce. Place chicken pieces in cold water. Let stand 30 minutes. In a pie plate, combine flour, salt and pepper. Spread breadcrumbs in a second pie plate. Drain each chicken piece. Roll a chicken piece in flour mixture; shake off excess. Roll chicken piece in breadcrumbs. Press breadcrumbs evenly onto chicken. Place coated chicken on a wire rack. Repeat with remaining chicken pieces. Let stand 20 to 30 minutes at room temperature to firm coating. Heat butter and oil in a deep heavy skillet over medium heat to 350F (175C). Place 4 to 5 chicken pieces in hot fat. Avoid crowding or chicken will not brown evenly. Fry, turning with tongs, 20 to 30 minutes or until evenly browned and cooked through. To test for doneness, remove 1 piece from hot oil. Pierce meat near bone with point of a knife. Meat should be white but still moist. Remove chicken; drain on paper towel. Serve on a platter garnished with lemon wedges. Makes 3 to 4 servings.

Variation

For added flavor, but no additional calories, season breadcrumbs with 1 teaspoon Italian herb seasoning or 1/4 teaspoon each of dried leaf basil, thyme and rosemary or 1 teaspoon Herbs of Provence or 1 teaspoon zest of orange or lemon.

How to Bone Legs with Thighs

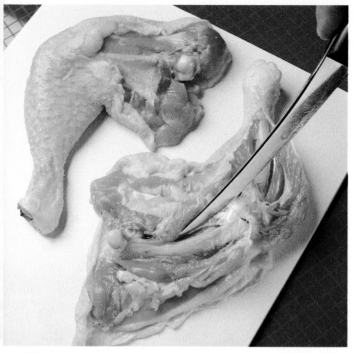

1/Place leg-thigh piece skin-side down on a work surface. Using the point of a sharp knife, cut along full length of bone. Repeat on other side of bone. Keep the meat in 1 piece.

2/Insert knife under end of bone in thigh portion. Cut completely under bone, removing it from meat. Remove any tendons or cartilage. Turn meat skin-side up. Smooth leg and thigh piece into original shape.

Spinach-Stuffed Thighs

Surprise your guests with this unusual treatment of thighs.

1 (10-oz.) pkg. frozen chopped spinach, thawed	1/2 teaspoon salt
1 cup dairy sour cream	1/4 teaspoon coarsely ground pepper
1 envelope dry onion-soup mix	1/8 teaspoon ground nutmeg
1 cup seasoned croutons	2 eggs
6 chicken legs with thighs, boned	1 tablespoon water
1 cup all-purpose flour	2-1/4 cups fine dry breadcrumbs
	Oil for deep-frying

Squeeze spinach to remove all moisture. In a medium bowl, combine spinach, sour cream and soup mix. Stir in croutons. Let stand 10 minutes or until croutons are softened. Stir mixture until smooth. Spoon mixture into each chicken piece. Overlap skin and press firmly together to enclose stuffing. Secure with a wooden pick, if desired. In a pie plate, combine flour, salt, pepper and nutmeg. In a shallow bowl, beat eggs with water. Spread breadcrumbs in a second pie plate. Roll a chicken piece in flour mixture; shake off excess. Dip chicken piece in egg mixture; drain over bowl. Roll chicken piece in breadcrumbs. Press breadcrumbs evenly onto chicken. Place coated chicken on a wire rack. Repeat with remaining pieces. Let stand 20 to 30 minutes at room temperature to firm coating. Or, refrigerate until ready to fry. Bring chicken to room temperature before frying. Preheat oven to 350F (175C). In a deep heavy skillet, pour oil to a 1-1/2-inch depth. Heat oil to 350F (175C). Fry 2 to 3 chicken pieces in hot oil 4 to 5 minutes, turning with tongs to brown evenly. Drain on paper towel. Repeat with remaining chicken. Place browned chicken on a baking sheet. Bake 15 to 20 minutes or until chicken tests done. To test for doneness, pierce meat near bone with point of a knife. Meat should be white but still moist. Makes 4 to 6 servings.

Russian Turkey Cutlets

Turkey takes on a different form in this delicious dish.

2 slices soft white bread, crust removed
1/2 cup dairy sour cream
2 tablespoons butter
1/2 cup finely chopped mushrooms
1 lb. ground raw turkey
1 teaspoon salt
2 teaspoons prepared horseradish
1 cup all-purpose flour

2 eggs
2 tablespoons water
3 cups fine dry breadcrumbs
Oil for deep-frying
6 tablespoons mayonnaise
6 tablespoons dairy sour cream
Salt and coarsely ground pepper to taste
Paprika

Place sliced bread in a large bowl. Add 1/2 cup sour cream. Let stand until absorbed. Melt butter in a small skillet over low heat. Add mushrooms; sauté 5 minutes or until soft. To bread mixture, add sautéed mushrooms, turkey, 1 teaspoon salt and 1 teaspoon horseradish. Stir to blend. Cover and refrigerate 1 hour to firm for easy handling. Place flour in a pie plate. In a shallow bowl, beat eggs with water. Spread breadcrumbs in a second pie plate. Using a spoon, scoop out 2 tablespoons chilled-turkey mixture. Roll turkey mixture in flour mixture; shake off excess. Shape into a flat cutlet or pattie. Dip cutlet in egg mixture; drain over bowl. Dip cutlet in breadcrumbs. Press breadcrumbs evenly onto cutlet. Place coated cutlet on a wire rack. Repeat with remaining turkey mixture. Let stand 20 to 30 minutes at room temperature to firm coating. Preheat oven to 425F (220C). In a deep heavy skillet, pour oil to a 1/2-inch depth. Heat oil to 375F (190C). Place 3 to 4 cutlets in hot oil. Fry 3 to 4 minutes or until evenly browned. Drain on paper towel. Repeat with remaining cutlets. Add more oil as needed. Place browned cutlets on a heatproof platter or in a 13" x 9" baking dish. Bake 8 to 10 minutes. In the top of a double boiler, combine mayonnaise, 6 tablespoons sour cream and remaining 1 teaspoon horseradish. Place over simmering water. Stir until heated through. Season with salt and pepper. Place cutlets on a serving platter or plates. Top each cutlet with 1 tablespoon hot sour-cream mixture. Sprinkle with paprika. Serve hot with cherry or gooseberry sauce. Makes 4 to 6 servings.

Schnitzel Chicken

A German favorite, easy to prepare and rather spectacular.

6 chicken-breast halves, skinned, boned
2 eggs
2 tablespoons all-purpose flour
1/2 teaspoon salt
1 tablespoon grated Parmesan cheese
2 tablespoons minced parsley
3 tablespoons butter

3 tablespoons vegetable oil
1 tablespoon lemon juice
Paprika
Lemon wedges
Hot cooked flat noodles
2 tablespoons poppy seeds

Using a cleaver or meat mallet, flatten each breast piece to about 1/4 inch thick. In a small bowl, beat eggs until foamy. Stir in flour, salt, cheese and parsley. Heat butter and oil in a heavy skillet until foamy. When foam subsides, dip 3 chicken pieces in egg mixture; drain over bowl. Place 3 chicken pieces in hot fat. Cook 2 to 3 minutes or until lightly browned. Placed browned chicken on a heatproof platter. Keep warm until remaining pieces have been fried. Sprinkle with lemon juice and paprika. Garnish with lemon wedges. Serve over noodles sprinkled with poppy seeds. Makes 4 to 6 servings.

Neopolitan Chicken-Breast Rolls

If you love Italy and all things Italian, this is for you.

Tomato Sauce, see below
8 chicken-breast halves, skinned, boned
8 thin slices prosciutto or
  other dry-cured ham
8 (3- to 4-inch) strips mozzarella cheese
1 cup all-purpose flour
1/2 teaspoon salt

1/4 teaspoon coarsely ground pepper
2 eggs
1 tablespoon water
1-1/2 cups Italian-seasoned breadcrumbs
Vegetable oil
1 (8-oz.) pkg. very fine noodles, cooked
Grated Parmesan or Romano cheese

Tomato Sauce:
2 tablespoons olive oil or butter
1 small onion, chopped
1 garlic clove, minced
1/4 teaspoon Italian herb seasoning
1 (1-lb.) can Italian tomato sauce
  with basil

1/4 cup water
1 tablespoon red-wine vinegar
Dash hot-pepper sauce
Salt and coarsely ground pepper to taste

Prepare Tomato Sauce. Preheat oven to 350F (175C). Using a heavy cleaver or meat mallet, flatten each chicken breast to about 1/4 inch thick. Place a slice of ham on a breast piece. Place a strip of cheese on ham. Roll up from long side to enclose ham and cheese. Press firmly to seal closed. Repeat with remaining breasts, ham and cheese. In a pie plate, combine flour, salt and pepper. In a shallow bowl, beat eggs with water. Spread breadcrumbs in a second pie plate. Roll a chicken breast in flour mixture; shake off excess. Dip breast in egg mixture; drain over bowl. Roll breast in breadcrumbs. Press breadcrumbs evenly onto breast. Place coated breast on a wire rack. Repeat with remaining chicken breasts. Let stand at room temperature 20 to 30 minutes to firm coating. In a deep heavy skillet, pour oil to 1-1/2-inch depth. Heat oil to 350F (175C). Fry 3 or 4 chicken-breast rolls in hot oil 2 to 3 minutes. Turn, using tongs, until evenly browned. Place browned rolls on a baking sheet. Bake 10 to 15 minutes. To serve, place noodles on a large platter. Spoon about 3/4 of Tomato Sauce over noodles. Top with chicken-breast rolls and remaining sauce. Sprinkle with grated cheese. Makes 6 to 8 servings.

Tomato Sauce:
Heat olive oil or butter over low heat in a medium saucepan. Add onion and garlic. Sauté 3 to 4 minutes or until tender. Stir in herb seasoning, tomato sauce and water. Bring to a boil, stirring constantly. Reduce heat and simmer 10 to 15 minutes. Stir in vinegar and hot-pepper sauce. Season with salt and pepper. Keep warm until ready to use.

When shopping for food, pick up meat, poultry and dairy items last. Get them home and into the refrigerator or freezer promptly.

1/Place a slice of prosciutto or dry-cured ham on a flattened chicken-breast half. Place a strip of mozzarella cheese on ham.

2/Place a rolled chicken breast in flour mixture; then dip in egg. Roll piece in breadcrumbs. Let coated chicken breasts stand to firm coating.

Cantonese Chicken Wings

A flavorful Oriental marinade is used as part of the batter.

18 chicken wings
6 tablespoons soy sauce
3 tablespoons rice vinegar or white vinegar
1 garlic clove, crushed

1 (1-inch) cube gingerroot, crushed or
   1 teaspoon ground ginger
1 egg, beaten
3/4 cup rice flour or all-purpose flour

Remove small wing-tip section from each chicken wing. Reserve for another use. Place chicken wings in a 13" x 9" baking dish. In a small bowl, combine soy sauce, vinegar, garlic and ginger. Pour soy mixture over chicken wings. Marinate at room temperature, 1 to 2 hours, turning wings occasionally. Remove wings from marinade; set wings aside. Remove garlic and gingerroot from marinade; discard. Stir beaten egg into remaining marinade. Place flour on a pie plate. Dip a wing in marinade mixture; drain over bowl. Roll wing in flour; shake off excess. Repeat with remaining wings. In a deep heavy skillet or wok, pour oil to a 1-1/2-inch depth. Heat oil to 350F (175C). Fry 5 to 6 wings in hot oil, turning with tongs, until golden brown on all sides. Drain on paper towel. Repeat with remaining wings. Serve warm or hot. Makes 18 chicken wings.

Rice flour is generally available in Oriental markets and in the gourmet section of some supermarkets.

Pan-Fried Chicken & Brandied Gravy

Enjoy this flavorful gravy over potatoes or biscuits.

1-1/2 to 2 cups all-purpose flour
1-1/2 teaspoons salt
1 teaspoon coarsely ground pepper
1/4 teaspoon paprika, if desired

1/4 teaspoon ground cinnamon, if desired
1 (2-1/2- to 3-lb.) chicken, cut-up
Peanut oil for deep-frying
Brandied Gravy, see below

Brandied Gravy:
2 tablespoons brandy
1 egg

1 cup whipping cream
Salt and coarsely ground pepper to taste

In a pie plate, combine flour, salt and pepper. Add paprika and cinnamon, if desired. Roll a chicken piece in flour mixture; shake off excess. Place coated chicken on a wire rack. Repeat with remaining chicken. Let stand 20 to 30 minutes at room temperature to firm coating. In a deep heavy skillet, pour oil to a 1-1/2-inch depth. Heat oil to 350F (175C). Place breast and wing pieces in hot oil. Avoid crowding or chicken will not brown evenly. Brown each side lightly. Reduce heat and cover. Cook 15 to 20 minutes or until cooked through. To test for doneness, remove 1 piece from hot oil. Pierce meat near bone with point of a knife. Meat should be white but still moist. Preheat oven to 200F (95C). Remove chicken using tongs or a slotted spoon. Place on a heatproof platter lined with paper towel. Place in warm oven. Increase heat under skillet until oil is reheated to 350F (175C). Fry remaining chicken, 4 to 5 pieces at a time, until evenly browned. Reduce heat and cover. Cook 20 to 25 minutes or until meat tests done. Place on platter to keep warm. Prepare Brandied Gravy. Spoon gravy over each piece or serve gravy in a separate dish. Makes 3 to 4 servings.

Brandied Gravy:
Pour off oil from skillet; discard. Add brandy to skillet. Cook over low heat, scraping up brown bits from bottom of skillet, until brandy is reduced to 1 tablespoon. Remove from heat. In a small bowl, beat egg until blended. Stir in cream. Add egg mixture to skillet, stirring as added. Place skillet over low heat. Cook, stirring constantly, until thickened. Season with salt and pepper.

Dody's Oven-Fried Chicken

This is lazy-day cooking at its best.

8 chicken thighs or 4 chicken-breast halves
1/2 cup mayonnaise
2 teaspoons honey

1-1/2 teaspoons Dijon-style mustard
1 cup soda-cracker crumbs
1/4 teaspoon salt

Preheat oven to 350F (175C). Blot chicken pieces dry. In a small bowl, combine mayonnaise, honey and mustard. Blend well. In a pie plate, combine crumbs and salt. Dip each chicken piece in mayonnaise mixture; drain over bowl. Roll chicken pieces in crumb mixture. Press crumbs evenly onto chicken. Place coated pieces, skin-side up, in a single layer in a 13" x 9" baking dish. Bake 1-1/2 hours or until tender. Makes 4 servings.

Stir-Fried Chicken

If you enjoy today's style of cooking lighter, low-calorie foods, you are undoubtedly aware of Oriental stir-frying. It can be lower in calories than other types of cooking because little oil is needed in its preparation. Cooking over high heat for a short time retains the natural flavors and juices—and most of the nutrients.

Stir-fry in a wok with a rounded or flat bottom and flaring sides or in a deep heavy skillet. Meat is stir-fried only until cooked through. Vegetables are cooked until crisp-tender. Foods are minced, diced, sliced or chopped into bite-size pieces, ideal for quick uniform cooking. And best of all, everything is cooked in the same pan. When ingredients require different cooking times, those requiring longer time go in first. Those needing the least time are added last.

Chicken or turkey breast is great for stir-frying. Place a boned skinned breast in the freezer until very firm. Then slice lengthwise, across the grain. Make thin strips or cut into cubes, according to recipe directions. Prepare all ingredients before beginning to cook. Assemble all ingredients near the wok in the order in which they will be added.

To begin, heat a wok or skillet over high heat 1 minute. Slowly pour about 1 to 2 tablespoons of oil in a thin stream around the rim. The oil will slide down, coating the sides, and collect in a small pool at the bottom. Heat until the oil has nearly reached the smoking point. Then, add ingredients as called for in the recipe. Begin to stir-fry immediately. It's fun, fast and delicious.

One of the most popular stir-fry dishes is Almond Chicken. For variety use walnuts or cashews. Sweet-and-sour dishes combine the flavor of pineapple and the crunch and color of green pepper. Chicken & Mushroom Salad is perfect for any luncheon.

Each recipe is a splendid combination of flavorful ingredients. For additional recipes and information on stir-frying poultry, refer to *Wok Cookery* or *More Wok Cookery,* published by HPBooks.

Oriental Treats
Egg-Drop Soup
Chicken with Cashews, page 91
Hot Steamed Rice
Mini-Egg Rolls
Almond Cookies
Chinese Tea

Chicken with Eggplant

Fresh tomatoes make this stir-fry especially flavorful.

Fresh Tomato Sauce, see below

4 chicken-breast halves, skinned, boned

1 medium eggplant, peeled

2 teaspoons salt

1 cup all-purpose flour

1/4 teaspoon coarsely ground pepper

1/4 cup olive oil

1/2 cup vegetable oil

2 tablespoons butter

Fresh Tomato Sauce:

2 tablespoons butter

1 medium onion, chopped

1 garlic clove, minced

3 tablespoons water

4 to 5 large ripe tomatoes, peeled, chopped

1 teaspoon tomato paste

1 teaspoon sugar

1/4 teaspoon dried leaf rosemary

1/2 teaspoon dried leaf basil

1/2 teaspoon salt

1/4 teaspoon coarsely ground pepper

1 tablespoon dry red wine

Prepare Fresh Tomato Sauce. Slice chicken breasts lengthwise in 1/2-inch strips. Cut eggplant in 1/3-inch slices. Cut slices in 1/4-inch strips. Place eggplant strips in a single layer on paper towel. Sprinkle eggplant with 2 teaspoons salt. Let stand 20 minutes. Rinse eggplant strips to remove salt. Pat dry with paper towel. In a pie plate, combine flour and pepper. Roll eggplant strips in flour mixture; shake off excess. Heat olive oil and vegetable oil in a wok or large heavy skillet over high heat. Fry eggplant strips in hot oil, a few at a time, until evenly browned. Drain on paper towel. Pour off oil; discard. Wipe wok or skillet clean with paper towel. Melt butter in wok or skillet over medium heat until foamy. When foam subsides, add chicken. Stir-fry 1 to 2 minutes or until firm and white. Add Fresh Tomato Sauce and eggplant. Reduce heat and simmer until bubbly hot. Serve hot. Makes 4 to 6 servings.

Fresh Tomato Sauce:

Melt butter in a large heavy skillet over medium heat. Add onion; sauté 1 minute. Add garlic; sauté 30 seconds. Add water, tomatoes, tomato paste, sugar, rosemary, basil, salt, pepper and wine. Reduce heat and simmer 15 to 20 minutes, stirring often. Set aside until ready to use.

Chop Suey

This Chinese-American dish first made its appearance in San Francisco in the 19th century.

3 chicken-breast halves, skinned, boned

2 tablespoons vegetable oil

1 large onion, chopped

3 to 4 celery stalks,
   thinly sliced on diagonal

1 cup fresh bean sprouts

6 to 8 water chestnuts, thinly sliced

1/4 cup chicken stock

2 tablespoons dry sherry

1/4 cup soy sauce

2 teaspoons cornstarch

1/2 teaspoon sugar

Hot cooked rice

Slice chicken breasts lengthwise in narrow strips. Heat oil in a wok or large heavy skillet over high heat. When hot, add chicken; stir-fry until firm and white. Add onion, celery, bean sprouts and water chestnuts. Stir-fry about 30 seconds. Add stock and sherry. Blend well. Cover and steam about 1 minute. In a small bowl, combine soy sauce, cornstarch and sugar. Blend well. Add soy mixture to chicken mixture, stirring until thickened. Serve over rice. Makes 4 to 6 servings.

1/Place eggplant strips in a single layer on paper towel. Sprinkle eggplant with salt. Let stand 20 minutes.

2/In a wok or heavy skillet, stir-fry chicken strips, a few at a time, 1 to 2 minutes or until firm and white.

Chicken with Cashews

Crisp, deep-fried cashews and chicken strips are delicious in a flavorful Oriental sauce.

3 tablespoons vegetable oil
1 cup raw cashews
About 1/4 teaspoon salt
1 tablespoon cornstarch
2 tablespoons soy sauce
2 tablespoons rice wine or dry sherry
1 teaspoon sesame oil
6 chicken thighs, skinned, boned,
   page 47, steps 1 and 2
1/4 lb. mushrooms, thinly sliced
1 tablespoon vegetable oil

1 cup shredded bok choy or Chinese cabbage
1/4 lb. fresh pea pods or
   1 (10-oz.) pkg. frozen pea pods,
   broken apart
1/2 cup slivered Smithfield, Westphalian
   or other highly seasoned ham
6 to 8 green onions, thinly sliced
3/4 cup chicken stock
Hot cooked rice or thin noodles
Minced green-onion tops for garnish

Place 3 tablespoons vegetable oil in a wok or large heavy skillet over high heat. Heat oil to 350F (175C). Add cashews; fry until lightly browned, stirring occasionally. Drain on paper towel. Sprinkle cashews lightly with salt; set aside. Cashews may be fried several hours ahead. Pour off oil; discard. In a small bowl, combine cornstarch and soy sauce. Add wine or sherry and sesame oil. Blend well; set aside. Cut chicken in strips. Place wok or skillet over high heat. Add 1 tablespoon vegetable oil. When hot, add chicken strips. Stir-fry until chicken is firm. Add mushrooms, bok choy or cabbage, pea pods, ham and green onions. Stir-fry 1 minute. Cover and steam 30 seconds. Add stock. Reduce heat and bring to a gentle simmer. Stir cornstarch mixture into simmering liquid. Cook, stirring constantly, until thickened. Stir in cashews. Serve over rice or noodles. Sprinkle with green-onion tops. Makes 4 to 6 servings.

Almond Chicken

Perhaps the most popular of all Oriental stir-fry combinations.

1/2 cup slivered almonds
2 tablespoons vegetable oil
4 chicken-breast halves,
  skinned, boned, diced
1/4 lb. mushrooms, thinly sliced
2 celery stalks, thinly sliced diagonally
1 small green pepper, cut in narrow strips
1/4 cup bamboo shoots, cut in narrow strips
1 garlic clove, minced

2 tablespoons chicken stock
3/4 cup chicken stock
1 tablespoon cornstarch
1 teaspoon sugar
1/4 cup dry sherry
2 tablespoons soy sauce
1/4 cup minced parsley
Hot cooked rice or fine noodles

Preheat oven to 350F (175C). Spread almonds evenly in a pie plate. Bake almonds, shaking frequently, 5 minutes or until lightly browned and crisp; set aside. Heat oil in a wok or large heavy skillet over high heat. Add chicken; stir-fry 1 to 2 minutes or until firm and white. Add mushrooms, celery, green pepper and bamboo shoots. Stir-fry about 1 minute. Add garlic; stir-fry 30 seconds. Add 2 tablespoons stock. Cover and steam about 1 minute. Add remaining 3/4 cup stock; bring to a simmer. In a small bowl, combine cornstarch, sugar, sherry and soy sauce. Stir cornstarch mixture into simmering stock. Cook until thickened, stirring constantly. Stir in almonds and parsley. Serve hot over rice or noodles. Makes 4 to 6 servings.

Stir-Fried Chicken & Shrimp

Bamboo shoots can be substituted for water chestnuts.

4 chicken-breast halves, skinned, boned
2 tablespoons vegetable oil
1 medium onion, chopped
1 small green pepper, cut in 1-inch squares
1/4 lb. mushrooms, thinly sliced
1/4 cup sliced water chestnuts
1 cup chopped Chinese cabbage or bok choy

1/4 cup dry sherry
1/4 cup soy sauce
1 lb. deveined shelled shrimp
1 cup chicken stock
1 tablespoon cornstarch
3 cups hot cooked rice
Chow mein noodles for garnish

Slice chicken breasts lengthwise in narrow strips. Heat oil in a wok or large heavy skillet over high heat. Add chicken. Stir-fry 1 to 2 minutes or until firm and white. Add onion, green pepper, mushrooms, water chestnuts and cabbage or bok choy. Stir-fry 1 minute. Add sherry. Cover and steam 1 minute. Add soy sauce, shrimp and 3/4 cup stock. Cook, stirring constantly, 30 seconds or until shrimp are firm and pink. In a small bowl, combine cornstarch and remaining 1/4 cup stock. Stir cornstarch mixture into chicken mixture. Cook, stirring constantly, until thickened. Serve hot over rice. Sprinkle with chow mein noodles. Makes 4 to 6 servings.

Use fresh-chilled poultry within 1 to 2 days.

Stir-Fried Turkey

Leftover turkey becomes a superb Oriental dish in less than 10 minutes.

1 tablespoon vegetable oil
2 celery stalks,
   cut diagonally in 1/4-inch slices
1 small onion, chopped
1 small garlic clove, minced
2 cups diced cooked turkey or chicken
1 (8-oz.) can water chestnuts,
   drained, thinly sliced

1 (1-lb.) can tomato sauce
2 tablespoons soy sauce
1/4 teaspoon dried red-pepper flakes
1 teaspoon sesame oil, if desired
1/2 cup mung-bean sprouts
Hot cooked rice or fine noodles

Heat vegetable oil in a wok or large heavy skillet over high heat. Add celery and onion. Stir-fry 1 minute. Cover and steam 30 seconds. Add garlic; stir-fry 30 seconds. Stir in turkey or chicken, water chestnuts, tomato sauce, soy sauce, red-pepper flakes and sesame oil, if desired. Reduce heat; simmer 5 to 6 minutes. Stir in bean sprouts. Cook, stirring constantly, 30 seconds. Serve hot over rice or noodles. Makes 4 to 6 servings.

Chinese Sweet & Sour Chicken

A pot of tea and almond cookies complete your Chinese dinner.

3 chicken-breast halves, skinned, boned
Oil for deep-frying
1 egg white
3 tablespoons cornstarch
1 (8-oz.) can unsweetened pineapple
   chunks with juice
1 tablespoon vegetable oil

2 green peppers, cut in strips
1-1/2 cups chicken stock
1 tablespoon light-brown sugar
1 tablespoon vinegar
2 tablespoons soy sauce
1/4 cup water
Hot cooked rice or chow-mein noodles

Slice chicken breasts lengthwise in narrow strips. In a wok or deep heavy skillet, pour oil to a 1-1/2-inch depth. Heat oil to 350F (175C). In a small bowl, beat egg white until frothy. Add 1 teaspoon cornstarch; continue beating. Gradually add 1 tablespoon plus 2 teaspoons cornstarch, beating until egg whites form soft peaks. Dip chicken strips, 1 at a time, in egg-white mixture; drain over bowl. Fry strips in hot oil, a few at a time, until evenly browned. Drain on paper towel. Repeat with remaining chicken. Pour oil from wok or skillet; discard. Wipe wok or skillet clean with paper towel. Drain pineapple, reserving juice. Place wok or skillet over high heat. Add 1 tablespoon oil. When hot, add green peppers. Stir-fry 2 to 3 minutes or until crisp-tender. Pour in reserved pineapple juice and stock. Add sugar, vinegar and soy sauce. Stir to blend. In a small bowl, combine water and remaining 1 tablespoon cornstarch. Stir cornstarch mixture into simmering pineapple-juice mixture. Add pineapple chunks and fried chicken strips, stirring until sauce has thickened. Serve hot over rice. Makes 4 to 6 servings.

Indonesian Rice & Chicken

In Indonesia, this is known as Nasi Goreng.

1/4 cup hot chicken stock
1 teaspoon dark corn syrup
2 tablespoons soy sauce
3 tablespoons vegetable oil
4 chicken-breast halves,
   skinned, boned, diced
1 small onion, chopped
1 (1-inch) cube gingerroot,
   minced or 1 teaspoon ground ginger

1 fresh hot red chili, seeded, minced
2 teaspoons curry powder
3 cups cold cooked rice
1/2 cup chopped peanuts
1/4 cup minced green onion
1/4 cup minced parsley

In a small bowl, combine stock, corn syrup and soy sauce; set aside. In a wok or large heavy skillet, heat oil over high heat. When hot, add chicken. Stir-fry 1 to 2 minutes or until firm and white. Add onion, ginger and chili. Stir-fry 30 seconds. Stir in curry powder and rice. Stir-fry 1 minute. Pour in stock mixture. Stir and lift with a spatula or 2 forks until liquid is absorbed. Stir in peanuts, green onion and parsley. Serve hot. Makes 4 to 6 servings.

Chicken Chow Mein

Mandarin-style chicken and noodles.

2 qts. (8 cups) water
1/2 teaspoon sesame oil or vegetable oil
1 (8-oz.) pkg. dry Chinese noodles or
   thin spaghetti
1 tablespoon sesame oil or vegetable oil
3 chicken-breast halves, skinned, boned
2 tablespoons peanut oil, safflower oil or
   vegetable oil
1 medium onion, chopped

6 to 8 fresh mushrooms, thinly sliced
1 cup shredded Chinese cabbage or
   1 cup fresh bean sprouts
6 to 8 water chestnuts, thinly sliced
1/4 cup chicken stock
2 tablespoons dry sherry
1/4 cup soy sauce
2 teaspoons cornstarch

In a large pot, bring water to a full boil. Stir in 1/2 teaspoon sesame oil or vegetable oil. Add noodles or spaghetti, about 1/4 at a time so water continues to boil. Cook until al dente, 3 to 5 minutes depending on pasta used. Drain well. Place cooked noodles in a large bowl. Stir in 1 tablespoon sesame oil or vegetable oil; set aside. Slice chicken breasts lengthwise in narrow strips. Place a wok or large heavy skillet over high heat. Add peanut oil, safflower oil or vegetable oil. When hot, add chicken. Stir-fry until meat is firm and white. Stir in onion, mushrooms, cabbage or bean sprouts and water chestnuts. Stir-fry 30 seconds. Pour in stock and sherry. Stir-fry 30 seconds. Cover and steam 1 minute. Pour soy sauce in a small bowl. Add cornstarch; stir to blend. Add soy mixture to chicken mixture. Stir until thickened. Remove vegetables and chicken from wok or skillet; set aside. Wipe wok clean with paper towel. Add 2 tablespoons oil. When hot, add noodles. Lift and toss until hot. Add chicken mixture. Stir-fry 1 minute, mixing well. Serve hot. Makes 4 to 6 servings.

Chicken & Mushroom Salad

Impress your luncheon guests with this totally different and delicious salad.

4 chicken-breast halves, skinned, boned
Salt to taste
3 tablespoons vegetable oil
1/2 lb. mushrooms, whole if small,
   cut in halves or quarters if large
1 (1-oz.) can caper-stuffed anchovies

1/2 cup mayonnaise
1 tablespoon lemon juice
1/2 teaspoon Dijon-style mustard
Crisp lettuce leaves
Minced parsley

Using a heavy cleaver or meat mallet, flatten chicken pieces to about 1/4 inch thick. Slice chicken breasts lengthwise in 1/2-inch strips. Lightly pound each strip. Season chicken with salt. Heat 2 tablespoons oil in a wok or large heavy skillet over high heat. Add chicken; stir-fry 1 to 2 minutes or until firm and white. Place cooked chicken strips in a medium bowl. Add remaining 1 tablespoon oil to wok or skillet. When hot, add mushrooms. Stir-fry 1 minute. Place mushrooms in bowl with chicken. Add anchovies to chicken mixture. In a small bowl, combine mayonnaise, lemon juice and mustard. Add mayonnaise mixture to chicken mixture. Toss lightly to coat. Arrange lettuce leaves on individual plates. Spoon warm salad onto lettuce. Sprinkle salads with parsley. Serve at room temperature. Makes 4 to 6 servings.

Stir-Fried Chicken & Vegetables

A different combination of vegetables makes this dish special.

3 chicken-breast halves, skinned, boned
1/2 cup soy sauce
1/3 cup cornstarch
1/2 cup dry sherry
1 garlic clove, crushed
4 small turnips, peeled,
   cut in 1/4-inch slices
3 tablespoons vegetable oil

2 medium, sweet potatoes, peeled,
   cut in 1/4-inch strips
1 medium onion, chopped
2 tablespoons water
1/2 lb. fresh spinach or
   1 (10-oz.) pkg. frozen spinach,
   thawed, drained well
Hot cooked rice

Slice chicken breasts lengthwise in narrow strips. Place chicken in a 13'' x 9'' baking dish. In a small bowl, combine soy sauce and cornstarch. Stir in sherry and garlic. Pour soy mixture over chicken. Toss chicken to coat evenly. Let stand 25 to 30 minutes at room temperature. Cut each turnip slice in 4 wedges. Heat 2 tablespoons oil in a wok or large heavy skillet over high heat. When very hot, add turnip wedges, sweet potatoes and onion. Stir-fry 2 minutes. Remove vegetables from wok or skillet; place in a medium bowl. Using tongs or a slotted spoon, remove chicken from soy mixture. Remove and discard garlic from soy mixture; set soy mixture aside. Add 1 tablespoon oil to wok or skillet. When oil is hot, add chicken strips. Stir-fry 1 to 2 minutes or until firm and white. Return vegetables to wok or skillet. Add reserved soy mixture and water. Cover and steam 1 minute. Place spinach on top of other vegetables. Cover and steam 30 seconds. Remove cover; stir spinach into other ingredients. Serve hot over rice. Makes 4 to 6 servings.

Easy Casserole & Oven Cookery

Now and then we all want the easy way out. *Easy* is the word for these casseroles and baked-chicken dishes. Casserole cookery is one of the most satisfactory ways of turning out grand, almost one-dish meals with a minimum of effort and in relatively short time. Because they are simple to prepare and serve, they lend themselves nicely to casual entertaining. To complete the meal, add a tasty bread and fresh fruit. If time permits, create a more elaborate dessert.

Baked Chicken Pilaf is a satisfying and economical dish with just a touch of tomato. For a colorful one-dish meal, try Chicken with Oriental Vegetables. An elegant, yet inexpensive dish to serve is Turkey-Mushroom Loaf. Several recipes use tasty pastry. How about doing chicken in your clay pot? Try Bombay Chicken, seasoned with dried fruit and served with a yogurt sauce. Serve with hot couscous or rice.

These casseroles are usually made in two stages. First, the chicken is baked to remove excess fat. Then, other ingredients are added and baked. Personalize your casseroles by using different herbs and vegetables. I am certain you will be pleased with the results. They have excellent flavor and you will enjoy them.

Thanksgiving-Weekend Dinner
Turkey-Mushroom Loaf,
pages 102-103
Souffléed Rice Casserole, page 153
Coleslaw
Fruit Sorbet

Sweet & Sour Chicken Puff

A puffy pastry-like shell holds this savory mixture.

1 (13-1/2-oz.) can unsweetened pineapple
   tidbits with juice
1 tablespoon butter
1 tablespoon vegetable oil
6 chicken-breast halves,
   skinned, boned, diced
1/2 lb. fresh mushrooms, sliced
2 large green peppers,
   cut in 1/4-inch strips

5 tablespoons soy sauce
1/4 cup vinegar
2 tablespoons sugar
1-1/2 teaspoons salt
1 tablespoon cornstarch
3 tablespoons water
1 (8-oz.) can sliced water chestnuts,
   drained
Pastry Puff, see below

Pastry Puff:
2/3 cup milk
2 eggs
2/3 cup all-purpose flour

1/4 teaspoon salt
1 tablespoon butter

Drain pineapple, reserving juice. Set pineapple and juice aside. Heat butter and oil in a heavy skillet over medium-high heat until foamy. When foam subsides, add chicken. Sauté 3 to 4 minutes or until firm and white. Add mushrooms and green peppers. Stir-fry 2 to 3 minutes or until crisp-tender. Add pineapple juice, soy sauce, vinegar, sugar and salt. Bring mixture to a boil. Reduce heat and simmer 1 to 2 minutes. In a small bowl, combine cornstarch and water until smooth. Add cornstarch mixture to skillet. Cook, stirring constantly, until thickened. Add water chestnuts and pineapple. Cook 4 to 5 minutes, stirring occasionally. Prepare Pastry Puff. Reheat chicken mixture and spoon into hot Pastry Puff. Serve immediately. Makes 6 to 8 servings.

Pastry Puff:
Preheat oven to 450F (230C). In a small bowl, combine milk, eggs, flour and salt. Melt butter in a 9-inch ovenproof skillet until very hot. Swirl skillet to distribute butter evenly. Pour pastry batter into skillet. Bake 10 minutes. Reduce temperature to 350F (175C). Bake 10 minutes longer or until puff is firm and golden brown.

Pineapple Chicken

A perfect dish to serve at your Hawaiian luau.

4 chicken legs with thighs
Salt and coarsely ground pepper to taste
1 (8-oz.) can unsweetened pineapple
   slices with juice
1/2 cup honey
3 tablespoons ketchup

2 tablespoons soy sauce
2 tablespoons vegetable oil
1/2 cup chopped cashews
1/2 cup diced celery
1 small garlic clove, minced
3 cups hot cooked rice

Preheat oven to 350F (175C). Place chicken, skin-side down, in a single layer in a 13'' x 9'' baking dish. Bake 30 minutes. Pour fat from baking dish; discard. Season with salt and pepper. Drain juice from pineapple, reserving juice. Combine 1/2 cup pineapple juice, honey, ketchup, soy sauce, oil, cashews, celery and garlic. Pour juice mixture over chicken. Cover tightly with foil. Bake 30 minutes. Turn chicken skin-side up. Bake, uncovered, 15 to 20 minutes or until tender. Top chicken with pineapple slices. Bake 5 minutes or until pineapple is warmed through. Serve hot over rice. Makes 3 to 4 servings.

Italian Chicken & Zucchini

A grand way to use up the last of the summer zucchini.

3 to 4 medium (about 2 lbs.) zucchini,
   thinly sliced
1 medium onion, thinly sliced
6 chicken-breast halves, skinned, boned
1/2 cup bottled Italian salad dressing

1/4 cup lemon juice
1/2 teaspoon sugar
2 to 3 dashes hot-pepper sauce
Salt and coarsely ground pepper to taste
Grated Parmesan cheese, if desired

Preheat oven to 350F (175C). Heavily butter a 13" x 9" baking dish. Arrange zucchini evenly in dish. Break onion slices in rings. Place onion over zucchini. Place chicken breasts over vegetables. In a small bowl, combine Italian dressing, lemon juice, sugar and hot-pepper sauce. Pour dressing mixture over chicken. Season lightly with salt and pepper. Bake, uncovered, 25 to 30 minutes or until chicken and vegetables are tender. Sprinkle with cheese, if desired. Makes 4 to 6 servings.

Glazed Chicken

East meets West in this tangy sauce that coats the chicken as it bakes.

2 (2-1/2- to 3-lb.) chickens, cut-up
2 tablespoons butter
1 medium onion, chopped

1 (8-oz.) can tomato sauce
2 tablespoons soy sauce
1/4 cup dark corn syrup

Preheat oven to 350F (175C). Place chicken, skin-side up, in a single layer in 2 (13" x 9") baking dishes. Bake 30 minutes. Pour fat from baking dishes; discard. Melt butter in a large heavy skillet over low heat. Add onion; sauté 3 to 4 minutes or until tender. Add tomato sauce, soy sauce and corn syrup. Stir until blended. Pour sauce over chicken. Bake 15 to 20 minutes or until chicken is tender and glazed. Serve hot. Makes 6 to 8 servings.

Baked Chicken Pilaf

Personalize by adding curry powder, raisins, nuts, pimiento, red pepper, peas or mushrooms.

1 (2-1/2- to 3-lb.) chicken, cut-up
Garlic salt to taste
2 tablespoons tomato paste
Salt and coarsely ground pepper to taste
1/2 cup water, room temperature

2 cups boiling water
1 tablespoon butter
1 teaspoon salt
1 cup uncooked long-grain white rice

Preheat oven to 350F (175C). Place chicken, skin-side up, in a single layer in a 13" x 9" baking dish. Season with garlic salt. Bake 20 minutes. Pour fat from baking dish; discard. Coat each chicken piece with a thin film of tomato paste. Season with salt and pepper. Return chicken to baking dish. Pour 1/2 cup water around chicken. Bake 10 minutes. Remove chicken from pan. Increase oven temperature to 400F (205C). Add boiling water to pan. Stir in butter and 1 teaspoon salt. Stir in rice. Arrange chicken over rice. Cover tightly with foil. Bake 30 minutes or until rice and chicken are tender. Makes 3 to 4 servings.

How to Make Chicken Tarts

1/Fill each chilled shell with chicken mixture.

2/Press pastry edges together. Crimp to seal in filling.

Indonesian-Style Chicken Casserole

A tasty combination of chicken, sweet potatoes and fruit spiced with cinnamon and curry.

8 chicken thighs
1 large navel orange
3 tablespoons thawed frozen
    unsweetened orange-juice concentrate
Water
3 tablespoons bitter-orange marmalade
1 teaspoon curry powder

1/4 teaspoon ground cinnamon
1/4 cup raisins
1/4 cup slivered almonds
4 medium, sweet potatoes,
    peeled, finely diced
1 large banana, thickly sliced
Salt to taste

Preheat oven to 425F (220C). Place chicken, skin-side up, in a single layer in a 13" x 9" baking dish. Bake 25 minutes. While chicken is baking, cut orange in 8 wedges. Working over a bowl to catch all the juice, cut peel from orange pieces. Squeeze peel to extract any remaining juice. Set orange pieces aside. Pour fresh juice into a 1-cup measure. Add orange-juice concentrate. Add water to make 1 cup liquid. Pour orange-juice mixture into a small bowl. Stir in marmalade, curry powder, cinnamon, raisins and almonds; set aside. Pour fat from baking dish; discard. Reduce oven temperature to 300F (150C). Place potatoes around chicken. Pour orange-juice mixture over chicken. Cover tightly with foil. Bake 30 to 35 minutes or until potatoes and chicken are tender. Stir orange pieces and banana slices gently down between potatoes and chicken. Season lightly with salt. Bake 5 minutes. Arrange chicken, potatoes and fruit on a platter. Spoon sauce over chicken or serve separately. Makes 4 to 6 servings.

For a sweeter flavor, substitute sweet-orange marmalade for bitter marmalade.

Chicken Tarts

Double this recipe and store extra tarts in the freezer.

Tart-Shell Pastry, see below
1 cup chicken stock
1 cup milk
1/4 cup dry sherry
1/4 cup butter
1 medium onion, chopped
3 tablespoons all-purpose flour

1 teaspoon salt
1/4 teaspoon coarsely ground pepper
1 (10-oz.) pkg. frozen mixed vegetables,
   thawed
3 to 4 chicken-breast halves,
   skinned, boned, diced

Tart-Shell Pastry:
2 cups all-purpose flour
1/2 teaspoon salt
3 tablespoons vegetable shortening

1/4 cup butter
3 to 4 tablespoons cold water, more if needed

Prepare Tart-Shell Pastry. Bring stock to a full boil in a medium saucepan. Add milk and sherry. Stir until mixture simmers; set aside. Melt butter in a medium skillet over low heat. Add onion; sauté 5 to 6 minutes or until transparent. Stir in flour, salt and pepper. Pour in stock mixture. Cook, stirring constantly, until thickened. Add mixed vegetables and chicken. Cool to room temperature. Divide chilled Tart-Shell-Pastry dough into 8 portions. Roll 4 portions into 7-inch rounds. Place each round in a 5-inch tart pan. Refrigerate. Roll 4 remaining portions into 6-inch rounds. Place between sheets of waxed paper. Refrigerate until ready to use. Preheat oven to 400F (205C). Remove tart shells from refrigerator. Fill each shell with chicken mixture. Lightly moisten rims of pastry shells. Cover each shell with a chilled 6-inch pastry round. Press edges together and crimp to seal in filling. Using a knife, make a criss-cross slash in the top of each pastry. Place tarts on a baking sheet. Bake 35 to 40 minutes or until lightly browned. Serve hot. Makes 4 tarts.

Tart-Shell Pastry:
In a large bowl, combine flour and salt. Add shortening and butter, working mixture together until it resembles coarse meal. Sprinkle with 3 to 4 tablespoons cold water. Work dough together in a ball. Add more water, if necessary, to hold dough together. Dough should be moist, but not sticky. If too moist, sprinkle lightly with flour. Cover and refrigerate until ready to use.

Chicken with Oriental Vegetables

Here's the easy dish everyone wants today. Serve with crusty French bread and fresh fruit.

1 (2-1/2- to 3-lb.) chicken, cut-up
Garlic salt to taste
1 (1-lb.) pkg. frozen Oriental-style
   vegetables or other mixed vegetables,
   broken apart

1 teaspoon soy sauce
2 tablespoons water
Soy sauce, if desired

Preheat oven to 350F (175C). Place chicken, skin-side up, in a single layer in a 13" x 9" baking dish. Season with garlic salt. Bake 30 minutes. Remove chicken from pan. Pour all but a thin coating of fat from baking dish. Add vegetables to baking dish. Stir to coat. Stir in soy sauce and water. Place chicken over vegetables. Cover tightly with foil. Bake 30 minutes or until chicken is tender. Serve with additional soy sauce, if desired. Makes 3 to 4 servings.

Turkey-Mushroom Loaf

Festive and elegant; garnish this beautiful molded loaf with mushrooms and cherry tomatoes.

2 tablespoons butter
1 lb. mushrooms, sliced
1 garlic clove, minced
1/4 teaspoon dried leaf thyme
1 small onion, chopped
2 lbs. ground raw turkey
1 cup fresh breadcrumbs

2 eggs
1/4 cup tomato juice
2 to 3 dashes hot-pepper sauce
1-1/2 teaspoons salt
1/2 teaspoon coarsely ground pepper
Creamy Tomato Sauce, see below

Creamy Tomato Sauce:
2 tablespoons butter
2 tablespoons all-purpose flour
1 cup milk

1/2 cup dry white wine
1 (6-oz.) can tomato paste
Salt and coarsely ground pepper to taste

Preheat oven to 350F (175C). Melt butter in a small skillet over medium heat. Add mushrooms, garlic, thyme and onion. Sauté 2 to 3 minutes or until tender. Place sautéed mixture in a medium bowl; cool slightly. Add turkey, breadcrumbs, eggs, tomato juice, hot-pepper sauce, salt and pepper. Blend thoroughly. Pack turkey mixture in 2 (7" x 3") loaf pans. Smooth top. Bake 1 hour. Let stand at room temperature 10 minutes. Prepare Creamy Tomato Sauce. Turn onto a platter. Slice thickly. Serve with Creamy Tomato Sauce. Makes 8 to 10 servings.

Creamy Tomato Sauce:
Melt butter in a medium saucepan over medium heat. Stir in flour. Slowly add milk, stirring as added. Cook, stirring constantly until smooth. Add wine and tomato paste. Season with salt and pepper. Cook, stirring constantly, until thickened. Set aside until ready to use.

Bombay Chicken in a Clay Pot

Tangy fruit sauce with yogurt gives this chicken the flavor of that fabled Indian city.

1/4 cup diced mixed dried fruit and raisins
1/4 cup apple brandy, applejack or brandy
1 (3- to 3-1/2-lb.) chicken,
    cut-up, skinned
Juice from 1 small lemon
Salt to taste

1 tablespoon cold butter, slivered
1 (8-oz.) pkg. pineapple-orange or
    apricot yogurt
Paprika to taste
Hot cooked couscous or rice

Soak unglazed clay cooking pot in water to cover for 15 minutes. Place fruit and raisins in a small bowl. Cover with brandy. Let stand at room temperature 15 minutes. Place chicken in a shallow pan. Sprinkle with lemon juice. Turn pieces to moisten evenly. Season with salt. Let stand at room temperature 15 minutes. Drain clay pot well. Place butter in bottom of clay pot. Add chicken pieces; cover pot. Place in a cold oven. Set oven temperature at 450F (230C). Bake chicken 30 minutes. Add soaked fruit and any excess brandy to chicken. Stir fruit down between chicken pieces. Spoon liquid in pot over chicken surface. Cover and return to oven. Bake 30 minutes. Pour yogurt over chicken. Stir to mix with liquid in pot. Spoon liquid over chicken. Sprinkle with paprika. Bake, uncovered, 10 minutes or until sauce is heated. Serve hot over couscous or rice. Makes 4 to 6 servings.

Turkey Casserole with Mornay Sauce

A great way to use leftover turkey and stuffing.

2 cups leftover turkey stuffing or
  Curried Rice, see below
Mornay Sauce, see below
1 tablespoon butter, softened

2 tablespoons cold butter, slivered
8 thin slices cooked turkey breast
4 teaspoons grated Parmesan,
  Swiss or Gruyère cheese

Curried Rice:

3 tablespoons butter
1 small onion, chopped
1 small tart apple, peeled, chopped
1/2 cup chopped almonds

1 to 2 teaspoons curry powder
1 cup uncooked long-grain white rice
1-1/2 cups water
1/4 teaspoon salt

Mornay Sauce:

2 tablespoons butter
2 tablespoons all-purpose flour
1/2 cup hot chicken stock
1/2 cup half and half, room temperature

2 tablespoons light beer,
  room temperature
1/4 teaspoon salt
1/4 cup grated Swiss or Gruyère cheese

Prepare Curried Rice, if desired. Prepare Mornay Sauce. Preheat oven to 350F (175C). If you have a second oven, preheat broiler to high. Grease 4 individual au gratin dishes or a long shallow baking dish with 1 tablespoon soft butter. Divide stuffing or Curried Rice in 4 equal portions. Shape each portion into a mound; place in au gratin dishes or in baking dish. Top each mound with 1/2 tablespoon cold slivered butter. Cover each mound with 2 slightly overlapping turkey slices. Bake 5 minutes or until warm. Preheat broiler, if necessary. Spoon 1/4 of the Mornay Sauce over each pair of turkey slices. Sprinkle each with grated cheese. Place 3 inches below heat. Broil until bubbly hot and flecked with brown. Makes 4 servings.

Curried Rice:
Melt butter in a large saucepan over low heat. Add onion; sauté 3 minutes or until softened. Stir in apple, almonds and curry powder. When blended, stir in rice. Cook, stirring constantly, 30 seconds. Add water and salt. Bring to a boil. Reduce heat and cover. Simmer 18 to 20 minutes or until rice is tender and liquid has been absorbed.

Mornay Sauce:
Melt butter in top half of a double boiler over low heat. Stir in flour until blended. Slowly stir in stock. Add half and half and beer. Blend well. Add salt and cheese. Cook, stirring constantly, until thickened. Sauce may be prepared 1 hour ahead. Cover sauce; set over hot water. Let stand at room temperature. When ready to use, reheat over simmering water.

Most kinds of ready-to-cook poultry are available whole or as parts, halves or quarters. Some kinds are also available as boneless roasts and rolls.

Chicken with Turmeric Pilaf

Serve this easy, elegant oven-baked chicken over turmeric-flavored rice.

1 cup all-purpose flour
1/2 teaspoon salt
1/4 teaspoon coarsely ground pepper
1/4 cup peanut oil, safflower oil or
 vegetable oil
1 garlic clove, crushed

4 chicken-breast halves
1/4 teaspoon ground rubbed sage
1/4 teaspoon ground allspice
8 thin bacon slices, cut in half crosswise
Turmeric Pilaf, see below

Turmeric Pilaf:
2 tablespoons butter
2 tablespoons minced onion
1/2 cup uncooked long-grain rice
1/2 cup vermicelli or thin spaghetti

2 teaspoons powdered turmeric
1/2 cup hot chicken stock
1 cup hot water

Preheat oven to 375F (190C). In a pie plate, combine flour, salt and pepper. Roll each breast half in flour mixture; set aside. Pour oil in a 12-inch skillet. Add garlic. Place over low heat and cook until garlic is lightly browned. Remove garlic; discard. Increase heat to medium-high. When oil begins to shimmer or move back and forth in skillet, add chicken, skin-side down. Cook until lightly browned. Turn and brown other side. Remove chicken; drain on paper towel. Arrange chicken, skin-side up, in a single layer, not touching, in a 13'' x 9'' baking dish. Sprinkle with sage and allspice. Cover each breast half with 4 slightly overlapping bacon slices. Cover tightly with foil. Bake 40 minutes. Remove cover; bake 20 minutes longer or until bacon is crisp. Prepare Turmeric Pilaf while chicken bakes. To serve, spoon rice onto a platter. Top with chicken pieces. Makes 4 servings.

Turmeric Pilaf:
Melt butter in a large saucepan over low heat. Add onion; sauté until tender. Stir in rice, vermicelli and turmeric. Add chicken stock and water. Increase heat to high; bring mixture to a full boil. Cover and reduce heat. Simmer 18 minutes or until tender and liquid has been absorbed. Fluff with a fork just before serving.

Garlic Chicken with Oranges

This highly seasoned chicken is mellowed by brown-sugar-coated orange slices.

1/2 cup Dijon-style mustard
2 to 3 dashes hot-pepper sauce
2 large garlic cloves, minced
1 teaspoon dried leaf oregano, crushed
1/2 teaspoon salt
1 navel orange, thickly sliced

1 (2-1/2- to 3-lb.) chicken,
 cut in quarters, page 14
1 tablespoon brown sugar
Salt to taste
1 tablespoon cold butter, slivered

Preheat oven to 350F (175C). In a small bowl, combine mustard, hot-pepper sauce, garlic, oregano and salt. Spread mustard mixture over chicken quarters. Place chicken, skin-side up, in a single layer in a 13'' x 9'' baking dish. Bake 35 to 40 minutes. Pour fat from baking dish; discard. Top each chicken quarter with an orange slice. Sprinkle orange slices with sugar, salt and butter. Bake 10 to 15 minutes or until chicken is tender. Serve hot. Makes 3 to 4 servings.

Chicken Véronique

Green grapes, slivered almonds, mellow sherry and cream add up to a spectacular dish.

1 (2-1/2- to 3-lb.) chicken, cut-up
1/2 cup seedless green grapes
1/2 cup toasted slivered almonds
2 tablespoons butter
2 tablespoons all-purpose flour
1-1/2 cup hot chicken stock

1/4 cup dry sherry
1/2 cup half and half
Salt and coarsely ground pepper to taste
Paprika to taste
1/4 cup green grapes for garnish

Preheat oven to 350F (175C). Place chicken, skin-side up, in a single layer in a 13'' x 9'' baking dish. Bake 30 minutes. Pour fat from baking dish; discard. Sprinkle grapes and almonds over chicken. Melt butter in a large heavy skillet over high heat. Stir in flour. Cook 1 to 2 minutes, stirring constantly. Add stock; stir until smooth. Pour in sherry and half and half. Cook, stirring until thickened. Season with salt and pepper. Pour sauce over chicken. Cover tightly with foil. Bake 30 minutes. Season with paprika. Garnish with green grapes. Serve hot. Makes 3 to 4 servings.

Easy Chicken & Rice

Combine your favorite chicken parts for this dinner speciality.

4 chicken thighs, skinned
4 chicken legs, skinned
4 chicken-breast halves, skinned
1 garlic clove, crushed
1 tablespoon honey
2 tablespoons tomato paste
2 to 3 dashes hot-pepper sauce
1/2 teaspoon dry mustard
1 teaspoon salt

1/4 teaspoon coarsely ground pepper
1/4 cup cold butter, slivered
1/2 cup water
3 cups hot chicken stock
1/2 teaspoon salt
1-1/2 cups uncooked white rice
1/2 cup raisins
1/4 cup slivered almonds

Preheat oven to 375F (190C). Lightly grease a 13'' x 9'' baking dish. Remove any excess fat from chicken; discard. Rub each chicken piece with garlic. Place chicken in a single layer in greased baking dish. In a small bowl, combine honey, tomato paste, hot-pepper sauce, mustard, 1 teaspoon salt and pepper. Using a pastry brush or your fingers, coat the top of each chicken piece with honey mixture. Sprinkle chicken with butter. Pour water around chicken. Bake 30 minutes. Using tongs, remove chicken pieces; set aside. Pour hot stock into baking dish. Sprinkle with 1/2 teaspoon salt. Stir in rice, raisins and almonds. Arrange chicken on top of rice mixture. Cover tightly with foil. Increase oven temperature to 400F (205C). Bake 1 hour or until rice and chicken are tender. Makes 4 to 6 servings.

Keep frozen poultry hard-frozen until time to thaw; cook promptly after thawing.

How to Make Stuffed Chicken Quarters

1/Lift skin and spoon spinach stuffing into each pocket.

2/Gently press on skin to spread stuffing evenly.

Stuffed Chicken Quarters

Flavorful stuffing goes under the skin to create a special entree.

1 (10-oz.) pkg. frozen chopped spinach,
  thawed
3 tablespoons butter
1 small onion, minced
1 garlic clove, minced
1 cup soft white breadcrumbs
1 egg, slightly beaten

3 tablespoons apricot yogurt,
  well blended
Salt to taste
1/2 teaspoon coarsely ground pepper
1 (2-1/2- to 3-lb.) chicken,
  cut in quarters, page 14

Preheat oven to 425F (220C). Squeeze spinach to remove all moisture; set aside. Melt butter in a small skillet over low heat. Add onion and garlic. Sauté 3 to 4 minutes or until tender. Remove from heat. Stir in spinach, breadcrumbs, egg and yogurt. Season with salt and pepper. Carefully loosen skin on each chicken piece by pushing your fingers between skin and meat to form a pocket. Lift skin and push spinach stuffing into each pocket. Smooth skin back in place. Gently press on skin to spread stuffing evenly over meat. Place stuffed quarters, skin-side up, in a 13'' x 9'' baking dish. Bake 15 minutes. Reduce temperature to 375F (190C). Continue baking 45 minutes or until tender. Makes 4 servings.

Country-Style Chicken in a Pot

This low-calorie dish is reminiscent of the classic French Poulet au Pot.

1 (4- to 4-1/2-lb.) chicken
Salt to taste
Vegetable oil
Paprika
3 tablespoons butter
1 small garlic clove, minced
1 medium onion, chopped

1/4 lb. mushrooms, sliced
3 medium carrots, cut in 1-inch pieces
1/4 lb. fresh green beans,
   cut in 1-inch pieces
2 large baking potatoes, peeled,
   cut in 1/2-inch cubes

Preheat oven to 450F (230C). Season cavity of chicken with salt. Rub chicken skin with vegetable oil; season generously with salt and paprika. Place chicken on a rack in a shallow roasting pan. Bake 20 minutes or until skin is crisp and lightly browned. Melt butter in a large heavy pot over low heat. Add garlic, onion and mushrooms. Sauté 3 to 4 minutes until vegetables are tender. Place chicken in pot with sautéed vegetables. Cover and place pot in center of oven. Reduce oven temperature to 350F (175C). Bake chicken and sautéed vegetables 30 minutes. Bring a large saucepan of water to a boil. Add carrots, green beans and potatoes. Cook 5 minutes. Drain vegetables; add to pot of chicken. Stir to coat vegetables with pan juices. Season with salt. Cover and bake 30 minutes or until chicken and vegetables are tender. Makes 4 to 6 servings.

Brunswick-Stew Casserole

Kentucky-style chicken with vegetables.

1 (2-1/2- to 3-lb.) chicken, cut-up
2 tablespoons butter
1 small white onion, chopped
1 small green pepper, chopped
1 (1-lb.) can tomato sauce
1 tablespoon red-wine vinegar

1 teaspoon brown sugar
Coarsely ground pepper to taste
1 (10-oz.) pkg. frozen lima beans,
   broken apart
1 (10-oz.) pkg. frozen whole-kernel corn,
   broken apart

Preheat oven to 400F (205C). Place chicken, skin-side up, in a single layer in a 13" x 9" baking dish. Bake 20 to 25 minutes or until browned. Pour off any fat; discard. While chicken bakes, melt butter in a large heavy skillet over low heat. Add onion and green pepper. Cover and cook 10 minutes or until vegetables are tender. Add tomato sauce, vinegar and sugar. Season with pepper. Increase heat to medium-high. Bring to a simmer. Add lima beans. Cook 10 minutes, stirring frequently. Remove from heat. Stir in corn. Pour vegetable mixture over chicken. Cover tightly with foil. Bake 20 to 25 minutes or until chicken and vegetables are tender and sauce is bubbly hot. Makes 6 servings.

For convenience, make casserole ahead. Bring to room temperature before baking.

Cooked Poultry Used Great Ways

A "chicken in every pot" was a popular political slogan. Why not extend that? Let's include cooked chicken and turkey in every refrigerator. They are great for preparing quick and delectable dishes.

It's as simple as this. Buy more than enough for one planned menu. For example, buy two or three whole chickens when they are on sale. You save both time and energy. It takes no more effort to steam, poach or roast two or three birds than to prepare one. The results will be good food with less work and more imaginative meals.

Many classic culinary creations require cooked poultry as a base.

In doubt about what to serve? A favorite of mine is old-fashioned Chicken a la King. For a more elegant meal, I name it Chicken in Velouté Sauce. No matter what you call it, it's delicious. What about hash? Chicken Hash Blindbrook has made my reputation as the cook who provides the best Sunday brunch in town.

Don't want to cook, but don't want to eat out? Try the Easy, Easy Tetrazzini. This delightful combination of turkey or chicken, pasta and sauce can be assembled quickly.

On a diet, but hungry for a satisfying meal? Prepare low-calorie Chicken with Pasta in Primavera Sauce. Pasta is not high-calorie. Sauces generally add those unwanted calories. This sauce is made without butter, eggs, cream or other rich ingredients—just what dieters need.

Poached, steamed or roasted, chicken or turkey can be used interchangeably in these recipes. If your roasted bird has become dry from a long stay in the refrigerator or freezer, here's a way you can turn it into juicy, flavorful meat. Remove skin and bones. Dice or thinly slice meat. Place in the top of a double-boiler. Add half and half or whipping cream to cover meat. Place over simmering water. Cook, stirring occasionally, until liquid has been absorbed. Then, proceed with your recipe. I guarantee it will be excellent.

This collection of cooked-poultry recipes is one you are sure to refer to frequently. The convenience of cooked poultry is hard to beat.

Kids' Cooking
Easy, Easy Tetrazzini, page 125
Colorful Tossed Salad
Do-It-Yourself Sundaes

Chicken Couscous

A North African speciality that is enjoyed in many countries.

1/2 cup raisins
1/4 cup dry sherry
3 tablespoons butter
1 large onion, chopped
1 cup chicken stock
1/2 cup water
1/2 cup orange juice

1/4 teaspoon ground turmeric
1/2 teaspoon salt
1 cup couscous
1-1/2 to 2 cups packed minced
 cooked chicken or turkey
1/4 cup toasted slivered almonds

In a small bowl, soak raisins in sherry until ready to use. Melt butter in a large saucepan over low heat. Add onion; sauté 4 to 5 minutes or until tender. Add stock, water, orange juice, turmeric and salt. Bring to a boil. Slowly add couscous. Reduce heat and cook about 2 minutes, stirring until liquid has been absorbed. Remove from heat. Stir in chicken or turkey and almonds. Cover pan tightly. Let stand about 10 minutes. Fluff with a fork just before serving. Makes 3 to 4 servings.

Variation

Foods often served with or included in couscous are mango chutney, slivered almonds, sliced water chestnuts, crisp-cooked crumbled bacon, chopped green onion, chopped parsley and chopped peanuts.

Chicken Hash for a Buffet

An all-time crowd-pleaser that is easy on the hostess as well as the budget.

7 tablespoons butter
1/2 cup chopped celery
1/4 cup water
1-1/4 teaspoons salt
1 (10-oz.) pkg. frozen peas and carrots,
 broken apart
1/4 cup all-purpose flour
1 pint (2 cups) hot chicken stock

1 pint (2 cups) milk, room temperature
2 egg yolks, beaten
3 to 3-1/2 cups diced cooked chicken
 or turkey
1 medium boiled potato, peeled, diced
1 (2-oz.) can drained chopped pimientos,
 if desired
1/2 cup grated Parmesan cheese (1-1/2 oz.)

Lightly grease a 13" x 9" baking dish. Melt 1 tablespoon butter in a small saucepan over low heat. Add celery; sauté 4 to 5 minutes or until crisp-tender. Add water and 1/4 teaspoon salt. Bring to a full boil. Add peas and carrots. Cover and cook 5 minutes or until tender; set aside. Melt remaining 6 tablespoons butter in a large heavy saucepan over low heat. Stir in flour and 1 teaspoon salt. Cook, stirring constantly, 4 to 5 minutes or until flour has lost its raw taste. Add stock; stir with a whisk until smooth. Slowly add milk, stirring as added. Cook, stirring, until thickened. Remove from heat and let stand, stirring occasionally, about 10 minutes. Quickly stir in beaten egg yolks, chicken or turkey, celery mixture including any remaining cooking liquid, potato and pimientos, if desired. Spoon mixture into greased baking dish. Sprinkle cheese evenly over surface. Cover and refrigerate until ready to bake or bake immediately. Preheat oven to 375F (190C). Bake 8 to 10 minutes or until bubbly hot. Serve immediately. Makes 6 to 8 servings.

Chicken Hash Blindbrook

This is an old recipe from a once-famous country club in New England.

1 cup whipping cream
2 cups diced cooked chicken or turkey
1/2 teaspoon salt
1/4 teaspoon coarsely ground pepper
Pinch of ground nutmeg

1/4 cup butter, room temperature
1 egg yolk
2 tablespoons dry sherry
Dry toast or patty shells

In a medium saucepan, heat cream over medium heat, stirring constantly; DO NOT BOIL. Add chicken or turkey, salt, pepper and nutmeg. Reduce heat and simmer 5 minutes, stirring often. Remove from heat. In a small bowl, beat together butter and egg yolk until smooth. Slowly add butter mixture to meat mixture, stirring as added. Stir in sherry. Return saucepan to low heat. Cook, stirring constantly, until thickened. Do not boil. Serve hot over toast or in patty shells. Makes 3 to 4 servings.

Parker-House Chicken Omelettes

A classic French omelette filled with a flavorful mixture of chicken, olives and sour cream.

Tomato Sauce, see below
3/4 to 1 cup diced cooked chicken or turkey
1/2 cup cooked cocktail shrimp
6 to 8 pimiento-stuffed olives, chopped
1/4 cup dairy sour cream

4 large eggs
2 tablespoons water
Salt
2 to 3 drops hot-pepper sauce
2 teaspoons butter

Tomato Sauce:
2 tablespoons butter
1 small onion, chopped
1 bay leaf
1/2 teaspoon dried leaf tarragon

1 (8-oz.) can tomato sauce
1/4 teaspoon salt
Dash hot-pepper sauce

Prepare Tomato Sauce. In a small bowl, combine chicken or turkey, shrimp, olives and sour cream. Blend well; set aside. In a small bowl, beat 2 eggs with 1 tablespoon water. Season with salt and hot-pepper sauce. In a 6-inch omelette pan, melt 1 teaspoon butter over medium heat until foamy. Pour in beaten eggs. Stir once, as if making scrambled eggs. Cook, without stirring, shaking pan back and forth over heat, until eggs have set on the bottom but are still moist on top. Spoon about 3 tablespoons chicken or turkey mixture onto center of omelette. Tilt pan away from you, and with the help of a spatula, roll omelette over filling and onto a warm plate. Cover loosely with foil to keep warm while you quickly prepare a second omelette with remaining ingredients. Roll omelette onto second plate. Stir any remaining filling into hot Tomato Sauce. Bring to a boil over direct heat. Spoon over omelettes. Serve immediately. Makes 2 servings.

Tomato Sauce:
Melt butter in top half of double boiler over medium heat. Stir in onion; sauté until tender. Add bay leaf, tarragon, tomato sauce, salt and hot-pepper sauce. Bring to a boil, stirring constantly. Place over simmering water while preparing omelette.

Curried Chicken in Avocado Shells

Beautiful to look at—delightful to eat.

5 tablespoons butter
1 small tart apple, chopped
1 small onion, minced
1 tablespoon curry powder
1/4 cup all-purpose flour
1 cup chicken stock
1 cup milk

2 dashes hot-pepper sauce
1/2 cup fruity sweet wine or Sauternes
1 teaspoon salt
2-1/2 to 3 cups diced cooked chicken or turkey
3 large avocados
3 cups hot cooked white rice
Chopped dry-roasted peanuts

Toppings:
Chopped preserved ginger
Minced parsley

Minced green onion

Preheat oven to 350F (175C). Melt butter in a large heavy skillet over low heat. Add apple and onion. Cook, stirring frequently, 10 minutes or until tender. Stir in curry powder and flour. Gradually add stock, milk, hot-pepper sauce, wine or Sauternes and salt. Add chicken or turkey. Stir until heated. Cut avocados in half. Remove pits and peel. Place avocado halves in an 8-inch square baking dish. Bake 5 minutes. Spoon rice onto 6 serving plates. Top each serving with half an avocado. Spoon curried chicken or turkey over each serving. Top with chopped peanuts. Serve with various toppings. Makes 6 servings.

Double-Delicious Chicken Soufflé

Flavorful curried chicken topped with a light cheese soufflé.

4 eggs
1 (10-1/2-oz.) can condensed cream of
 mushroom or cream of chicken soup
2 tablespoons dry sherry
1 teaspoon curry powder
1/4 teaspoon salt
Coarsely ground pepper to taste
2 cups diced cooked chicken or turkey

2 tablespoons butter
2 tablespoons all-purpose flour
1 cup hot milk
1/2 teaspoon salt
1/4 teaspoon coarsely ground pepper
1/4 cup grated Swiss or
 Cheddar cheese (1 oz.)
1/8 teaspoon cream of tartar

Preheat oven to 375F (190C). Place oven rack at center position. Lightly butter a 1-1/2-quart soufflé dish or round baking dish. Refrigerate dish until butter is firm. Separate eggs, placing yolks in a small bowl and whites in a large bowl; set aside. In a medium bowl, combine mushroom or chicken soup, sherry, curry powder and 1/4 teaspoon salt. Season with pepper. Add chicken or turkey; stir until blended. Spoon into buttered soufflé dish; set aside. Melt butter over low heat in a large saucepan. Stir in flour; cook until frothy. Slowly add hot milk, stirring constantly until it becomes a smooth thick sauce. Remove from heat. Season with 1/2 teaspoon salt and 1/4 teaspoon pepper. Beat in egg yolks. Stir in cheese; set aside until slightly cooled, stirring occasionally to keep a film from forming over surface. Beat egg whites until frothy. Add cream of tartar; beat until soft peaks form. Using a spatula, fold about 1/4 of beaten egg whites into cheese mixture. Gently fold cheese mixture into remaining beaten egg whites. Spoon over chicken or turkey mixture in soufflé dish. Bake 30 to 35 minutes or until lightly browned and set in the center. Serve immediately. Makes 4 to 6 servings.

How to Make Turkey Enchiladas

1/Spoon turkey filling onto center of each tortilla or Mexican Crepe.

2/Roll each crepe. Place filled tortillas or crepes in a 13" x 9" baking dish.

Chicken Aspic

Perfect for a summer luncheon buffet.

1/2 cup dry white wine
3 (1/4-oz.) envelopes unflavored gelatin
1 cup chicken stock
1 hard-cooked egg, thinly sliced
8 pimiento-stuffed olives, thinly sliced
1/2 cup cold water

3/4 cup mayonnaise
1 to 1-1/2 cups diced cooked chicken
   or turkey
1 cup finely diced celery
1/2 cup pimiento-stuffed olives, chopped
1/2 cup chopped walnuts or pecans

Refrigerate a 1-1/2 quart (8-1/2" x 4-1/2" x 2-1/2") loaf pan and a platter or serving plate. Pour wine in a small bowl. Sprinkle 1 envelope gelatin over wine. Let stand 5 minutes to soften. In a small saucepan, bring stock to a boil. Pour boiling stock over softened gelatin. Stir until dissolved. Chill until mixture thickens. Rinse chilled loaf pan with cold water; drain well. Pour a thin layer of thickened gelatin into chilled pan. Arrange egg and olive slices over gelatin layer. Refrigerate until firm. Place remaining gelatin mixture in refrigerator until firm; reserve for garnish. Pour cold water in top of a double boiler. Sprinkle remaining 2 envelopes of gelatin over water. Stir over low heat until dissolved. Place mayonnaise in a small bowl. Stir gelatin mixture into mayonnaise. Add chicken or turkey, celery, chopped olives and nuts. Blend well. Spoon mayonnaise mixture into gelatin-lined pan. Refrigerate until firm. Unmold onto a chilled platter. Dice reserved chilled gelatin mixture. Garnish mold with diced gelatin. Makes 6 servings.

Turkey Enchiladas

Perfect to make ahead for a Mexican Fiesta; bake just before serving.

16 flour or corn tortillas, or
   Mexican Crepes, see below
Enchilada Sauce, see below
3 cups chopped cooked turkey or chicken

1 pint (2 cups) dairy sour cream
1-1/2 cups grated Cheddar cheese (6 oz.)
1/2 cup shredded Cheddar cheese (2 oz.)

Mexican Crepes:
2 eggs
1/2 cup all-purpose flour
3/4 cup Masa Harina or cornmeal
1/4 teaspoon salt

About 1 cup milk
1/4 cup butter, melted
Vegetable oil for frying

Enchilada Sauce:
2 tablespoons vegetable oil
1 medium onion, chopped
1 to 2 teaspoons chili powder
1 (1-lb.) can tomato sauce

1/2 cup water
1 jalapeño pepper, chopped
Salt to taste

Prepare Mexican Crepes, if desired. Prepare Enchilada Sauce. Preheat oven to 350F (175C). In a medium bowl, combine turkey or chicken, sour cream and grated cheese. Fill tortillas or crepes with turkey or chicken mixture. Roll tortillas or crepes and place in a single layer in a 13'' x 9'' baking dish. Bake 15 minutes or until bubbly hot. Pour Enchilada Sauce over tortillas or crepes. Sprinkle with shredded cheese. Bake until cheese is slightly melted. Serve immediately. Makes 16 enchiladas.

Mexican Crepes:
In a medium bowl, beat eggs until well blended. Stir in flour, Masa Harina or cornmeal and salt. Slowly stir in 1 cup milk until mixture is smooth. Add melted butter. Let batter stand about 30 minutes before preparing crepes. Batter may also be refrigerated overnight. Be sure to remove batter from refrigerator 30 minutes before preparing crepes. If necessary, stir in additional milk to make a thin batter. Lightly oil a 7- or 8-inch crepe pan. Heat over medium-high heat. When hot, pour in 2 to 3 tablespoons crepe batter. Immediately tilt pan to spread batter evenly. Cook crepe until bottom is lightly browned. Turn and cook until second side is lightly flecked with brown. Place crepe on a large platter. Repeat with remaining batter, adding oil as needed. Set aside until ready to use.

Enchilada Sauce:
Heat oil in a large heavy skillet over medium heat. Add onion; sauté 2 to 3 minutes until tender. Add chili powder, tomato sauce, water and jalapeño pepper. Simmer over low heat until thickened. Stir in salt. Set aside until ready to use.

Masa Harina is cornmeal treated with lime water and ground finely.

Parmesan Crepes with Chicken

Very flavorful and especially attractive.

12 Parmesan Crepes, see below
1/4 cup butter
1 small onion, chopped
2 tomatoes, chopped
5 tablespoons all-purpose flour
1 pint (2 cups) chicken stock
1 cup milk, room temperature

2 tablespoons dry sherry, if desired
2-1/2 to 3 cups chopped cooked chicken
   or turkey
1 small avocado
1 teaspoon lemon juice
2 to 3 dashes hot-pepper sauce
Grated Parmesan cheese

Parmesan Crepes:
3 eggs
1/2 cup all-purpose flour
1/2 teaspoon salt
1-1/2 cups milk

1/4 cup butter, melted
1/4 cup grated Parmesan or
   Romano cheese (3/4 oz.)
2 to 3 tablespoons butter

Prepare Parmesan Crepes. Preheat oven to 300F (150C). Melt butter in a large heavy skillet over medium heat. Add onion and tomatoes. Sauté 2 to 3 minutes or until tender. Stir in flour. Cook, stirring constantly, 2 to 3 minutes or until flour has lost its raw taste. Slowly add stock, stirring to blend. Add milk and sherry, if desired. Cook, stirring until thickened and smooth. Remove from heat. Divide sauce in half, reserving half the sauce. Add chicken or turkey to remaining sauce. Spoon 2 tablespoons meat mixture into center of each crepe. Roll crepes; place in a single layer in a 13" x 9" baking dish. Place in preheated oven to keep warm while finishing sauce. Peel and coarsely chop avocado. Place avocado in a blender or food processor fitted with a steel blade. Add 1/2 cup reserved sauce. Blend until pureed. Add avocado mixture to remaining sauce. Stir in lemon juice and hot-pepper sauce. Stir over low heat until hot. Do not boil. Spoon some sauce over center of heated crepes in baking dish. Sprinkle with Parmesan cheese. Serve remaining sauce separately. Makes 6 to 8 servings.

Parmesan Crepes:
In a medium bowl, beat eggs until light and frothy. Add flour and salt. Stir until blended. Slowly add milk, beating with whisk as added. Beat until smooth. Add melted butter and cheese. Stir until blended. Let batter stand about 1 hour before preparing crepes. Melt 2 teaspoons butter in a 7-inch crepe pan over medium-low heat. When butter is bubbly, pour in 2-1/2 to 3 tablespoons batter. Immediately tilt pan to spread batter evenly. Cook crepe until bottom is lightly browned, about 3 minutes. Turn and cook until second side is lightly flecked with brown. Place crepe on a platter. Repeat with remaining batter, adding butter as needed. Crepes may be kept in a warm oven until all are prepared.

Completely cook poultry at one time. NEVER partially cook, then store and finish cooking at a later date.

Chicken Quiche

A flavorful French-custard pie—great as an appetizer, for lunch or even a main course.

Basic Pastry Shell, see below
1 cup finely diced Swiss cheese (4 oz.)
3/4 to 1 cup packed minced cooked chicken
   or turkey
2 tablespoons all-purpose flour
1-1/2 cups half and half
4 eggs, slightly beaten

2 tablespoons chopped green onion
1/2 cup chopped baked lean ham
1/2 teaspoon salt
Dash hot-pepper sauce
1/2 cup chopped cooked artichoke hearts,
   if desired

Basic Pastry Shell:
1-1/4 cups all-purpose flour
1/4 teaspoon salt
1/8 teaspoon baking soda
1/4 cup chilled butter
2 tablespoons lard or
   vegetable shortening, chilled

1 egg
1 tablespoon ice water
1 tablespoon lemon juice
1/2 teaspoon prepared mustard
   or mayonnaise

Prepare Basic Pastry Shell. Preheat oven to 375F (190C). In a small bowl, combine cheese, chicken or turkey and flour. Add half and half, eggs, onion, ham, salt, hot-pepper sauce and artichoke hearts, if desired. Mix well. Pour cheese mixture into pastry shell. Bake 45 minutes or until set. Center will be slightly soft when it is done. Makes 8 servings.

Basic Pastry Shell:
In a large bowl, combine flour, salt and baking soda. Cut butter and lard or shortening into small pieces; add to flour mixture. Using a pastry blender, 2 knives or your fingers, work fat into flour until mixture resembles coarse meal. In a small bowl, beat egg with ice water and lemon juice. Pour egg mixture over flour mixture, stirring with a fork until blended, Mixture should form a soft moist dough. Turn dough out onto a lightly floured square of waxed paper. Shape dough in a ball. Wrap dough loosely in waxed paper. Refrigerate 1 hour or longer. On a lightly floured surface, roll chilled dough in an 11- or 12-inch circle, about 1/4 inch thick. Roll dough loosely but carefully over rolling pin. Lift rolling pin and carefully unroll dough in a 9-inch pie plate. Lightly pat dough in a pie plate. Avoid stretching dough. Press dough onto sides of pan. Trim edges with a knife or scissors, allowing a 1/2-inch overlap. Crimp dough edges by pinching dough between your fingers, making a firm edge. Refrigerate 10 to 15 minutes. Preheat oven to 425F (220C). Line pastry shell with foil, shiny-side down. Press foil onto pastry. Place lined pastry shell on a baking sheet. Bake 14 to 15 minutes. Remove foil from partially baked pastry shell. Using a pastry brush, coat bottom of pastry shell with mustard or mayonnaise. Bake pastry shell 2 minutes longer. This seals the crust and prevents it from becoming soggy. Set aside until ready to use.

Serve poultry often—it is a nutritious, delicious taste-treat the year round.

Creamy Blue Cheese & Chicken Quiche

Quick, delicious and creamy—perfect for any luncheon.

Basic Pastry Shell, page 117
1 (8-oz.) pkg. cream cheese
1 cup milk
1/2 cup crumbled blue cheese (2 oz.)
4 eggs

1 cup packed minced cooked chicken
  or turkey
1/4 cup crumbled crisp-cooked bacon
1 (2-oz.) can chopped pimientos, drained
Salt and coarsely ground pepper to taste

Prepare pastry shell; set aside until ready to use. Preheat oven to 375F (190C). In a saucepan, combine cream cheese and milk. Stir over low heat until smooth. Stir in blue cheese. Gradually add cheese mixture to eggs, stirring with a whisk as added. Add chicken or turkey, bacon and pimientos. Season to taste with salt and pepper. Pour into partially baked pastry shell. Bake 40 to 45 minutes or until set. Center will be slightly soft when it is done. Makes 8 servings.

Frittata di Pollo

An Italian open-face omelette—great with green salad and hard rolls.

Quick Tomato Sauce, if desired
6 eggs
1/2 teaspoon salt
1/4 teaspoon coarsely ground pepper
1/2 to 3/4 cup diced cooked chicken,
  or turkey
2 thin slices Italian salami,
  cut in narrow strips

1/4 cup thinly sliced zucchini
1/4 cup freshly grated Parmesan cheese
  (3/4 oz.)
1 tablespoon butter
2 tablespoons peanut oil,
  safflower oil or vegetable oil

Quick Tomato Sauce:
2 tablespoons olive oil or butter
1 small onion, chopped
1 small garlic clove, minced
1 (16-oz.) can Italian tomatoes with basil
1 tablespoon tomato paste

1/4 teaspoon salt
Coarsely ground pepper to taste
2 teaspoons chopped parsley
1/4 teaspoon Italian herb seasoning

Prepare Quick Tomato Sauce, if desired; set aside. Place oven rack 2 inches below heat. Preheat broiler to high. In a large bowl, beat eggs until blended. Add salt, pepper, chicken or turkey, salami, zucchini and cheese. Heat butter and oil in a 12-inch ovenproof skillet over medium heat until foamy. When foam subsides, add egg mixture. Reduce heat to low. Cook egg mixture 10 minutes, sliding skillet back and forth over heat until eggs have set on the bottom but are still moist on top. Place skillet under broiler, leaving oven door open. Broil until top is puffy and firm. Using a spatula, loosen frittata and slide onto a platter. Cut in wedges. Serve warm, topped with Quick Tomato Sauce, if desired. Makes 4 to 6 servings.

Quick Tomato Sauce:
Heat oil or butter in top half of a double boiler over low heat. Add onion; cook 3 to 4 minutes or until tender. Add garlic; cook 30 seconds to 1 minute or until fragrant. Pour in tomatoes and juice. Break up tomatoes with a spoon or spatula. Stir in tomato paste, salt, pepper, parsley and herb seasoning. Increase heat to high; stir until mixture begins to boil. Place over simmering water. Cook, stirring occasionally, 10 to 15 minutes. Keep warm over hot water until ready to use.

Deluxe Croquettes

An all-time favorite that will never go out of style.

1/4 cup Madeira wine or dry sherry
1/4 lb. turkey ham, minced
2 tablespoons butter
2 tablespoons vegetable oil or corn oil
3 tablespoons all-purpose flour
1 cup hot chicken stock
1 large egg yolk
1/4 cup milk, room temperature

1 tablespoon lemon juice
1/2 teaspoon salt
2 cups packed minced cooked chicken
  or turkey
1 cup all-purpose flour
2 eggs
2 cups fine dry breadcrumbs
Oil for deep-frying

In a small saucepan, combine wine or sherry and turkey ham. Cook over medium-low heat, stirring occasionally, until liquid has evaporated; set aside. Heat butter and 1 tablespoon oil in a deep heavy skillet over medium heat until foamy. When foam subsides, stir in 3 tablespoons flour. Cook, stirring constantly, 2 to 3 minutes or until flour has lost its raw taste. Slowly stir in stock, cooking until mixture has slightly thickened. Remove from heat. In a small bowl, beat egg yolk with milk. Add 1/4 cup stock mixture to egg-yolk mixture. Stir with whisk until blended. Stir egg-yolk mixture into remaining stock mixture. Cook, stirring constantly, until thickened. Add lemon juice, salt, chicken or turkey and turkey ham. Place skillet over medium heat, stirring until thickened. Pour meat mixture in a 13" x 9" baking dish. Refrigerate until cold and firm. Place 1 cup flour in a pie plate. In a shallow bowl, beat 2 eggs with 1 tablespoon oil until blended. Spread breadcrumbs on a second pie plate. Shape chilled chicken mixture into 2-1/2-inch patties or croquettes. Roll each croquette in flour; shake off excess. Dip each croquette in egg mixture; drain over bowl. Roll croquettes in breadcrumbs. Press breadcrumbs evenly onto croquettes. Place croquettes, not touching, on a baking sheet. Refrigerate until coating is firm, about 30 minutes, or until ready to use. Pour oil in skillet to a 1-1/2-inch depth. Heat oil to 375F (190C). Fry 3 to 4 croquettes in hot oil until golden brown. Repeat with remaining croquettes. Place on baking sheet in warm oven to keep warm. Serve hot. Makes 4 to 6 servings.

Turkey Divan with Spinach

You'll love this easy version of a classic French dish.

2 (10-oz.) pkgs. frozen chopped spinach
2 tablespoons butter
2 tablespoons all-purpose flour
1-1/2 cups hot chicken stock
1/2 cup milk, room temperature
2 tablespoons dry sherry

Salt and coarsely ground pepper to taste
10 to 12 thin slices cooked turkey or
  chicken breast
2 tablespoons mayonnaise
1/3 cup grated Swiss cheese (1 oz.)

Preheat oven to 375F (190C). Cook spinach according to package directions; drain well. Place cooked spinach in a medium bowl; set aside. Melt butter in a heavy saucepan over low heat. Stir in flour. Cook, stirring constantly, 4 to 5 minutes or until flour has lost its raw taste. Add stock; stir with a whisk until smooth. Add milk and sherry. Cook, stirring constantly, until thickened. Season with salt and pepper. Pour 3/4 of the sauce over cooked spinach. Stir to blend well. Spoon mixture into a 13" x 9" baking dish. Cover with slightly overlapping slices of turkey or chicken. Stir mayonnaise into remaining sauce. Spoon evenly over meat. Sprinkle with cheese. Bake 5 to 10 minutes or until cheese melts and sauce is glazed with cheese. Makes 5 to 6 servings.

How to Make Deluxe Croquettes

1/Shape chilled chicken mixture into croquettes.

2/Fry 3 or 4 croquettes in hot oil until golden brown.

Upside-Down Chicken Pie

A flaky crust with fried onions and a hearty filling make this a favorite.

2 tablespoons butter
1 medium onion, chopped
1 small green pepper, chopped
1 small tart apple, peeled, chopped
1 (10-1/2-oz.) can condensed tomato soup
2 tablespoons chopped mango chutney or
   orange marmalade
1 teaspoon prepared mustard
1/4 teaspoon Worcestershire sauce

1-1/2 teaspoons water
3 cups diced cooked chicken or turkey
1-1/2 cups biscuit mix
1/2 cup finely chopped canned
   French-fried onions
1/3 cup water
3 thin slices American or
   brick cheese

Preheat oven to 425F (220C). Melt butter in a large heavy ovenproof skillet. Add onion, green pepper and apple. Sauté 4 to 5 minutes or until tender. Stir in soup, chutney or marmalade, mustard, Worcestershire sauce and 1-1/2 teaspoons water. Add chicken or turkey. Blend well; set aside. In a medium bowl, combine biscuit mix and fried onions. Stir in 1/3 cup cold water to make a soft dough. On a lightly floured surface, roll dough in a circle slightly smaller than skillet. Spread meat mixture evenly in skillet. Position biscuit dough over top of skillet. Bake 5 minutes. Reduce oven temperature to 350F (175C). Bake 15 minutes longer. Invert on a large round platter. Top with cheese. Cut in wedges. Serve hot. Makes 6 servings.

Cheese Puff with Chicken

Pretty as a picture; serve this as a main course for your next luncheon.

Cheese Puff, see below
6 tablespoons butter
1/4 cup all-purpose flour
2-1/2 cups hot chicken stock
1-1/2 cups milk, room temperature
1/4 cup grated mild Cheddar cheese (1 oz.)
2 large egg yolks
2 tablespoons dry sherry

1 (3-oz.) can sautéed-in-butter mushrooms
1-1/2 to 2 cups packed minced cooked chicken or turkey
1 (2-oz.) can chopped pimientos, drained
1 teaspoon salt
Coarsely ground pepper to taste
1 teaspoon chopped pimiento, if desired
2 teaspoons chopped parsley, if desired

Cheese Puff:
2/3 cup milk
2 eggs
2/3 cup all-purpose flour

1 tablespoon grated Parmesan cheese
1/4 teaspoon salt
1-1/2 tablespoons butter

Prepare Cheese Puff. Melt butter in a saucepan over low heat. Stir in flour; cook, stirring constantly, 5 minutes or until flour has lost its raw taste. Add stock; stir with a whisk. Stir in milk and cheese. Cook, stirring until smooth. In a small bowl, beat egg yolks and sherry until blended. Add 1 to 2 tablespoons hot-stock mixture to egg-yolk mixture. Stir with whisk until blended. Stir egg-yolk mixture into remaining stock mixture. Cook over low heat, stirring until thickened. Stir in mushrooms, chicken or turkey, pimientos, salt and pepper. Pour meat mixture into puff, or cover and place over hot water to keep warm. Reheat, stirring frequently, over boiling water when ready to use. Garnish with pimiento and parsley, if desired. Makes 6 to 8 servings.

Cheese Puff:
Preheat oven to 450F (230C). In a small bowl, combine milk, eggs, flour, cheese and salt. Melt butter in a 9-inch ovenproof skillet until very hot. Swirl skillet to distribute butter evenly. Pour puff batter into skillet. Bake 10 minutes. Reduce temperature to 350F (175C). Bake 10 minutes longer or until puff is firm and golden brown.

Chicken-Broccoli Casserole

Crisp colorful broccoli and juicy chicken with a seafood-sauce surprise.

2 tablespoons butter
1/2 cup soft breadcrumbs from French bread
2 tablespoons grated mild Cheddar cheese
2 (10-oz.) pkgs. frozen chopped broccoli
1 cup thinly sliced celery
2 cups packed diced cooked chicken or turkey

1 (13-oz.) can seafood, crab or lobster bisque (not condensed)
1/4 cup milk
1/4 cup dairy sour cream
1 egg yolk

Preheat oven to 375F (190C). Lightly grease a 13" x 9" baking dish. Melt butter in a small skillet over low heat. Stir in breadcrumbs. Cool to room temperature. Stir in cheese; set aside. Cook broccoli according to package directions; drain well. In a medium bowl, combine cooked broccoli and celery. Spread broccoli mixture in greased baking dish. Cover with chicken or turkey. In a medium bowl, combine bisque, milk, sour cream and egg yolk. Pour bisque mixture over meat. Sprinkle with breadcrumb mixture. Bake 20 to 25 minutes or until bubbly hot. Serve hot. Makes 4 to 6 servings.

1/Spoon chicken mixture over hot Cheese Puff.　　2/Garnish Cheese Puff with pimiento and parsley.

Chicken Soufflé with Olives

A beautiful dish that rises to any occasion.

6 eggs
1/3 cup butter
1/3 cup all-purpose flour
1 cup hot milk
1/2 cup chicken stock
1/2 teaspoon dried dill weed

1/4 teaspoon salt
2 cups finely shredded sharp Cheddar,
　Swiss or Gruyère cheese (8 oz.)
1 cup packed minced cooked chicken or turkey
8 to 10 pimiento-stuffed olives,
　thinly sliced

Generously butter a 2-quart soufflé dish. Separate eggs while cold, placing yolks in a small bowl, whites in a large bowl. Let yolks and whites stand 15 to 20 minutes to bring to room temperature. Preheat oven to 300F (150C). Melt butter in a large saucepan over low heat. Stir in flour until smooth. Cook, stirring constantly, 4 to 5 minutes or until flour has lost its raw taste. Add hot milk; stir vigorously with a whisk until smooth. Stir in stock, dill weed, salt and cheese. Stir until cheese has melted. Add chicken or turkey and olives. Remove from heat; cool slightly. Stir in egg yolks; set aside. Beat egg whites until firm peaks form. Stir in about 1/4 cup yolk mixture. Fold remaining yolk mixture into egg whites. Pour egg mixture into buttered dish. With the tip of a spoon, make a slight indentation around top of soufflé, about 1 inch in from edge to form a "top hat." Bake 1 hour and 15 minutes or until center is set. Serve hot. Makes 6 servings.

Deep-Dish Chicken Pie

Old-fashioned deep-down goodness, just like grandma's.

6 tablespoons butter
1/4 lb. large mushrooms, cut in quarters
3 medium carrots, cut in 1/2-inch slices
1/4 cup all-purpose flour
1 teaspoon curry powder
1-1/2 cups chicken stock
1 egg yolk

1/2 cup whipping cream
1 (3-1/2- to 4-lb.) cooked chicken,
   skinned, boned, cut in large pieces
1/4 lb. baked ham, slivered
1 cup cooked green peas
Salt and coarsely ground pepper to taste
Onion Biscuits, see below

Onion Biscuits:
1 cup all-purpose flour
1-1/2 teaspoons baking powder
1/2 teaspoon salt
1/4 teaspoon poultry seasoning

1/3 cup cold butter, slivered
2 tablespoons chopped canned
   French-fried onion rings
1/3 cup milk

Melt 2 tablespoons butter in a small skillet over medium heat. Add mushrooms; sauté 2 to 3 minutes or until tender; set aside. Place carrots in a medium saucepan. Cover with water. Cook carrots 10 to 12 minutes or until tender. Drain well; cool to room temperature. Melt 1/4 cup butter in a large heavy skillet over low heat. Stir in flour and curry powder. Cook, stirring constantly until smooth. Slowly whisk in stock until blended. Remove from heat. In a small bowl, beat egg yolk and cream until blended. Stir 1/4 cup stock mixture into egg-yolk mixture. Stir egg-yolk mixture into remaining stock mixture. Add chicken, ham, peas, mushrooms and carrots. Blend well. Season with salt and pepper. Pour mixture into a 3-quart baking dish. Preheat oven to 425F (220C). Prepare Onion Biscuits. Arrange biscuits in a single layer on top of meat mixture. Bake 20 minutes or until filling is bubbly hot and biscuits lightly browned. Serve hot. Makes 6 to 8 servings.

Onion Biscuits:
In a medium bowl, combine flour, baking powder, salt and poultry seasoning. Cut in butter until mixture resembles coarse meal. Add onions and milk, all at once, stirring to form a smooth dough. Turn out on a lightly floured surface. Knead lightly. Roll or pat to 1/2 inch thick. Cut with a biscuit cutter.

Do not thaw commercially frozen stuffed poultry before cooking.

Chicken & Ham Tarts

A rich meaty filling in a flaky cheese pastry.

Parmesan Tart Shells, see below
1/4 cup butter
1/2 lb. mushrooms, sliced
1/4 lb. baked or boiled ham, chopped
3 tablespoons all-purpose flour
1 pint (2 cups) chicken stock

1 cup milk
2 tablespoons vermouth or dry white wine
2-1/2 to 3 cups diced cooked chicken
   or turkey
Salt and coarsely ground pepper to taste

Parmesan Tart Shells:
1-1/4 cups all-purpose flour
3 tablespoons Parmesan cheese
1/4 teaspoon salt

6 tablespoons cold butter, slivered
1/4 cup ice water
1 teaspoon prepared mustard

Prepare Parmesan Tart Shells. Melt butter in a medium saucepan over low heat. Add mushrooms; sauté 4 to 5 minutes or until tender. Add ham; stir until heated through. Stir in flour. Slowly add stock, milk and vermouth or wine, stirring until thickened. Add chicken or turkey. Season with salt and pepper. Spoon into tart shells. Serve immediately. Makes 6 tarts.

Parmesan Tart Shells:
In a medium bowl, combine flour, cheese and salt. Add butter; work mixture with fingertips into small, flaky particles. Sprinkle with ice water, 1 tablespoon at a time. Mix lightly with a fork until pastry holds together when gently pressed into a ball. Cover and refrigerate 30 minutes. Divide chilled pastry into 6 equal pieces. On a lightly floured surface, roll each piece in a 7-inch circle. Fit each circle into a 5-inch tart pan. Prick bottom of tart shells with a fork. Refrigerate or freeze tart shells while preheating oven to 425F (220C). Place tarts on a baking sheet. Bake 5 minutes. If dough puffs up, gently press it down with your fingertips. Bake 10 minutes longer or until lightly browned. Spread a thin film of mustard over bottom of each tart shell. Bake 2 minutes. Cool tarts slightly. Gently remove tarts from pans. Let stand at room temperature until ready to fill.

Variation
Add 1 (10-ounce) package frozen cut asparagus, cooked, when adding chicken.

Easy, Easy Tetrazzini

You don't have to precook the pasta in this delicious dish.

3 tablespoons butter
1 (8-oz.) pkg. uncooked fine egg noodles
2 (10-1/2-oz.) cans condensed cream
   of mushroom soup
1/2 cup pimiento-stuffed olives, sliced

1 (3-oz.) can sliced mushrooms, undrained
1 cup diced cooked chicken or turkey
1 pint (2 cups) milk
1/2 cup fine breadcrumbs
1/4 cup grated Parmesan cheese (3/4 oz.)

Preheat oven to 350F (175C). Coat bottom and sides of a 13" x 9" baking dish with 1 tablespoon butter. In buttered baking dish, layer half the following ingredients: noodles, soup, olives, mushrooms and chicken or turkey. Pour 1 cup milk over top. Repeat layering with remaining noodles, soup, olives, mushrooms and chicken or turkey. Pour remaining 1 cup milk over top. Press noodles into liquid. Sprinkle breadcrumbs over top. Dot with remaining butter. Sprinkle with cheese. Bake 40 minutes or until noodles are tender. Serve hot. Makes 6 servings.

Chicken with Pasta in Primavera Sauce

A dieter's dream—rich, flavorful and filling, yet low in calories.

3 ripe tomatoes, cut in wedges
1 medium onion, coarsely chopped
1 medium zucchini, ends trimmed, chopped
1 medium, yellow crookneck squash,
   ends trimmed, chopped
4 to 6 large mushrooms, cut in quarters
1/4 cup dry sherry
1/2 cup chicken stock or water
1/2 teaspoon salt or to taste
1/4 teaspoon crushed red-pepper flakes or
   to taste

Coarsely ground black pepper to taste
1 to 1-1/2 cups cooked chicken or
   turkey strips
1 cup drained canned peas or frozen peas,
   thawed
2 teaspoons tomato paste, if desired
Hot cooked flat noodles or
   other cooked pasta

In a large saucepan, combine tomatoes, onion, zucchini, crookneck squash, mushrooms, sherry and stock or water. Cook over medium-high heat, stirring frequently. Bring liquid to a boil. Reduce heat. Add salt, red pepper and black pepper. Cover and simmer 10 minutes. Stir vegetables from bottom of saucepan to top. Cover and simmer 20 minutes or until vegetables are reduced to a chunky sauce. Stir in chicken or turkey and peas. Cook, stirring frequently, 5 minutes or until heated through. Add tomato paste, if desired. Cook until thickened, stirring frequently. Serve hot with noodles or other pasta. Makes 3 to 4 servings.

Chicken a la King

Popular in the '50s, a la king makes a comeback with fewer calories and a rich flavor.

2 tablespoons butter
2 tablespoons all-purpose flour
1/2 teaspoon salt
1 pint (2 cups) hot chicken stock
1 egg yolk
1/2 cup milk
2 to 3 dashes aromatic bitters or
   hot-pepper sauce

2 to 2-1/2 cups diced cooked chicken
   or turkey
1 (2-oz.) can chopped pimientos, drained
1 (3-oz.) can sautéed-in-butter mushrooms
2 tablespoons dry sherry
Salt and coarsely ground pepper to taste
Buttermilk biscuits or toast tips

Melt butter in a medium, heavy saucepan over low heat. Stir in flour and salt. Cook, stirring constantly, 4 to 5 minutes or until flour has lost its raw taste. Add stock; stir with a whisk. In a small bowl, beat egg yolk and milk. Stir in bitters or hot-pepper sauce. Add 1/4 cup stock mixture to egg-yolk mixture. Stir with whisk until blended. Stir egg-yolk mixture into remaining stock mixture. Cook, stirring constantly, until thickened. Add chicken or turkey, pimientos, mushrooms and sherry. Season with salt and pepper. Cook 5 minutes, stirring frequently. Serve hot over biscuits or toast tips. Makes 4 servings.

Variations

Sauté 1 pint drained small oysters in 1 tablespoon butter until oyster edges begin to curl. Add to sauce when adding chicken or turkey. Serve over split hot popovers.

Add 1/2 cup slivered Smithfield or similar dry-cured ham to sauce when adding chicken or turkey. Serve over split toasted Cornbread Squares, page 153.

Salads and sandwiches have finally arrived. No longer are they just side dishes and light luncheon fare. They have become a respectable main-course entree to be served at noon, midnight or any time in between.

To prepare a main-course salad or sandwich, you need only a few basic cooking skills, an eye for color and texture and a feeling for flavorful combinations. Try such great go-togethers as California Chicken Salad with avocado and crumbled bacon, or Chicken & Fruit Salad with crisp celery and colorful grapes. Experience the surprising sweet-tart taste of green grapes with chicken. Sound good? They are, indeed, as are chicken sandwiches made with a blend of rich cream and blue cheese or smoky-baked Smithfield ham.

For the best of all salads and sandwiches, start with juicy, cooked poultry. If your meat has become dry, don't despair. Marinate it in a simple dressing of 3 parts olive oil to 1 part white-wine vinegar, plus salt and coarsely ground pepper. Marinate in the refrigerator for several hours. Drain well before using. Your salad or sandwich will taste positively superb.

Here are three tips you may not know about salad and sandwich-making. First, don't over-dress a salad. The mixture will taste best when each ingredient is only lightly coated with dressing. Second, make mixed salads without adding lettuce or other greens. Refrigerate mixture several hours to allow flavors to mellow and blend. Add greens just before serving. And lastly, when preparing sandwiches ahead, first freeze the bread. Spread each slice evenly, but lightly, with softened butter. Place the buttered slices in a single layer on a baking sheet. Place in freezer until firm. Then spread with filling. This prevents fillings from making your sandwiches soggy and limp.

For a variety of sandwiches, use Basic Chicken Salad as a filling. Then, create Chicken Tea Sandwiches, Brown-Bag Chicken Sandwiches or Open-Face Chicken Sandwiches.

Although cooked turkey and chicken can be used interchangeably, try a salad specially developed for the flavor of turkey. Turkey & Apple Salad has a nice crunchy texture with a bright-red apple color. Try a molded salad such as the Cranberry-Turkey Mold, perfect as a follow-up to the holiday season. Need a late-night snack after the movie? Grilled Chicken & Cheese Sandwiches will hit the spot.

Whatever the need, salads and sandwiches are made special with cooked poultry.

Superb Salads & Sandwiches

Bridge Luncheon
Singhalese Soup, page 35
Chicken Tea Sandwiches, page 128
Raw Vegetable Slices
Creamy Smooth Lemon Mousse

Basic Chicken Salad

Here's a multipurpose chicken mixture, great for salads and sandwiches of any size.

2-1/2 to 3 cups coarsely chopped
   cooked chicken or turkey
1/2 green pepper, coarsely chopped
4 to 6 celery stalks, coarsely chopped
1/2 cup mixed sweet pickles, drained

1 tablespoon lemon juice
1/2 teaspoon dry mustard
1/2 cup mayonnaise
2 tablespoons minced chives
1 teaspoon prepared horseradish, if desired

In a food processor fitted with a steel blade, combine chicken or turkey, green pepper, celery and pickles. Process until finely chopped. Or, place ingredients on a chopping board and chop finely. Mixture should hold together firmly before dressing is added. Place chicken or turkey mixture in a large bowl. Add lemon juice, mustard, mayonnaise, chives and horseradish, if desired. Mix well. Cover and refrigerate several hours. Makes about 4 cups sandwich filling, sufficient for 8 large sandwiches or 16 tea sandwiches.

Variations

Chicken Tea Sandwiches: Place 1 (1-pound) loaf thinly sliced whole-wheat or white bread in freezer until firm. Reserve end pieces for another use. Stack remaining slices, 4 or 6 to a stack. Using a bread knife, trim off crust. Spread each slice lightly with butter. Butter will keep sandwiches from becoming soggy. Spread half the slices with salad mixture. Top with remaining slices. Press each sandwich firmly together. Wrap, in stacks of 4, in damp, clean kitchen towels or linen napkins. Sandwiches will stay much fresher this way than if wrapped in foil or plastic wrap. Refrigerate up to 3 days before serving. To serve, unwrap stack. Slice each sandwich, lengthwise or diagonally, in half. Makes 16 to 18 sandwiches.

Brown-Bag Chicken Sandwiches: Slice 8 French rolls in half. Remove center from top and bottom slices. Spread both halves lightly with butter. Fill bottom half with chicken-salad mixture, mounding it high. Add a slice of tomato, if desired. Cover with top half of roll. Secure each sandwich with wooden picks. Wrap each sandwich in foil. Refrigerate until ready to pack a lunch bag or to take for a picnic. Makes 8 sandwiches.

Open-Face Chicken Sandwiches: Lightly toast 6 thin slices whole-wheat or white bread. Place each slice of bread on a salad plate. Top each slice with Basic Chicken Salad. Sprinkle with crumbled crisp-cooked bacon. Surround with watercress. Makes 6 servings.

Turkey-Cranberry Salad

Turkey and cranberries go together naturally and are delicious in this beautiful salad.

1 cup fresh or frozen cranberries
1/2 cup water
1/4 cup sugar
2-1/2 to 3 cups diced cooked turkey
1 cup sliced celery
2 crisp tart apples, peeled, diced

Salt to taste
1/2 cup mayonnaise
1 tablespoon Dijon-style mustard
2 tablespoons lemon juice
Crisp lettuce leaves
2 tablespoons minced chives

In a medium saucepan, combine cranberries, water and sugar. Bring to a boil over medium heat. Reduce heat and simmer 10 minutes; drain. Cool to room temperature. In a medium bowl, combine cooked cranberries, turkey, celery and apples. Season with salt. In a small bowl, combine mayonnaise, mustard and lemon juice. Pour mayonnaise mixture over turkey mixture. Toss lightly. Cover and refrigerate 2 to 3 hours. To serve, line a salad bowl with lettuce. Spoon salad into lined bowl. Sprinkle with chives. Makes 6 to 8 servings.

1/Hold a cooked potato on a fork. Peel under cold running water, or plunge potato in a bowl of ice water. Then remove peel.

2/Arrange chicken, potatoes and bean salad on lettuce leaves. Top each serving with anchovy fillets. Garnish with tomato wedges.

Chicken Salad Niçoise

Substitute chicken for tuna in this classic French salad.

Vinaigrette Dressing, see below
2 cups packed cooked chicken or
   turkey strips
8 very small new potatoes
Crisp lettuce leaves

1 (1-lb.) can mixed-bean salad,
   chilled, drained
8 anchovy fillets
Tomato wedges for garnish
Small oil-cured black olives for garnish

Vinaigrette Dressing:
1 teaspoon salt
1/2 teaspoon coarsely ground pepper
1/2 teaspoon sugar

1 teaspoon Dijon-style mustard
1/4 cup white-wine vinegar
3 tablespoons vegetable oil

Prepare Vinaigrette Dressing; set aside. In a medium bowl, combine chicken or turkey and half the Vinaigrette Dressing. Toss to mix. Cover and refrigerate 30 minutes to 1 hour. Bring a large saucepan of water to a boil. Drop whole potatoes into boiling water. Cook until tender when pierced with a fork; drain well. Using a fork, hold a cooked potato under cold running water or plunge potato in a bowl of ice water. Quickly remove peel. Repeat with remaining potatoes. Place peeled potatoes in a medium bowl. Pour remaining dressing over potatoes. Toss to blend. Cover and refrigerate 30 minutes to 1 hour. Arrange lettuce on 4 salad plates. Drain chicken or turkey strips and potatoes. Place an equal portion of meat in center of each plate. Place 2 potatoes beside meat on each plate. Place bean salad on opposite side of meat, dividing it equally between 4 plates. Top each mound of meat with 2 criss-crossed anchovy fillets. Garnish with tomato wedges and olives. Makes 4 servings.

Vinaigrette Dressing:
In a blender, small bowl or jar, combine all ingredients. Blend until sugar is completely dissolved.

California Chicken Salad

Chicken with bacon, avocado and Roquefort cheese—with a light, tangy dressing.

California Dressing, see below
1 large tomato
1 (2-1/2- to 3-lb.) cooked chicken,
 skinned, boned, diced
1/2 cup crumbled Roquefort or
 other blue cheese (2 oz.)
1 Belgian endive, shredded

1 small bunch watercress,
 tough stems removed
1 small head Boston lettuce,
 torn in bite-size pieces
1 avocado, cut in wedges
4 slices crisp-cooked bacon, crumbled

California Dressing:
1/2 cup mayonnaise
1 tablespoon vegetable oil
2 teaspoons Dijon-style mustard

2 tablespoons lemon juice
1/2 teaspoon salt

Prepare California Dressing. Cut tomato in half. Gently squeeze out juice and seeds. Cut tomato in narrow strips. Blot dry with paper towel. In a large bowl, combine tomato strips, chicken, cheese and 2 tablespoons California Dressing. Toss gently to mix. In a medium bowl, toss endive, watercress and lettuce with remaining California Dressing. Place greens in a salad bowl. Arrange avocado wedges around edge of salad bowl. Spoon chicken mixture in center of bowl. Sprinkle with crumbled bacon. Serve immediately. Makes 5 to 6 servings.

California Dressing:
In a blender, small bowl or jar, combine all ingredients. Blend well. Set aside until ready to use.

Italian Chicken Salad

A different salad that's especially suitable for summer entertaining.

1/2 lb. large fresh mushrooms,
 thinly sliced
1/4 cup fresh lemon juice
1/2 teaspoon dried leaf oregano
1 small garlic clove, minced
1/4 cup olive oil
1 to 1-1/2 cups diced cooked chicken
 or turkey

1 teaspoon salt
1/4 teaspoon coarsely ground pepper
1 (8-oz.) pkg. elbow macaroni, cooked
2 medium tomatoes, peeled, cut in quarters
8 pitted black olives
1 bunch watercress
Capers, if desired

In a large bowl, combine mushrooms, lemon juice, oregano, garlic, olive oil and chicken or turkey. Toss to blend. Cover and let stand 1 hour at room temperature, stirring occasionally. Season with salt and pepper. Add cooked macaroni to chicken mixture. Gently toss mixture with a fork. Adjust seasonings as needed. Let stand at room temperature 30 minutes before serving. Spoon salad onto a large platter. Surround salad alternately with tomato wedges, olives and watercress. Garnish with capers, if desired. Makes 4 to 6 servings.

California Chicken Salad with Chicken Tea Sandwiches, page 128

1/Beat chilled mixture at high speed until fluffy.

2/Spoon salad mixture into a 6-cup ring mold.

Waldorf Chicken Mold

Perfect for your next buffet party.

1 crisp tart red apple, chopped	**2 to 3 dashes hot-pepper sauce**
1 tablespoon lemon juice	**2 tablespoons lemon juice**
1 (1/4-oz.) envelope unflavored gelatin	**1-1/2 cups chopped cooked chicken or turkey**
1/2 cup chicken stock	**1/2 cup chopped dates**
1/2 teaspoon salt	**1/2 cup chopped walnuts**
1 cup mayonnaise	**Crisp lettuce leaves**
1 cup dairy sour cream	**Cherry tomatoes, if desired**

Sprinkle apple with lemon juice; set aside. In a small saucepan, combine gelatin, stock and salt. Stir over low heat until gelatin dissolves. Remove from heat. Add mayonnaise, beating with a whisk until smooth. Pour into a 13" x 9" baking dish. Cover and place in freezer about 20 minutes or until mixture becomes firm around the edges but is still soft in the center. Spoon mixture into a large bowl. Beat with an electric mixer at high speed until fluffy. Fold in sour cream, hot-pepper sauce, lemon juice, chicken or turkey, dates and walnuts. Spoon mixture into a 6-cup ring mold. Cover and refrigerate until firm, 4 to 6 hours. To serve, line a large platter with lettuce. Unmold salad on lettuce. Fill center of salad with tomatoes, if desired. Makes 6 to 8 servings.

Turkey & Apple Salad

Here's a great way to use leftover dark meat from your holiday bird.

Creamy Chive Dressing, see below
3 to 3-1/2 cups diced cooked turkey
2 Red-Delicious apples, diced

1 small head romaine lettuce,
   torn in bite-size pieces
Crisp lettuce leaves

Creamy Chive Dressing:
1 egg yolk
2 tablespoons white-wine vinegar
1/2 teaspoon dry mustard
Dash hot-pepper sauce

6 tablespoons olive oil or vegetable oil
1 teaspoon salt
1/4 teaspoon coarsely ground pepper
2 to 3 tablespoons minced chives

Prepare Creamy Chive Dressing. In a medium bowl, combine turkey, apples and romaine lettuce. Add Creamy Chive Dressing. Toss lightly. Cover and refrigerate 30 minutes to 1 hour. Line a salad bowl with lettuce. Spoon salad into lined bowl. Makes 5 to 6 servings.

Creamy Chive Dressing:
In a small bowl, beat together egg yolk, vinegar, mustard and hot-pepper sauce until doubled in volume. Slowly add oil, beating with a whisk until thickened. Stir in salt, pepper and chives. Set aside until ready to use.

Cranberry-Turkey Mold

A colorful molded salad and a quick new way to prepare it.

1/4 cup lemon juice
2 (1/4-oz.) envelopes unflavored gelatin
1 (8-oz.) can jellied cranberry sauce
1/2 cup water
1 cup mayonnaise
1/2 teaspoon salt

1-1/2 cups chopped cooked turkey
1/2 cup chopped celery
1/2 cup chopped walnuts
1 (1-lb.) can whole-cranberry sauce, chilled
Crisp lettuce leaves

Place lemon juice in a large bowl. Sprinkle gelatin over lemon juice. Stir to dissolve gelatin. In a medium saucepan, combine jellied cranberry sauce and water. Stir over low heat until mixture begins to boil. Pour boiling cranberry mixture over gelatin mixture. Stir until blended. Add mayonnaise and salt to gelatin mixture. Beat until smooth. Pour into a 9'' x 5'' loaf pan. Cover and place in freezer 20 minutes or until firm around edges but still soft in center. Remove from freezer. Spoon mixture into a large bowl. Beat with electric mixer at high speed until fluffy. Fold in turkey, celery and nuts. Spoon mixture into a 4-cup ring mold. Cover and refrigerate until firm, about 3 hours. To serve, line a platter with lettuce. Unmold salad onto lettuce. Fill center of salad with whole-cranberry sauce. Makes 5 to 6 servings.

Chicken Salad for Singles

Dine alone and enjoy it.

1 cup diced cooked chicken or turkey
1 hard-cooked egg, chopped
1/4 cup mayonnaise
1 teaspoon Dijon-style mustard
1 teaspoon lemon juice
1 teaspoon prepared horseradish, if desired

1/4 teaspoon salt
Coarsely ground pepper to taste
Crisp lettuce leaves
Slivered almonds or
    chopped walnuts for garnish

In a small bowl, combine chicken or turkey, egg, mayonnaise, mustard, lemon juice and horse-radish, if desired. Blend well. Season with salt and pepper. Place lettuce on a plate. Spoon salad onto lettuce. Garnish with almonds or walnuts. Makes 1 serving.

Chicken-Rice Salad

Simple ingredients made very elegant.

1 (3- to 3-1/2 lb.) cooked chicken,
   skinned, boned, diced
2 cups cold cooked rice
1/2 cup sliced celery
1/2 cup chopped pecans
1 cup chopped tomato
1/4 cup chopped green pepper

1/2 cup pimiento-stuffed olives, sliced
2 tablespoons red-wine vinegar
1 tablespoon Dijon-style mustard
1/4 cup vegetable oil
2 to 3 drops hot-pepper sauce
Salt and coarsely ground pepper to taste
Crisp lettuce leaves

In a large bowl, combine chicken, rice, celery, pecans, tomato, green pepper and olives. In a small bowl, combine vinegar and mustard. Beat in oil. Season with hot-pepper sauce, salt and pepper. Pour dressing over chicken mixture. Toss lightly with a fork. Line a large salad bowl with lettuce. Spoon salad into lettuce-lined bowl. Serve at room temperature. Makes 6 to 8 servings.

Chicken & Fruit Salad

For a delightful luncheon, serve in scooped-out papaya halves.

1 (3- to 3-1/2-lb.) cooked chicken,
   skinned, boned, diced
1 cooked chicken breast,
   skinned, boned, diced
1/4 cup minced parsley
1/2 cup chopped celery
3/4 cup slivered almonds
1/2 lb. seedless white grapes

3/4 cup mayonnaise
1 tablespoon lemon juice
1 cup diced papaya
1 cup diced cantaloupe
Salt and coarsely ground pepper to taste
Crisp lettuce leaves
Paprika for garnish

In a large bowl, combine chicken, parsley, celery, almonds, grapes, mayonnaise, lemon juice, papaya and cantaloupe. Toss to mix. Season with salt and pepper. Cover and refrigerate several hours to blend flavors. To serve, arrange lettuce on a platter. Spoon salad onto lettuce. Sprinkle with paprika. Makes 5 to 6 servings.

Chicken Rarebit Sandwich

A great, light feast after the game.

3/4 lb. grated sharp Cheddar cheese (3 cups)	1 tablespoon all-purpose flour
1/4 teaspoon dry mustard	3/4 cup milk, room temperature
2 tablespoons brandy	1 egg, slightly beaten
1 (8-oz.) can tomato sauce	6 to 8 thick slices French bread
1/8 teaspoon baking soda	6 to 8 slices roast chicken or turkey breast
2 tablespoons butter	

In a large bowl, combine cheese, mustard, brandy, tomato sauce and baking soda; set aside. Melt butter in a heavy skillet over low heat. Stir in flour until blended. Slowly add milk, stirring until smooth. Cool slightly. Stir in egg. Add cheese mixture; blend well. Place skillet over medium heat. Cook until bubbly hot. Place 1 slice bread on each of 6 or 8 serving plates. Cover each with a slice of chicken or turkey. Spoon sauce over each. Serve hot. Makes 6 to 8 servings.

Pocket-Bread Sandwich

Tasty pita bread filled with a Middle Eastern blend of chicken and fresh sprouts.

1 (3-oz.) pkg. cream cheese	2 medium cucumbers, peeled, seeded, chopped
3 tablespoons plain yogurt	3/4 cup soybean sprouts,
1 tablespoon lime juice or lemon juice	alfalfa sprouts or watercress
1/2 teaspoon salt	4 large pita breads
1 cup chopped cooked chicken or turkey	4 thin slices Swiss cheese

Preheat broiler. In a medium bowl, combine cream cheese, yogurt and lime juice or lemon juice. Beat with a fork until blended and smooth. Add salt, chicken or turkey, cucumbers and sprouts or watercress. Stir with fork to blend. Split each pita bread open at 1 side. Spoon chicken or turkey mixture into bread, dividing evenly between 4 breads. Place breads on a baking sheet. Top each with a slice of cheese. Place sandwiches 6 inches below heat. Broil until cheese begins to melt. Serve immediately. Makes 4 sandwiches.

Grilled Chicken & Cheese Sandwiches

For early or late supper, a tasty sandwich.

1 tablespoon tarragon vinegar	1/2 lb. fontina cheese, sliced
3 tablespoons mayonnaise	2 tablespoons butter
4 large slices Italian-style bread	2 to 3 tablespoons sliced almonds
8 to 12 slices roast chicken or	Mango chutney
turkey, room temperature	

Preheat broiler. In a small bowl, combine vinegar and mayonnaise. Spread mayonnaise mixture on 1 side of each slice of bread. Place bread, spread-side up, on a baking sheet. Cover each slice with 2 to 3 meat slices. Top with cheese. Melt butter in a small skillet over medium heat. Add almonds; sauté 4 to 5 minutes or until golden and crisp. Sprinkle almonds over sandwiches. Drizzle sandwiches with any remaining butter from sautéing almonds. Place sandwiches 6 inches below heat. Broil until cheese begins to melt. Serve with chutney. Makes 4 servings.

How to Make Croque Madame

1/In a pie plate, beat eggs with water until frothy. Dip each sandwich in egg mixture, turning to coat each side.

2/Fry sandwiches in hot butter, turning once, until browned on both sides. Serve sandwiches hot.

Croque Madame

A blend of cream cheese and chicken breast served hot from the skillet.

1 (3-oz.) pkg. cream cheese,
  room temperature
1 tablespoon dry onion-soup mix
1 tablespoon plain yogurt
4 (1/4-inch-thick) slices French bread
4 thin slices cooked chicken or
  turkey breast, room temperature

2 eggs
2 tablespoons water
2 tablespoons butter
1 tablespoon vegetable oil
Uncooked Cranberry-Orange Sauce,
  page 156, if desired

In a small bowl, combine cream cheese, soup mix and yogurt. Blend well. Spread mixture on 1 side of each bread slice. Place 2 slices of chicken or turkey over cheese spread on 2 slices of bread. Top with remaining bread slices, spread-side down. Press each sandwich together firmly. In a pie plate, beat eggs with water until frothy. Dip each sandwich in egg mixture, turning to coat each side. Heat butter and oil in a large heavy skillet over medium heat until foamy. When foam subsides, add sandwiches. Fry, turning once, until well-browned on both sides. Serve hot with Uncooked Cranberry-Orange Sauce, if desired. Makes 2 servings.

Croque à l'Américaine

A superbly flavored version of a classic French sandwich.

1 (2-1/4-oz.) can deviled ham
2 teaspoons mayonnaise
1/4 teaspoon dry mustard
1 to 2 dashes hot-pepper sauce
1 teaspoon prepared horseradish, if desired
4 slices firm white bread

4 thin slices roast chicken or
   turkey breast, room temperature
2 eggs
1 tablespoon water
1 tablespoon butter
1 tablespoon vegetable oil

In a small bowl, combine ham, mayonnaise, mustard, hot-pepper sauce and horseradish, if desired. Spread ham mixture on 1 side of each bread slice. Place 2 slices of chicken or turkey over ham spread on 2 slices of bread. Top with remaining bread slices, spread-side down. Trim off crusts. Press each sandwich together firmly. In a pie plate, beat eggs with water until frothy. Dip each sandwich in egg mixture, turning to coat each side. In a large heavy skillet, heat butter and oil over medium heat until foamy. When foam subsides, add sandwiches. Fry, turning once, until well-browned on both sides. Serve hot. Makes 2 servings.

Tostada-Salad Sandwich

Hearty enough for a main dish—festive enough for a party.

1 firm ripe tomato
1 small head iceberg lettuce,
   shredded (2 cups)
2 avocados
2 tablespoons lime juice or lemon juice
1 to 2 teaspoons grated onion
1/2 teaspoon salt
1 (10-oz.) can tomatillos with
   green chilies, chopped

1 tablespoon bottled or fresh Mexican salsa
12 to 16 thin slices cooked chicken
   or turkey
4 corn tortillas
1 to 2 tablespoons vegetable oil
1/2 lb. Monterey Jack cheese,
   coarsely grated
Black olives or
   pimiento-stuffed olives for garnish

Cut tomato in half. Gently squeeze out juice and seeds. Thinly slice tomato. Blot dry with paper towel. In a medium bowl, combine tomato slices and lettuce; set aside. Peel avocados. Place avocados in a medium bowl. Add lime juice or lemon juice. Using a fork, mash avocados until smooth. Stir in onion and salt; set aside. In a small skillet, combine tomatillos, salsa and chicken or turkey. Cook over medium heat, stirring, until bubbly hot; set aside. In another skillet, fry tortillas, 1 at a time, in a small amount of oil until heated, about 30 seconds each. Place 1 tortilla on each of 4 plates. Spread tortillas with avocado mixture. Top with equal portions of chicken or turkey mixture. Sprinkle each with equal amounts of lettuce and tomatoes. Top each with cheese. Garnish each serving with olives. Makes 4 servings.

Southern-Style Chicken Mousse

Beautiful and just perfect for a large party.

3 cups chicken stock
1 (6-oz.) pkg. lime-flavored gelatin
3 tablespoons white-wine vinegar
1 teaspoon salt
1 pint (2 cups) whipping cream, chilled
1 cup mayonnaise

2 cups diced cooked chicken or turkey
1-1/2 cups finely diced celery
1/2 cup pimiento-stuffed olives, sliced
Crisp lettuce leaves
Cherry tomatoes for garnish
Black olives for garnish

In a medium saucepan, bring 2 cups stock to a boil. Place gelatin in a large bowl. Add boiling stock. Stir until gelatin dissolves. Add remaining stock, vinegar and salt. Blend well. Cover and refrigerate 30 to 45 minutes or until it reaches the consistency of unbeaten egg whites. In a second large bowl, beat cream until stiff. Fold in mayonnaise, chicken or turkey, celery and stuffed olives. Cover and refrigerate until chilled. Fold chilled gelatin mixture into chilled meat mixture. Spoon into an 8-cup mold. Refrigerate until firm, 6 hours or overnight. To serve, line a large platter with lettuce. Unmold mousse onto lettuce. Garnish with cherry tomatoes and black olives. Makes 10 to 12 servings.

California Chicken Sandwich

Quick to prepare and just right for a festive luncheon party.

Russian Dressing, see below
1 medium avocado
2 tablespoons lemon juice
1/2 cup butter, room temperature
1/4 teaspoon salt

Russian Dressing:
1 cup mayonnaise
1/4 cup chili sauce

4 (1/4-inch-thick) slices sourdough bread
8 thin slices cooked chicken or
  turkey breast
1 large navel orange, peeled, thinly sliced
4 orange twists

2 tablespoons lemon juice
Dash hot-pepper sauce

Prepare Russian Dressing. Peel avocado; place in a medium bowl. Using a fork, mash avocado. Stir in lemon juice, butter and salt. Beat until smooth. Spread avocado mixture evenly on 1 side of each slice of bread. Cover each slice of bread with 2 slices meat. Cover meat with orange slices. Spoon dressing over orange slices. Garnish with an orange twist. Makes 4 servings.

Russian Dressing:
In a blender, small bowl or jar, combine all ingredients. Blend well. Set aside until ready to use.

To make orange twists, slice 1 navel orange. Make 1 cut from the rind-edge to the center of the slice. Twist each orange slice.

Flavorful Backyard-Cooked Poultry

Nothing tastes as great as food cooked outdoors over a charcoal fire. And, it's a simple way to prepare delicious chicken. There is something about it that sets it apart from indoor cooking. That "something" is the intensity of the charcoal heat. That is why it's so important to light the charcoal well ahead of cooking time so the coals will be ready when you are.

Here are a few ideas for making perfect grilled chicken. Select a small bird, preferably 2 to 3 pounds. Each chicken will provide two to three servings. Cut chicken in halves or quarters. Bring chicken almost to room temperature before grilling. This allows for faster, more even cooking. For added flavor, marinate chicken in a tasty sauce for several hours before grilling.

Light the charcoal at least 30 minutes before you plan to cook. Adjust the grate to about 6 inches above the heat. Coals should be reduced to a glowing hot ash before beginning to grill.

Blot chicken dry with paper towel. Rub each piece with a thin coating of vegetable oil. This helps to keep the chicken from sticking and seals in natural juices. When the chicken is first placed on a hot grill, skin-side down, a chemical reaction takes place. Natural sugars found in the skin caramelize, producing a beautifully crisp, golden-brown seal which holds in the natural moisture and flavor.

Grill chicken 10 minutes. Then, turn and grill 10 additional minutes. Baste, if desired, or use a little additional oil. Turn chicken again and grill 7 to 8 minutes. Turn again and coat with sauce, marinade or additional oil. Grill a final 7 to 8 minutes, turning and basting frequently. Total cooking time will be 35 to 40 minutes.

If a sauce or marinade is not used, season chicken with salt and coarsely ground pepper just before removing from grill. Sprinkle with lemon juice after removing from grill or serve with lemon wedges, if desired.

For variety, experiment with other sauces, marinades and grilling ideas. Try Barbecued Chicken Dinner for a total outdoor meal. Enjoy the spicy, south-of-the-border flavor of Taco Chicken Grill. Or, plan a luau and serve Polynesian Grilled Chicken. Tired of chicken? Try Chinese Grilled Turkey or Spit-Roasted Duck. All are delicious ways to enjoy backyard cooking.

Sunday Afternoon Cookout
Spit-Roasted Duck, page 146
Colorful Vegetable Salad
Grilled Corn-on-the-Cob
Ambrosia

Grilled Chicken with Herbs

Herb-flavored marinades give chicken a superb continental flavor.

Herb Marinade, see below
1 (2-1/2- to 3-lb.) chicken, cut in halves

2 tablespoons vegetable oil

Herb Marinade:
1/2 cup vegetable oil
1/4 cup dry red wine
1 tablespoon red-wine vinegar
1/2 teaspoon salt
1/4 teaspoon coarsely ground pepper
1/4 teaspoon dried leaf thyme

1 tablespoon chopped fresh rosemary or
  1/2 teaspoon dried leaf rosemary
1 tablespoon chopped fresh basil or
  1/2 teaspoon dried leaf basil
1 garlic clove, minced

Prepare Herb Marinade. Place chicken, skin-side down, in a single layer in a 13" x 9" baking dish. Pour marinade over chicken. Let stand at room temperature 1 hour, turning occasionally. Or, refrigerate several hours or overnight, turning occasionally. Prepare charcoal while chicken marinates. Drain chicken well, reserving marinade. Brush chicken with oil. Place chicken, skin-side down, on grill 4 to 6 inches above heat. Grill 10 minutes or until browned. Brush chicken with oil. Turn chicken. Continue grilling, turning and basting frequently with marinade, 20 to 25 minutes or until tender. Makes 2 servings.

Herb Marinade:
In a small bowl, combine oil, wine, vinegar, salt and pepper. Beat until blended. Stir in thyme, rosemary, basil and garlic. Set aside until ready to use.

Barbecued Chicken Texas-Style

This is sure to be everyone's favorite.

Texas Barbecue Sauce, see below
2 (2-1/2- to 3-lb.) chickens, cut in halves

2 tablespoons vegetable oil

Texas Barbecue Sauce:
3/4 cup ketchup
1/2 cup vinegar
1 garlic clove, crushed
1 tablespoon Worcestershire sauce

1/2 teaspoon dry mustard
1/4 teaspoon hot-pepper sauce
1 tablespoon sugar
1 teaspoon salt

Prepare Texas Barbecue Sauce. Prepare charcoal. Rub chicken halves lightly with oil. Place chicken, skin-side down, on grill 4 to 6 inches above heat. Grill 10 minutes or until browned. Brush with oil. Turn chicken and grill 8 to 10 minutes. Baste with Texas Barbecue Sauce. Grill 15 to 20 minutes longer, turning and brushing with sauce until chicken is tender. Brush generously with sauce just before removing from grill. Makes 4 servings.

Texas Barbeque Sauce:
In a small saucepan, combine all ingredients. Cook over low heat, stirring often, about 10 minutes. Set aside until ready to use.

Barbecued Chicken Dinner

Try this total meal cooked on the grill.

2 (2-1/2- to 3-lb.) chickens, cut in halves
1 (8-oz.) bottle Italian or
   French-style clear, thin salad dressing
3 medium zucchini, ends trimmed,
   cut in 1-inch cubes

3 medium, yellow crookneck squash,
   ends trimmed, cut in 1-inch cubes
1 small eggplant, cut in 1/4-inch slices
3 medium onions, cut in halves
1 loaf crusty Italian or French bread, sliced

Place chicken halves, skin-side down, in a single layer in 2 (13" x 9") baking dishes. Pour half the salad dressing over chicken, reserve remaining dressing. Let chicken stand at room temperature 30 minutes to 1 hour. Prepare charcoal while chicken marinates. Drain chicken well, discarding salad dressing. Place chicken, skin-side down, on grill 4 to 6 inches above heat. Grill 10 minutes or until browned. Turn chicken and continue grilling, turning and basting frequently with remaining salad dressing, 20 to 25 minutes or until tender. While chicken cooks, arrange zucchini and squash alternately on long metal skewers. Brush skewered vegetables, eggplant slices and cut-side of onions with salad dressing. Place vegetable skewers on grill. Place eggplant slices and onion halves, cut-side down, on grill. Grill vegetables, turning occasionally, 8 to 10 minutes or until tender but not overcooked. Brush with salad dressing while grilling. Toast bread slices on grill. Brush bread again with salad dressing. Makes 4 servings.

Taco Chicken Grill

South-of-the-border flavor.

Taco Sauce, see below
2 (2-1/2- to 3-lb.) chickens,
   cut in quarters

2 tablespoons vegetable oil
1/2 cup shredded mild Cheddar cheese (2 oz.)

Taco Sauce:
1 small onion, minced
1 (8-oz.) can tomato sauce
1 (4-oz.) can taco sauce
1/2 cup dark corn syrup
2 tablespoons vinegar

1 tablespoon vegetable oil
1 teaspoon salt
1/2 teaspoon dried leaf oregano
Coarsely ground pepper

Prepare Taco Sauce. Place chicken, skin-side down, in a single layer in 2 (13" x 9") baking dishes. Pour Taco Sauce over chicken. Let chicken stand at room temperature 30 minutes to 1 hour. Prepare charcoal while chicken marinates. Drain chicken well, reserving Taco Sauce. Blot dry with paper towel. Brush chicken with oil. Place chicken, skin-side down, on grill 4 to 6 inches above heat. Grill 7 minutes or until browned. Brush with oil. Turn skin-side up. Grill about 7 minutes. Turn and brush with Taco Sauce. Continue grilling white meat about 10 minutes longer, dark meat 15 to 20 minutes longer, turning and basting with sauce frequently. When tender, place chicken on a platter. Reheat remaining Taco Sauce. Pour sauce over chicken. Sprinkle with cheese. Serve immediately. Makes 4 to 6 servings.

Taco Sauce:
In a medium saucepan, combine all ingredients. Bring to a boil over medium heat. Reduce heat and simmer 5 minutes. Cool before using. Set aside until ready to use.

Oriental Chicken Kabobs

Serve as an appetizer or over rice as a main dish—either way, kabobs are delicious.

4 chicken-breast halves, skinned, boned
2 tablespoons soft butter
1/2 cup soy sauce
1/2 cup peanut oil
1 teaspoon sesame oil

2 garlic cloves, crushed
1 (1-inch) cube gingerroot,
    crushed or 1 teaspoon ground ginger
Hot cooked rice, if desired
Mango chutney, if desired

Using a heavy cleaver or meat mallet, flatten each breast to about 1/4 inch thick. Spread each flattened breast with butter. Roll each breast, jelly-roll fashion. Place chicken roll, seam-side down, on a flat tray or baking sheet. Refrigerate until butter is cold and firm. Cut each roll into 1/3-inch-thick slices. Place slices on small skewers, 3 to 4 per skewer. In a shallow baking dish, combine soy sauce, peanut oil and sesame oil. Add garlic and ginger. Place skewered chicken in soy mixture. Let stand at room temperature about 30 minutes or refrigerate up to 3 hours. Prepare charcoal while chicken marinates. Remove kabobs from marinade, reserving marinade. Grill kabobs, turning and basting occasionally with marinade, 4 to 5 minutes or until chicken is cooked through. Serve with hot cooked rice and chutney, if desired. Or, serve as appetizers. Makes 4 servings or 6 to 8 appetizer servings.

Polynesian Grilled Chicken

A speciality from the South-Sea Islands.

Polynesian Sauce, see below
12 chicken thighs

2 tablespoons vegetable oil

Polynesian Sauce:
1/2 cup pineapple juice
1/2 cup ketchup
2 tablespoons wine vinegar

2 tablespoons honey
2 to 3 dashes hot-pepper sauce
1 teaspoon dry mustard

Prepare Polynesian Sauce. Place chicken, skin-side down, in a single layer in a 13" x 9" baking dish. Pour Polynesian Sauce over chicken. Let chicken stand at room temperature 1 to 2 hours. Prepare charcoal while chicken marinates. Drain chicken well, reserving marinade. Brush chicken with oil. Place chicken, skin-side down, on grill 4 to 6 inches above heat. Grill 15 to 20 minutes, turning and basting frequently. Makes 6 servings.

Polynesian Sauce:
In a small bowl, combine all ingredients. Mix well. Set aside until ready to use.

California Barbecue Sauce

A sunny, sweet and sour flavor—great with chicken or turkey.

1 cup unsweetened pineapple juice
1/2 cup packed light-brown sugar
1/2 cup cider vinegar

1 (6-oz.) can tomato paste
1/4 cup vegetable oil

In a small saucepan, combine all ingredients. Cook over low heat, stirring, until sugar dissolves. Makes 3 cups.

1/Grill chicken, brushing occasionally with Yakitori Sauce.

2/Serve Yakitori with remaining sauce and lemon wedges.

Japanese-Style Grilled Chicken

Yakitori is a favorite snack food in Japan.

Yakitori Sauce, see below
1 chicken breast, cut in 1-inch cubes

6 chicken thighs, boned, page 47, steps 1 and 2
1 to 2 tablespoons vegetable oil

Yakitori Sauce:
1/2 cup saké, rice wine or dry white wine
1/4 cup honey
3/4 cup soy sauce

1 garlic clove, crushed
Lemon wedges

Prepare Yakitori Sauce. Prepare charcoal. Cut each thigh in 3 or 4 strips. Arrange breast and thigh meat on separate skewers, 4 to 6 pieces per skewer. Brush meat with oil. Place skewers on grill, 4 to 6 inches above heat. Grill 2 minutes, turning often. Brush with Yakitori Sauce. Continue cooking until tender, 5 to 6 minutes for white meat, 10 minutes for dark meat. Brush generously with Yakitori Sauce before removing from grill. Serve hot with lemon wedges. Serve remaining Yakitori Sauce as a dip. Makes 8 to 10 appetizer servings.

Yakitori Sauce:
In a small saucepan, combine all ingredients. Cook over low heat, stirring until blended and hot through. Do not boil. Cool to room temperature. Set aside until ready to use.

Grilled Cornish Hens

A piquant basting sauce gives these small, quick-cooking birds an elegant flavor.

3/4 cup cider vinegar
1 teaspoon sugar
1 teaspoon salt
1/4 teaspoon coarsely ground pepper

2 teaspoons chili powder
1 teaspoon dry mustard
4 Cornish hens, thawed if frozen
2 tablespoons vegetable oil

In a small bowl, combine vinegar, sugar, salt, pepper, chili powder and mustard; set aside. Prepare charcoal. Split each hen in half lengthwise. Brush halves with oil. Place hens on grill, skin-side down, 4 inches above heat. Grill 5 minutes or until browned. Brush again with oil. Turn skin-side up. Grill 5 minutes. Turn and brush with vinegar mixture. Continue grilling 7 minutes, turning and brushing with vinegar mixture or until browned or to desired doneness. Makes 4 servings.

Grilled & Filled Franks

A backyard-party winner everytime.

10 turkey or chicken frankfurters
10 bacon slices

10 frankfurter rolls, toasted
Choice of filling, see below

Prepare charcoal. Cut a slit almost the length of each frank. Avoid cutting through franks. Stuff each frank with desired filling. Wrap with bacon, securing ends with wooden picks. Grill over hot coals 5 to 8 minutes or until browned. Turn occasionally during cooking. Serve hot on toasted frankfurter rolls with choice of condiments. Makes 10 servings.

Fillings:

1/4 cup diced Cheddar cheese mixed with 1 tablespoon thinly sliced pimiento-stuffed olives
2 tablespoons mayonnaise mixed with 1 tablespoon hot mustard and 2 to 3 dashes hot-pepper sauce
1/4 cup drained sauerkraut mixed with 1/2 teaspoon caraway seeds
1/4 cup baked beans mixed with 1 tablespoon chili sauce
1 tablespoon mayonnaise mixed with 2 tablespoons pickle relish and 1 tablespoon chili sauce
1/4 cup canned taco sauce mixed with 2 tablespoons shredded lettuce
1/4 cup canned chili mixed with 1 teaspoon Mexican salsa

Uncooked Barbecue Sauce

Easy, easy.

1/2 cup vegetable oil
2 tablespoons Worcestershire sauce
1/2 cup red-wine vinegar
2 tablespoons chili powder

1 tablespoon light-brown sugar
1/2 teaspoon salt
1/4 teaspoon coarsely ground pepper
1 (8-oz.) can tomato sauce

In a small bowl, combine all ingredients. Blend well. Use as a basting sauce for chicken or turkey. Makes 2 cups.

Spit-Roasted Duck

The perfect way to cook duck on a rotisserie.

1 (5- to 6-lb.) duck
Marmalade Sauce, see below

Marmalade Sauce:

3/4 cup orange marmalade	**1 tablespoon Dijon-style mustard**
1 teaspoon grated orange rind	**2 teaspoons cornstarch**
1/2 cup orange juice	**1/4 teaspoon salt**
1/4 cup cider vinegar	

Prepare Marmalade Sauce. Prepare charcoal. Position a 13'' x 9'' or larger baking pan under spit to catch drippings from duck. Insert rotisserie spit lengthwise through duck, balancing duck. Tighten holding prongs. Using string, tie wings firm against breast. Tie legs together loosely, looping string around tail. Attach spit to rotisserie. Roast duck 30 minutes per pound or until browned and tender. Brush duck with Marmalade Sauce several times during last 30 minutes of roasting. Serve remaining sauce with duck. Makes 4 servings.

Marmalade Sauce:
In a small saucepan, combine all ingredients. Mix well. Bring to a boil, stirring constantly until thickened. Set aside until ready to use.

Lemon Grilled Chicken

Tangy, sweet and sour chicken from the grill.

1/2 cup lemon juice	**1/2 teaspoon dried leaf basil**
1 tablespoon sugar	**1/2 teaspoon poultry seasoning**
1/4 cup olive oil	**1/4 teaspoon coarsely ground pepper**
1 bay leaf	**1 (2-1/2- to 3-lb.) chicken,**
1/2 teaspoon salt	**cut in quarters**

In a small saucepan, combine lemon juice, sugar, olive oil, bay leaf, salt, basil, poultry seasoning and pepper. Place over low heat and cook, stirring, 2 to 3 minutes. Cool to room temperature. Place chicken, skin-side down, in a single layer in a 13'' x 9'' baking dish. Pour lemon-juice mixture over chicken. Let stand at room temperature 2 to 3 hours. Prepare charcoal while chicken marinates. Drain chicken well, reserving marinade. Place chicken, skin-side down, on grill 4 to 6 inches above heat. Grill 7 minutes or until browned. Brush with marinade. Turn skin-side up. Grill about 7 minutes. Turn and brush with marinade. Continue grilling white meat about 10 minutes longer, dark meat 15 to 20 minutes longer, turning and basting with marinade frequently. Makes 2 to 4 servings.

Chinese Grilled Turkey

Oriental flavors transform inexpensive turkey steaks into party fare.

1 turkey breast or 6 turkey-breast steaks,
  cut 1 to 1-1/2 inches thick
1 (1-inch) cube gingerroot,
  crushed or 1 teaspoon ground ginger
1 teaspoon dry mustard

1 garlic clove, crushed
1 tablespoon honey
1/2 cup soy sauce
6 tablespoons vegetable oil
1 teaspoon sesame oil

If using a turkey breast, cut turkey crosswise into 1- to 1-1/2-inch-thick steaks. Place turkey steaks in a 13" x 9" baking dish. In a small bowl, combine ginger, mustard, garlic, honey, soy sauce, 1/4 cup vegetable oil and sesame oil. Mix well and pour over turkey. Cover and refrigerate several hours or overnight. Prepare charcoal while turkey marinates. Drain turkey well, reserving marinade. Remove garlic and gingerroot from marinade; discard. Brush turkey with remaining 2 tablespoons vegetable oil. Place turkey on grill 4 to 6 inches above heat. Grill 6 to 8 minutes on each side, brushing often with sauce, if desired. Makes 6 servings.

Middle Eastern Barbecue Sauce

Try this tart and tangy barbecue sauce at your next cookout.

3 tablespoons vegetable oil
1 small onion, chopped
2 garlic cloves, minced
1 teaspoon crushed hot red-pepper flakes
1 cup chicken stock

1 (6-oz.) can tomato paste
1/4 cup dark corn syrup
2 teaspoons soy sauce
1 teaspoon coarsely ground black pepper

Heat oil in a small skillet over medium heat. Add onion, garlic and red pepper. Sauté 2 to 3 minutes or until tender. Stir in stock, tomato paste, corn syrup, soy sauce and black pepper. Cook, stirring occasionally, until sauce comes to a gentle boil. Strain into a small bowl. Makes 2 cups.

Cranberry Barbecue Sauce

Cranberries with mustard and lemon juice make a zesty turkey-basting sauce.

1 (8-oz.) can jellied cranberry sauce
1/4 cup packed brown sugar
1/4 cup prepared mustard

2 tablespoons lemon juice
1 teaspoon Worcestershire sauce

In a small bowl, combine all ingredients. Mix well. During last hour of cooking, baste turkey with sauce every 15 minutes. Makes 1-1/2 cups.

Perfect Poultry
Accompaniments

The reason for certain food combinations is mysterious to me. Team efforts such as sour cream with black-bean soup, bacon and eggs, cranberry jelly with turkey and countless others have been around for a long time. Interestingly enough, I have found certain accompaniments not only taste right with chicken—they also make the chicken itself taste better. The right contrast of flavors may be part of the reason.

Chicken, no matter how prepared, goes extremely well with hot or cold cooked fruit such as Sugar & Cinnamon Baked Oranges or Spicy Pineapple Chunks. Roast chicken, with or without stuffing, demands a tart jelly or a sauce such as classic Cumberland Sauce. Try chicken curry, first without and then with a spicy-hot, sweet-tart chutney. You'll see exactly what I mean.

If you are looking for ideas to round out your menu, here are some interesting ones: French Potato Salad, perfect to serve with fried chicken, or, Tuscan Green Salad, great with chicken cooked on the outdoor grill. Sautéed-vegetable combinations include Neopolitan Vegetables or Caponata. Casseroles such as Souffléed Rice make a hot meal of leftover roasted chicken or turkey. In this chapter, there is an assortment of sure-to-please fruit creations guaranteed to get compliments. Try Stuffed Apricots or Cinnamon Peaches.

You will also find a number of matchless sauces which are easily prepared and praiseworthy when served. Apple-Curry Sauce served over sautéed chicken will draw raves from everyone. Or, for a very special treat, present your guests with Tropical Fruit Flambé.

Poultry goes with a wide assortment of food. This collection has something special that adds up to successful menus every time.

Neighbors for Dinner
Perfect Sautéed Chicken, page 38
Apple-Curry Sauce, page 156
Caponata, page 154
Herb Rolls
Fresh-Fruit Tray with Cheese

French Potato Salad

The perfect picnic salad with fried chicken.

2 lbs. new or red-skinned potatoes
1/4 cup dry white wine
3 tablespoons vegetable oil
1 garlic clove, minced
1/2 teaspoon Dijon-style mustard
1 teaspoon dried leaf tarragon or
   1 tablespoon fresh tarragon, minced

2 tablespoons red-wine vinegar
1/4 teaspoon sugar
1 teaspoon salt
1/2 teaspoon coarsely ground pepper
1 tablespoon chopped chives
Crisp lettuce leaves
Sweet paprika

Place potatoes in a large saucepan. Add water to cover. Bring to a boil over medium heat. Cook 15 to 20 minutes or until tender when pierced with a fork; drain well. Using a fork, hold each potato under cold running water and peel skin off. While still warm, cut potatoes in 1/4-inch slices. Place potato slices in a medium bowl. Add wine. Toss gently with a spatula until evenly moistened. Heat oil in a small skillet over low heat. Add garlic; sauté 1 minute or until fragrant. Stir in mustard, tarragon, vinegar, sugar, salt, pepper and chives. Pour over potatoes. Toss gently until ingredients are blended. Cool to room temperature. Line a salad bowl with lettuce. Add potato mixture. Sprinkle evenly with paprika. Serve at room temperature. Makes 6 to 8 servings.

Variation
Add 1 cup cooked green beans or peas.

Tuscan Green Salad

This salad tastes wonderful and, unlike most green salads, can be made ahead.

1 (1-lb.) loaf Italian-style bread
1 (12-oz. or 1-lb.) bunch fresh spinach
1 large tomato
1-1/4 teaspoons salt
6 to 8 large mushrooms, thinly sliced
1 fennel, chopped, if desired
1/4 cup tarragon vinegar

1/2 teaspoon sugar
3/4 cup olive oil or vegetable oil
1 garlic clove, minced
Coarsely ground pepper to taste
1/2 cup freshly grated Parmesan cheese
   (1-1/2 oz.)

Preheat oven to 200F (95C). Cut bread in 1/4-inch cubes. Place bread cubes on a baking sheet. Bake, turning occasionally, until dry but not browned; set aside. Wash spinach thoroughly in cold water; drain well. Remove any large stems. Blot spinach dry with paper towel. Tear spinach in bite-size pieces. Place spinach in a large salad bowl. Cut tomato in half. Squeeze out juice and seeds. Cut tomato in narrow strips. Place on paper towel. Sprinkle lightly with 1/4 teaspoon salt. Let stand 10 minutes. Blot tomato thoroughly dry. Add tomato strips, mushrooms, bread cubes and fennel, if desired, to spinach; set aside. In a blender or food processor fitted with a steel blade, combine vinegar, sugar and salt. Process until sugar has dissolved. With blender or processor running, slowly add oil. Add garlic; process 10 seconds. Pour vinegar mixture over salad. Season with pepper. Sprinkle with cheese. Toss gently. Bread will absorb dressing. Refrigerate up to 30 minutes before serving. Makes 6 to 8 servings.

Tropical Fruit Flambé

Prepare this sauce for a dramatic tableside presentation.

2 teaspoons cornstarch
1/4 cup water
1 large navel orange
1 (15-1/4-oz.) can pineapple chunks
   in natural juice
2 medium peaches, peeled, sliced

1/2 cup seedless white grapes
1 cup watermelon or cantaloupe balls
1 kiwi, peeled, sliced
1 teaspoon sugar
1/4 cup brandy

In a small bowl, combine cornstarch and water; set aside. Cut orange in 8 wedges. Working over a bowl to catch all the juice, cut peel from orange pieces. Squeeze peel to extract any remaining juice. Set orange pieces aside. In an electric skillet set on high or a chafing dish over a high flame, combine orange juice, orange sections, pineapple with juice, peaches, grapes, melon balls and kiwi. Bring to a boil, stirring constantly. Add cornstarch mixture, stirring until slightly thickened. Sprinkle surface evenly with sugar. Warm brandy in a small saucepan over low heat until bubbles begin to appear around edge of pan. Pour heated brandy over fruit mixture. Using a long match, carefully ignite brandy. Ladle flaming fruit and sauce over sautéed chicken. Serve immediately. Makes about 3 cups.

Spicy Pineapple Chunks

A fruit for all seasons and to go with any style of chicken.

1 (15-1/4-oz.) can pineapple chunks
   in natural juice
Cider vinegar
1/4 cup sugar

1 cinnamon stick, broken into
   several pieces
4 whole cloves

Drain juice from pineapple into a measuring cup. Pour juice into a saucepan. Add an equal amount of vinegar. Stir in sugar. Add cinnamon and cloves. Place over low heat and simmer 15 minutes. Add pineapple. Simmer 15 minutes. Remove from heat. Place in a storage bowl. Cover and refrigerate until chilled. Drain well. Serve with chicken sandwiches, barbecued chicken, roast chicken or turkey. Makes about 2 cups.

Cinnamon Peaches

Crimson red, spiked with old-fashioned red-hot cinnamon candy.

2 cups water
1 cup sugar
1 cup red-hot cinnamon candy

6 large ripe peaches
1 drop red food coloring, if desired

In a medium saucepan, combine water, sugar and candy. Place over medium heat. Simmer 10 minutes or until a light syrup forms. Peel peaches. Cut in half and remove pits. Add peach halves to simmering syrup. Simmer until peaches are tender when pierced with a fork. Place peaches in a medium bowl. Cook syrup 20 minutes. Remove from heat. Let stand at room temperature 20 to 30 minutes or until cooled. Stir in red food coloring, if desired. Pour sauce over peaches. Cover and refrigerate. Drain before serving. Makes 12 peach halves.

How to Make Stuffed Apricots

1/Cut each apricot to remove pit easily.

2/Stuff each apricot with cream-cheese mixture.

Stuffed Apricots

Beautiful and so delicious.

1/4 cup mango or peach chutney
12 whole ripe unblemished apricots

1 (3-oz.) pkg. cream cheese,
** room temperature**

Finely chop large pieces in chutney. In a medium bowl, beat cream cheese until light and fluffy. Stir in chutney. Cut each apricot to remove pit. Stuff each apricot with cream-cheese mixture. Refrigerate until firm. Serve with broiled chicken. Makes 4 to 6 servings.

Sugar & Cinnamon Baked Oranges

Here's a garnish that looks as pretty as it tastes.

2 large navel oranges, unpeeled
1/2 teaspoon salt
2 tablespoons sugar

1 tablespoon ground cinnamon
2 tablespoons cold butter, slivered
1/4 cup water

Preheat oven to 375F (190C). Cut thin slices from both ends of each orange; reserve for another use. Cut remaining portion of each orange into 4 equal slices. Place slices in a single layer in a 13'' x 9'' baking dish. Sprinkle with salt, sugar and cinnamon. Top each slice with butter. Pour water into baking dish around oranges. Bake 10 minutes or until soft. Makes 8 slices.

Souffléed Rice Casserole

A Southern favorite that's sure to become yours, too!

2 tablespoons butter
3 to 4 green onions, white part only,
   thinly sliced
2 cups cooked rice
1/4 cup minced parsley
2 egg yolks, slightly beaten

1/4 cup milk
1/2 cup grated Parmesan cheese (1-1/2 oz.)
1/2 teaspoon salt
1/4 teaspoon coarsely ground pepper
2 egg whites

Preheat oven to 350F (175C). Lightly butter a 1-quart soufflé dish or similar baking dish; set aside. Melt butter in a large heavy skillet over low heat. Add green onions; sauté 2 to 3 minutes or until tender. Stir in rice, parsley, egg yolks, milk, cheese, salt and pepper. In a large bowl, beat egg whites until soft peaks form. Fold beaten egg whites into rice mixture. Spoon into buttered baking dish. Place baking dish in a slightly larger pan. Pour in enough hot water to come halfway up side of baking dish. Bake 30 minutes or until slightly puffed and firm. Makes 4 to 6 servings.

Carrots, Turnips & Peas

Three simple vegetables combine to make a simply delicious dish.

3 medium carrots, thinly sliced
1 tablespoon butter
1 teaspoon sugar
1/2 teaspoon salt
1/4 cup water

2 small turnips, peeled,
   cut in 1/2-inch cubes
1 (10-oz.) pkg. frozen baby peas
Butter, if desired
Salt and coarsely ground pepper to taste

In a medium saucepan, combine carrots, 1 tablespoon butter, sugar, salt, water and turnips. Cover tightly; simmer 10 minutes or until tender. Place peas in a colander. Run hot water over peas until thawed, about 1 minute. Add peas to vegetable mixture. Season with butter, if desired. Heat to simmering. Season with salt and pepper. Serve hot. Makes 4 servings.

Cornbread Squares

Cornbread with melt-in-your-mouth flavor.

1-1/2 cups milk
1 tablespoon lemon juice or cider vinegar
1 cup yellow cornmeal
1/2 cup all-purpose flour
1 teaspoon salt

1 tablespoon baking powder
1/2 teaspoon baking soda
1 egg
1/4 cup butter, melted

Pour milk into a 2-cup measure. Add lemon juice or vinegar; set aside. Lightly grease a 10'' x 6'' baking dish. Place baking dish in cold oven. Preheat oven to 450F (230C). In a large bowl, combine cornmeal, flour, salt, baking powder and baking soda. Add egg to milk mixture; beat well. Pour milk mixture over cornmeal mixture. Stir quickly to make a smooth batter. Stir in butter. Carefully remove hot baking dish from oven. Immediately pour batter into hot dish. Bake 25 to 30 minutes or until lightly browned. Serve hot. Makes 6 to 8 servings.

Basic Roast Duck, page 70, served with Black-Forest Cherry Sauce, page 71; Souffléed Rice Casserole, above; and Carrots, Turnips & Peas, above.

Neopolitan Vegetables

A great dish to serve with leftover turkey or chicken.

3 tablespoons olive oil
1 large red onion, chopped
1 small garlic clove, minced
1 small eggplant, unpeeled,
  cut in 1-inch cubes
2 small zucchini, ends trimmed,
  cut in 1-inch cubes

1/2 teaspoon Italian herb seasoning
1/2 teaspoon salt
1 (1-lb.) can Italian-style plum tomatoes
1/4 lb. mozarella cheese,
  cut in 1-inch cubes
2 tablespoons freshly grated Parmesan cheese
Salt and coarsely ground pepper to taste

Heat oil in a large heavy skillet. Add onion; sauté 5 minutes or until soft. Add garlic; sauté 1 minute. Add eggplant, zucchini, herb seasoning and salt. Sauté 2 minutes. Add tomatoes and juice. Break up tomatoes with a wooden spoon. Stir to blend well. Bring to a boil. Reduce heat and partially cover. Simmer 20 minutes or until tender. Before serving, stir in cheeses. Cook, stirring only until cheese is partially melted. Season with salt and pepper. Makes 4 to 6 servings.

Variation

Prepare mixture ahead and pour into a small casserole. Do not add cheese until ready to reheat. Reheat in 350F (175C) oven until bubbly hot. Stir in cheeses; serve at once.

Caponata

A classic Italian vegetable mélange.

1/4 cup olive oil
1 medium onion, chopped
1 medium, green pepper, chopped
2 celery stalks, thinly sliced
1 medium eggplant, peeled,
  cut in 1/2-inch cubes
2 medium zucchini,
  ends trimmed, thickly sliced
1 cup cauliflowerets

1 (1-lb.) can Italian marinara sauce or
  spicy tomato sauce
1/4 cup chicken stock
1 tablespoon vinegar
1 tablespoon sugar
1 teaspoon salt
1/2 teaspoon coarsely ground pepper
6 to 8 pitted black olives, sliced
6 pitted green olives, sliced

Heat oil in a large heavy skillet over medium heat. Add onion and green pepper. Sauté 5 minutes or until tender. Add celery, eggplant, zucchini and cauliflowerets. Cook, stirring, 10 minutes. Add marinara sauce or tomato sauce, stock, vinegar, sugar, salt, pepper and olives. Simmer over low heat 20 to 25 minutes, stirring occasionally. Serve hot or warm. Makes 6 to 8 servings.

Mushroom Sauce

Mushrooms are a favorite of many—so make plenty of this sauce.

2-1/2 tablespoons butter
2 tablespoons all-purpose flour
1 cup hot chicken stock
1 cup milk, room temperature
2 tablespoons dry sherry

1 egg yolk
1/2 cup half and half
1 (3-oz.) can sautéed-in-butter mushrooms
Salt and coarsely ground pepper to taste

Melt butter in a heavy saucepan over low heat. Stir in flour. Add stock; stir with a whisk until smooth. Slowly add milk and sherry, stirring constantly until thickened. In a small bowl, beat egg yolk with half and half until blended. Stir in about 1/4 cup of hot sauce. Stir this mixture into remaining hot sauce. Add mushrooms; season with salt and pepper. Stir until heated through. Makes 2-1/2 cups.

Cumberland Sauce

A traditional sauce with cold roast turkey—equally good with roast or fried chicken.

1 navel orange
1/4 cup red-currant jelly
2 tablespoons Madeira wine
1 tablespoon lemon juice

1/2 teaspoon dry mustard
1/2 teaspoon ground ginger
1/2 teaspoon salt

Using a vegetable peeler or a knife, remove a 1-inch-wide strip of colored peel from orange. Cut in fine slivers. Place orange slivers in a saucepan. Cover with water and simmer 10 minutes over medium-low heat; drain well. Squeeze juice from orange. Combine orange slivers, orange juice, jelly, wine, lemon juice, mustard, ginger and salt in a saucepan over low heat. Stir until jelly has melted. Serve chilled or at room temperature. Makes about 3/4 cup.

Madeira Sauce

Madeira is a fortified wine from the Portuguese island of the same name.

3 tablespoons butter
2 tablespoons minced onion
1-1/2 cups chicken stock

1/3 cup Madeira wine
2 tablespoons all-purpose flour
1-1/2 cups hot milk

Melt 1 tablespoon butter in a medium saucepan over medium heat. Add onion; sauté 2 to 3 minutes or until tender. Stir in stock and wine. Bring to a boil. Reduce heat and simmer 20 to 25 minutes or until reduced by 1/2. Strain through a fine seive or cheesecloth; set aside. Melt remaining 2 tablespoons butter in top of a double boiler over simmering water. Stir in flour. Add milk; stir with a whisk until smooth. Slowly add strained wine mixture; stir until thickened. Serve hot. Makes about 1-1/2 cups sauce.

Uncooked Cranberry-Orange Sauce

A New England favorite to serve with turkey.

1 large navel orange
2 cups fresh or frozen cranberries

2 cups sugar
1 tablespoon brandy

Cut unpeeled orange in large chunks over a bowl to catch juices. In a blender or food processor fitted with a steel blade, combine orange chunks with juice and cranberries. Process until finely ground. Or, put mixture through a meat grinder. Place orange mixture in a large bowl. Add sugar and brandy. Stir well. Cover and refrigerate several hours to blend flavors. Makes about 4 cups.

Apple-Curry Sauce

A thick flavorful low-calorie sauce—great over sautéed chicken.

2 small tart cooking apples,
  peeled, coarsely chopped
1 cup chicken stock
2 teaspoons curry powder

1 tablespoon cornstarch
1/2 teaspoon salt
1/4 teaspoon coarsely ground pepper

Combine all ingredients in a blender or food processor fitted with a steel blade. Process until smooth. Pour sauce mixture into a large skillet. Cook over medium-high heat, stirring constantly until thick and hot. Spoon sauce over sautéed chicken. Serve hot. Makes about 1-1/4 cups.

White-Wine Sauce

Enjoy the tangy flavor with sautéed chicken.

1/2 cup dry white wine
1 tablespoon lemon juice

1 tablespoon butter, if desired
Salt and coarsely ground pepper to taste

In a heavy skillet, heat wine over medium-high heat until reduced to about 1/4 cup. Stir in lemon juice and butter, if desired. Season with salt and pepper. Serve hot. Makes about 1/4 cup.

Sauce Aurore

A colorful sauce with an intriguing flavor.

3 tablespoons butter
2 tablespoons all-purpose flour
1-1/2 cups hot chicken stock
1/2 cup whipping cream

1 tablespoon tomato paste
Salt and coarsely ground pepper to taste
Lemon juice to taste

Melt butter in a large heavy saucepan over low heat. Stir in flour, cooking about 2 minutes. Slowly add stock, stirring as added. Cook, stirring until smooth and slightly thickened. Add cream and tomato paste. Stir to blend. Cook 2 to 3 minutes. Season with salt, pepper and lemon juice. Makes about 2 cups.

Index

A
A la King, Chicken 126
After-Work Chicken 30
Almond Chicken 92
APPETIZERS 15-24
Apple:
   Apple-Curry Sauce 156
   Apple Stuffing 72
   Bourbon Chicken with Apples 43
   Turkey & Apple Salad 133
Apricots, Stuffed 151
Aspic, Chicken 114
Au Poivre, Chicken Thighs 38
Aurore, Sauce 156
Authentic Creole Chicken Gumbo 34-35
Avgolemono, Chicken Soup 34
Avocado Shells, Curried Chicken in 112-113

B
Bag, Roast Turkey in a 74
Baked Chicken Pilaf 99
Barbecue Sauce:
   California Barbecue Sauce 142
   Cranberry Barbecue Sauce 147
   Middle Eastern Barbecue Sauce 147
   Texas Barbecue Sauce 140
   Uncooked Barbecue Sauce 145
Barbecued Chicken Dinner 141
Barbecued Chicken Texas-Style 140
Basic Chicken Salad 128
Basic Chicken Stock 26
Basic Preparation 6
Basic Roast Duck 70, 152
Basic Roasting 58
Basics of Cutting-Up 9
Basics on Buying 5
Basque-Style Chicken 45
Batter-Fried Chicken 80
Bean Casserole, Ducky 71
Beer Batter 80
Biscuits, Onion 124
Black-Forest Cherry Sauce 71, 152
Bleu, Chicken Cordon 78
Blue Cheese & Chicken Quiche, Creamy 118-119
Bombay Chicken in a Clay Pot 103
Boning:
   Chicken Breasts 12
   Chicken-Breast Halves 13
   Legs with Thighs 83
   Thighs 47

Turkey Breast 73
Bourbon Chicken with Apples 43
BRAISED & STEAMED, SAUTEED 37-56
Brandied Gravy, Pan-Fried Chicken & 88
Breast Half, How to Bone a Chicken- 13
Breast, How to Bone a Chicken 12
Breast, Stuffed Turkey 72-73
Breasts Milanese, Chicken 44-45
Broccoli Casserole, Chicken- 122
BROILED, ROASTED & STUFFED 57-76
Broth, see Stock 7
Brown Chicken Stock 26
Brown-Bag Chicken Sandwiches 128
Brunswick Stew 31
Brunswick-Stew Casserole 108
Buffet Party Chicken 20-21
Buffet, Chicken Hash for a 110
Buttermilk Batter 80
Butters, Seasoned 62
Buying, Basics on 5

C
Cacciatore, Chicken 46
Cajun Chicken 42
California Barbecue Sauce 142
California Chicken 52
California Chicken Salad 130-131
California Chicken Sandwich 138
California Dressing 130
Calorie-Affordable Fried Chicken 82
Cantonese Chicken Wings 87
Caponata 154
Carrots, Turnips & Peas 152-153
Carving Poultry 60
Cashews, Chicken with 91
CASSEROLE & OVEN CHICKEN 97-108
   Chicken-Broccoli Casserole 122
   Ducky Bean Casserole 71
   Rice & Giblet Casserole 74
   Souffléed Rice Casserole 152-153
Champagne Sauce, Chicken in 50-51
Charleston Company Chicken 42
Cheese & Chicken Quiche, Creamy Blue 118-119
Cheese Puff with Chicken 122-123
Cheese Sandwiches, Grilled Chicken & 135
Cheesecloth-Covered Roast Turkey 75
Cherry Sauce, Black-Forest 71, 152

Chicken & Cream Sauce 56
Chicken & Ham Tarts 125
Chicken & Leek Soup 31
Chicken & Mushroom Salad 96
Chicken & Pineapple Spread 17, 21
Chicken & Red-Wine Sauce 39
Chicken & Sausage Ragout 56
Chicken a la King 126
Chicken Aspic 114
Chicken Breasts Milanese 44-45
Chicken-Broccoli Casserole 122
Chicken Cacciatore 46
Chicken Chow Mein 94
Chicken Cordon Bleu 78
Chicken Couscous 110
Chicken & Fruit Salad 134
Chicken Hash Blindbrook 111
Chicken Hash for a Buffet 110
Chicken in Champagne Sauce 50-51
Chicken Kiev 79
Chicken-Lettuce Rolls 24
Chicken-Liver Pâté 16, 21
Chicken Mole 38
Chicken-Mushroom Filling 22
Chicken Quiche 117
Chicken Rarebit Sandwich 135
Chicken-Rice Salad 134
Chicken Salad for Singles 134
Chicken Salad Nicoise 129
Chicken Soup Avgolemono 34
Chicken Stock 7
Chicken Tarts 100-101
Chicken Tea Sandwiches 128, 131
Chicken Thighs au Poivre 38
Chicken Véronique 106
Chicken Wings with Garden Vegetables 40
Chicken with Cashews 91
Chicken with Eggplant 90-91
Chicken with Green Noodles 43
Chicken with Oriental Vegetables 101
Chicken with Pasta in Primavera Sauce 126
Chicken with Taco Sauce 48
Chicken with Turmeric Pilaf 105
Chicken, Parmesan Crepes with 116
Chicken Soufflé with Olives 123
Chinese Chicken Mini-Drumsticks 18
Chinese Grilled Turkey 147
Chinese Sweet & Sour Chicken 93
Chive Dressing, Creamy 133
Chop Suey 90
Chopped Chicken Livers 16
Chow Mein, Chicken 94

Cinnamon Baked Oranges, Sugar & 151
Cinnamon Peaches 150
Classes of Poultry 4
Clay Pot, Bombay Chicken in a 103
Coated Chicken, Crumb- 41
Cock-a-leekie 31
COOKED POULTRY 109-126
Cooked Chicken Pointers 6
Cordon Bleu, Chicken 78
Cornbread:
    Cornbread Squares 153
    Sausage & Cornbread Stuffing 64
    Walnut-Cornbread Stuffing 63
Cornish Hens:
    Cornish Hens & Onion-Pineapple Stuffing 76
    Cornish Hens with Couscous Stuffing 76
    Grilled Cornish Hens 144-145
Cornmeal Dumplings 29
Cornmeal Batter 80
Country-Style Chicken in a Pot 108
Couscous Stuffing, Cornish Hens with 76
Couscous, Chicken 110
Cracker-Crumb Coating 81
Cranberry:
    Cranberry Barbecue Sauce 147
    Cranberry-Turkey Mold 133
    Turkey-Cranberry Salad 128
    Uncooked Cranberry-Orange Sauce 156
Cream of Chicken Soup 32
Cream Sauce, Chicken & 56
Cream Sauce, Quick Cutlets & 48
Creamed Turkey-Almond Soup 28
Creamy Blue Cheese & Chicken
    Quiche 118-119
Creamy Chive Dressing 133
Creamy Tomato Sauce 103
Creole Chicken Gumbo, Authentic 34-35
Crepes with Chicken, Parmesan 116
Croque à l'Américaine 137
Croque Madame 136
Croquettes, Deluxe 120-121
Crumb-Coated Chicken 41
Crumb-Crust Fried Chicken 81
Crunchy Chicken Nuggets 24
Culinary Injector 6
Cumberland Sauce 155
Currant-Jelly Glaze 71
Curried Chicken Soup 30
Curried Chicken in Avocado Shells
    112-113
Curried Rice 104
Curry Sauce, Apple- 156
Cutlets:
    Quick Cutlets & Cream Sauce 48
    Cutlets Italian-Style 49
    How to Make Chicken Cutlets 49
    Russian Turkey Cutlets 84-85
Cutting:
    Basics of Cutting-Up 9
    Cutting Chicken Halves 14
    Cutting Chicken Quarters 14
    Cutting-Up a Whole Chicken 10-11

D
Deep-Dish Chicken Pie 124
Defrosting 6
Defrosting Techniques for Microwave 8
Deluxe Croquettes 120-121
Dieter's Sautéed Chicken 52

Dinner in a Roasted Chicken 65
Divan with Spinach, Turkey 120
Dody's Oven-Fried Chicken 88
Double-Delicious Chicken Soufflé 112
Dressings:
    California Dressing 130
    Creamy Chive Dressing 133
    Russian Dressing 138
    Vinaigrette Dressing 129
Duck:
    Basic Roast Duck 70, 152
    Duck & Goose 7
    Ducky Bean Casserole 71
    Spit-Roasted Duck 146
Dumplings:
    Cornmeal Dumplings 29
    Herb Dumplings 29
    Neopolitan Chicken & Dumplings 54
    Sausage Dumplings 54

E
Easy Chicken & Rice 106
Easy, Easy Tetrazzini 125
Eggplant, Chicken with 90-91
Enchiladas, Turkey 114-115

F
Fat, Rendered Chicken 8
Filled Franks, Grilled & 145
Filling, Chicken-Mushroom 22
Filling, Florentine-Style 22
Fines Herbes, Turkey Scallops 52
Flambé, Tropical Fruit 150
Florentine-Style Filling 22
Franks, Grilled & Filled 145
French Potato Salad 149
Fresh Tomato Sauce 90
Fricassee, Old-Fashioned Chicken 50
FRIED CHICKEN 77-88
Frittata di Pollo 119
Fruit Flambé, Tropical 150
Fruit Salad, Chicken & 134
Fruit Stuffing 63
Fruit Stuffing, Roast Turkey with 75
Frying Temperatures 80

G
Garlic Chicken with Oranges 105
Garlic, Steamed Chicken & 55
Giblets:
    Giblet Gravy 61
    Giblets & Stock for Gravy & Stuffing 62
    Rice & Giblet Casserole 74
Glaze, Currant-Jelly 71
Glaze, Honey-Soy 72
Glazed Chicken 99
Goose & Duck 7
Goose & Peach Stuffing, Roast 67-69
Gravy, Giblet 61
Grebenes 8
Green Salad, Tuscan 149
GRILLED POULTRY 139-147
Grilled Chicken & Cheese Sandwiches 135
Gumbo, Authentic Creole Chicken 34-35

H
Ham Tarts, Chicken & 125
Hash Blindbrook, Chicken 111
Hash for a Buffet, Chicken 110
Hawaiian Chicken 39
Hens & Onion-Pineapple Stuffing,

Cornish 76
Hens with Couscous Stuffing, Cornish 76
Herbs:
    Herb Dumplings 29
    Herb Marinade 140
    Turkey Scallops Fines Herbes 52
    Grilled Chicken with Herbs 140
Honey-Soy Glaze 72
How To Make:
    Chicken Cutlets 49
    Mini-Drumsticks 19

I
India, Spicy Red Chicken from 66
Indonesian:
    Indonesian Oven-Fried Chicken 81
    Indonesian Rice & Chicken 94-95
    Indonesian-Style Chicken Casserole 100
Injector, Culinary 6
Italian:
    Cutlets Italian-Style 49
    Italian Chicken & Zucchini 99
    Italian Chicken Salad 130
    Italian-Style Crumb Coating 81

J
Japanese-Style Grilled Chicken 143
Jelly Glaze, Currant- 71

K
Kabobs, Oriental Chicken 142
Kiev, Chicken 79

L
Leek Soup, Chicken & 31
Lemon Grilled Chicken 146
Lemony Crumb Coating 81
Lettuce Rolls, Chicken- 24
Liver Pâté, Chicken- 16, 21
Livers, Chopped Chicken 16
Loaf, Turkey-Mushroom 102-103

M
Madeira Sauce 155
Marinade, Herb 140
Marmalade Sauce 146
Measuring Doneness 59
Meat Thermometer 59
Microwave Tips 8
Middle Eastern Barbecue Sauce 147
Mini-Drumsticks:
    Chinese Chicken Mini-Drumsticks 18
    How to Make Mini-Drumsticks 19
    Mustard-Honey Mini-Drumsticks 18
Miniature Chicken Strudels 23
Mold, Cranberry-Turkey 133
Mold, Waldorf Chicken 132
Mole, Chicken 38
Mornay Sauce, Turkey Casserole with 104
Mousse, Southern-Style Chicken 138
Mulligatawny Soup 27
Mushroom:
    Chicken & Mushroom Salad 96
    Mushroom Sauce 155
    Turkey-Mushroom Loaf 102-103
Mustard-Honey Mini-Drumsticks 18

N
Neopolitan Chicken & Dumplings 54
Neopolitan Chicken-Breast Rolls 86-87
Neopolitan Vegetables 154

New-Fashioned Chicken Soup 32-33
Nicoise, Chicken Salad 129
Noodle Supper, Simply Delicious Turkey- 30
Noodles or Rice, Chicken Soup with 32
Noodles, Chicken with Green 43
Nuggets, Crunchy Chicken 24

O
Old-Fashioned Chicken Fricassee 50
Old-Fashioned Stuffed Chicken 61
Old-Time Chicken Stew & Dumplings 29
Olive-Stuffed Turkey Rolls 53
Olives, Chicken Soufflé with 123
Omelette:
  Frittata di Pollo 119
  Parker-House Chicken Omelettes 111
Onion Biscuits 124
Onion-Pineapple Stuffing, Cornish Hens & 76
Open-Face Chicken Sandwiches 128
Orange:
  Garlic Chicken with Oranges 105
  Orange Sauce 70
  Sugar & Cinnamon Baked Oranges 151
  Uncooked Cranberry-Orange Sauce 156
Oriental:
  Chicken with Oriental Vegetables 101
  Oriental Chicken Kabobs 142
  Oriental Chicken Soup 36
  Stir-Fry 89-96
OVEN CHICKEN, CASSEROLES 97-108
Oven-Fried:
  Dody's Oven-Fried Chicken 88
  Indonesian Oven-Fried Chicken 81
  Oven-Fried Chicken Parma 82

P
Pan-Fried Chicken & Brandied Gravy 88
Parker-House Chicken Omelettes 111
Parma, Oven-Fried Chicken 82
Parmesan Crepes with Chicken 116
Parmesan Tart Shells 125
Party Chicken, Buffet- 20-21
Pasta Fagioli 36
Pasta in Primavera Sauce, Chicken with 126
Pastry Puff 98
Pastry, Tart-Shell 101
Pâté, Chicken-Liver 16, 21
Pâté, Smoked-Turkey 17
Peach Stuffing, Roast Goose & 67-69
Peaches, Cinnamon 150
Peas, Carrots, Turnips & 152-153
Perfect Sautéed Chicken 38
Pie, Deep-Dish Chicken 124
Pie, Upside-Down Chicken 121
Pilaf, Baked Chicken 99
Pilaf, Turmeric 105
Pineapple:
  Pineapple Chicken 98
  Spicy Pineapple Chunks 150
  Chicken & Pineapple Spread 17, 21
  Cornish Hens & Onion-Pineapple Stuffing 76
  Skewered Chicken with Pineapple 20
Poached Chicken & Rich Stock 27
Pocket-Bread Sandwich 135
Polynesian Grilled Chicken 142

Polynesian Sauce 142
Potato Salad, French 149
Potatoes & Onions, Steamed Chicken with 55
POULTRY ACCOMPANIMENTS 148-156
Poultry Classes 4
Poultry Types 4
Preparation Basics 6
Primavera Sauce, Chicken with Pasta in 126
Puff with Chicken, Cheese 122-123
Puff, Sweet & Sour Chicken Puff 98
Puffy Tarts 22

Q
Quarters, Stuffed Chicken 107
Quiche:
  Chicken Quiche 117
  Creamy Blue Cheese & Chicken Quiche 118-119
Quick Cutlets & Cream Sauce 48
Quick Tomato Sauce 119

R
Ragout, Chicken & Sausage 56
Raisin-Bread Stuffing 64
Rarebit Sandwich, Chicken 135
Red Chicken from India, Spicy 66
Red-Wine Sauce, Chicken & 39
Rendering Fat 8
Rice:
  Chicken-Rice Salad 134
  Curried Rice 104
  Easy Chicken & Rice 106
  Indonesian Rice & Chicken 94-95
  Rice & Giblet Casserole 74
  Souffléed Rice Casserole 152-153
Roast Duck, Basic 70, 152
Roast Goose & Peach Stuffing 67-69
Roast Turkey:
  Cheesecloth-Covered Roast Turkey 75
  Roast Turkey In a Bag 74
  Roast Turkey With Fruit Stuffing 75
ROASTED, STUFFED & BROILED 57-76
Roasting Timetable 59
Rolls, Neopolitan Chicken-Breast 86-87
Rolls, Olive-Stuffed Turkey 53
Rumaki 17
Russian Dressing 138
Russian Turkey Cutlets 84-85

S
SALADS & SANDWICHES 127-138
  Chicken & Mushroom Salad 96
  French Potato Salad 149
  Tuscan Green Salad 149
SANDWICHES & SALADS 127-138
Sauces:
  Sauce Aurore 156
  Apple-Curry Sauce 156
  Black-Forest Cherry Sauce 71, 152
  California Barbecue Sauce 142
  Cranberry Barbecue Sauce 147
  Cumberland Sauce 155
  Madeira Sauce 155
  Marmalade Sauce 146
  Middle Eastern Barbecue Sauce 147
  Mushroom Sauce 155

  Orange Sauce 70
  Polynesian Sauce 142
  Taco Sauce 141
  Tomato Sauce 86
  Uncooked Barbecue Sauce 145
  White-Wine Sauce 156
  Yakitori Sauce 143
Sausage:
  Chicken & Sausage Ragout 56
  Sausage & Apple Stuffing 65
  Sausage & Cornbread Stuffing 64
  Sausage Dumplings 54
SAUTEED, BRAISED & STEAMED 37-56
Scallops Fines Herbes, Turkey 52
Schnitzel Chicken 85
Seasoned Butters 62
Shrimp, Stir-Fried Chicken & 92
Simply Delicious Turkey-Noodle Supper 30
Singhalese Soup 35
Singles, Chicken Salad for 134
Skewered Chicken with Pineapple 20
Slow-Cooking Pot:
  After-Work Chicken 30
  Hawaiian Chicken 39
Smoked-Turkey Pâté 17
Soufflé:
  Double-Delicious Chicken Soufflé 112
  Soufflé with Olives, Chicken 123
  Souffléed Rice Casserole 152-153
SOUPS & STEWS 25-36
Southern Fried Chicken 78, cover
Southern-Style Chicken Mousse 138
Soy Glaze, Honey- 72
Spiced Chicken Wings 24
Spicy Pineapple Chunks 150
Spicy Red Chicken from India 66
Spinach, Turkey Divan with 120
Spinach-Stuffed Thighs 83
Spit-Roasted Duck 146
Spread, Chicken & Pineapple 17, 21
STEAMED, SAUTEED & BRAISED 37-56
Steamed:
  Steamed Chicken & Garlic 55
  Steamed Chicken 55
  Steamed Chicken with Potatoes & Onions 55
Stew:
  Brunswick Stew 31
  Brunswick-Stew Casserole 108
  Old-Time Chicken Stew & Dumplings 29
  Pasta Fagioli 36
STEWS & SOUPS 25-36
STIR-FRIED CHICKEN 89-96
Stock:
  Basic Chicken Stock 26
  Brown Chicken Stock 26
  Chicken Stock 7
  Giblets & Stock for Gravy & Stuffing 62
  Poached Chicken & Rich Stock 27
Storage 5
Storage Timetables 6
Strudels, Miniature Chicken 23
STUFFED & BROILED, ROASTED 57-76
Stuffed:
  Old-Fashioned Stuffed Chicken 61

Spinach-Stuffed Thighs 83
Stuffed Apricots 151
Stuffed Chicken Quarters 107
Stuffed Chicken Thighs 46-47
Stuffed Cornish Hens 76
Stuffed Goose 67-69
Stuffed Turkey 75
Stuffed Turkey Breast 72-73
Stuffed Turkey Rolls 53
Stuffings:
   Apple Stuffing 72
   Couscous Stuffing 76
   Fruit Stuffing 63
   Onion-Pineapple Stuffing 76
   Peach Stuffing 67
   Raisin-Bread Stuffing 64
   Sausage & Cornbread Stuffing 64
   Walnut-Cornbread Stuffing 63
Sugar & Cinnamon Baked Oranges 151
Sweet & Sour:
   Chinese Sweet & Sour Chicken 93
   Sweet & Sour Chicken 40
   Sweet & Sour Chicken Puff 98
   Sweet & Sour Sauce 40

T
Taco Chicken Grill with Taco Sauce 141
Taco Sauce, Chicken with 48
Tarts:
   Chicken & Ham Tarts 125
   Chicken Tarts 100-101
   Parmesan Tart Shells 125
   Puffy Tarts 22
   Tart-Shell Pastry 101
Tea Sandwiches, Chicken 128, 131
Tetrazzini, Easy, Easy 125
Texas Barbecue Sauce 140
Texas-Style, Barbecued Chicken 140

Thermometer, Meat 59
Thighs au Poivre, Chicken 38
Thighs, Spinach-Stuffed 83
Thighs, Stuffed Chicken 46-47
Tips on Vertical Roasting 66
Tips, Microwave 8
Tomato Sauce 86
Tomato Sauce, Creamy 103
Tomato Sauce, Fresh 90
Tomato Sauce, Quick 119
Tostada-Salad Sandwich 137
Tropical Fruit Flambé 150
Trussing Poultry 58-59
Turkey:
   Cheesecloth-Covered Roast Turkey 75
   Chinese Grilled Turkey 147
   Cranberry-Turkey Mold 133
   Creamed Turkey-Almond Soup 28
   Olive-Stuffed Turkey Rolls 53
   Roast Turkey in a Bag 74
   Roast Turkey with Fruit Stuffing 75
   Russian Turkey Cutlets 84-85
   Simply Delicious Turkey-Noodle Supper 30
   Smoked-Turkey Pâté 17
   Stir-Fried Turkey 93
   Stuffed Turkey Breast 72-73
   Turkey & Apple Salad 133
   Turkey Casserole with Mornay Sauce 104
   Turkey-Cranberry Salad 128
   Turkey Divan with Spinach 120
   Turkey Enchiladas 114-115
   Turkey-Mushroom Loaf 102-103
   Turkey Scallops Fines Herbes 52
   Turkey Tips 7
Turmeric Pilaf, Chicken with 105
Turnips & Peas, Carrots 152-153

Tuscan Green Salad 149
Types of Glazes 71
Types of Poultry 4

U
Uncooked Barbecue Sauce 145
Uncooked Cranberry-Orange Sauce 156
Upside-Down Chicken Pie 121

V
Vegetable:
   Chicken & Vegetable Soup 32
   Chicken Wings with Garden Vegetables 40
   Chicken with Oriental Vegetables 101
   Neopolitan Vegetables 154
   Stir-Fried Chicken & Vegetables 96
Véronique, Chicken 106
Vertical Roasting Tips 66
Vinaigrette Dressing 129

W
Waldorf Chicken Mold 132
Walnut-Cornbread Stuffing 63
White-Wine Sauce 156
Wine Sauce, Chicken & Red- 39
Wine Sauce, White- 156
Wings:
   Cantonese Chicken Wings 87
   Chicken Wings with Garden Vegetables 40
   Spiced Chicken Wings 24

Y
Yakitori Sauce 143

Z
Zucchini, Italian Chicken & 99